Bottom of the

Tanya A. Rich

Bill
Go Red-Sox
Best Wishes
Rich

Tanya
Rehart

a.
2009

Llumina
Press

Rich

Requests for permission to make copies of any part of this work should be mailed to Permissions Department, Llumina Press, PO Box 772246, Coral Springs, FL 33077-2246

ISBN: 978-1-60594-085-4 (PB)
      978-1-60594-086-1 (HC)
      978-1-60594-087-8 (Ebook)

Printed in the United States of America by Llumina Press

Library of Congress Control Number: 2008905603

Chapter 1

"It's the Bottom of the Ninth."

"D-o-l-l-a-r ... B-i-l-l-l-l! D-o-l-l-a-r ... B-i-l-l-l-l!"

Bill "No Chance" LaChance seemed oblivious to the venomous onslaught coming from the very bowels of Wrigley Field.

LaChance glanced into the home dugout and then ejected an eight-inch jet of discharge between his upper incisors.

"Listen to the crowd as No Chance throws his final warm-up pitch to catcher Dan Greene. The crowd is really into it, Richie. What started from the right-field bleachers in the top of the fifth inning, when LaChance questioned a called third strike when he was at the plate, has turned into a roaring crescendo here in the ninth. Well, it's better than the 'S...O...B' chant that echoed throughout the ballparks and stadiums of the National League every time LaChance pitched last season. Can I say 'S.O.B.' on the radio, Richie?"

"I think you just did, Ceder—twice. This is your WMET sportscaster, Rich Cleary, assisted by my able statistician, cohort and sidekick, D.W. Cederquist, bringing you our final Mets broadcast of the season from Chicago's Wrigley Field on the final day of September. Believe it or not, ladies and gents, boys and girls, it's the bottom of the ninth of the last game of the 2002 baseball season for both the New York Mets and the lowly Chicago Cubs. With a 5–1 lead, looks like the Mets are about to pick up their eleventh win of September."

"D-o-l-l-a-r ... B-i-l-l-l-l! D-o-l-l-a-r ... B-i-l-l-l-l!"

"Well, Richie, my friend, I'm not sure what the crowd meant by S.O.B., but I'm sure it wasn't 'Sweet Old Bill.' It's been said that No Chance LaChance is the most despised player in baseball. That may or may not be an accurate statement. However, today he demonstrated just how dominating he can be. Here in the bottom of the ninth, in a meaningless game for both teams, LaChance is gunning for his twenty-third win and league-leading sixteenth complete game of the year on a team that, four weeks ago, seemed to be headed for post-season play. An extremely disappointing 10–19 record in the month of September has closed the door on the 2002 season for the Mets, but the Mets' collapse can't be put on LaChance. He gave maximum effort with each start."

"LaChance throws down the rosin bag and spits again as Greene fires the baseball down to Natola at second, over to first. First baseman Dennis McHugh walks the ball to the mound. And we are ready to go."

"Attention-n-n-n-n! Pinch hitting-g-g-g for third baseman Jerry Keung-g-g-g, Number 36, Edgar-r-r-r-r Toto-o-o-o-o! Toto-o-o-o-o batting for Keung-g-g-g-g."

"Ceder, what do you think of LaChance's performance this afternoon? I know you're not a huge No Chance fan. Where do you see him next year?"

"Well, Richie, my friend, you can boot up your laptop, click on the Tools button, and open your thesaurus, and I don't mean the dinosaur. Then you can add reviled, detested, and loathed to the word 'despised.' Also include abhorrent and despicable, that will give you some of the words that have been used to describe Bill LaChance. But Rich, being honest, today LaChance made a believer out of me. In a game that means nothing to nobody, it seems to be a big deal to No Chance LaChance. Then again, when it comes to LaChance, everyone says, 'It's all about the moolah,' you know? 'Show me the money!' Everyone calls him 'Dollar Bill,' and perhaps we now appreciate why. He probably gets a bonus for every complete game and that's the reason why he's still on the mound. But no one can ignore the fact that LaChance can pitch. All you have to do is look at the record."

"You are correct, Ceder! No Chance's statistics speak for themselves. LaChance seems destined for the Hall of Fame in Cooperstown. Here's the first pitch of the bottom half of the ninth. Outside, ball one. LaChance's pitch count is at 120. We'll be watching the Mets' bullpen to see if there's any action. Looking in The Baseball Encyclopedia, LaChance is already in the top twenty-five in almost every pitching category. Today's performance only adds, positively, to those totals."

A sudden cool zephyr blew in from Lake Michigan, scattering Cederquist's notes. There was a long pause of dead air. Rich Cleary glared at Cederquist. Cleary hated dead air. Ceder re-sorted his notes and tried to regain his composure.

"Poor Ed Toto has had a rough year—broke his right-hand pinky finger in early May. On June 8, Edgar was in Boston during interleague play and was involved in a taxi accident, the result being a shoulder injury. Toto returned to Manager Herman Sherman's lineup on July 13, right after the All-Star break, and promptly fouled a pitch off of his big toe of the left foot. The busted toe put him on the bench until the end of August. Too bad, Toto is a true gentleman in every sense of the word.

Rubbing the baseball, LaChance is ready, winds … a bit low. Ball two. Toto taps his shoes with his bat and now steps back into the box. Here comes LaChance's third pitch. It's a slow roller to Natola, over to first. One away."

"Attention-n-n-n-n! Now batting-g-g-g-g, the center fielder, Number 6, Bill-l-l-l-l Clifford-d-d-d-d."

"Well, Rich, I didn't answer your question. Everyone I've talked with thinks it's a done deal. Next year, LaChance will be playing for the Red Sox in the American League. No Chance has made no bones about telling anyone and everyone that the Yankees reneged on his contract and that was his reason for going to the Mets. He'd like nothing better than to come back to be a thorn in the Yankee's side, I'm sure. Hey, Rich, did you know that Big Bill Clifford's great-grandfather was George 'Tex' Gore? Played fourteen years in the majors."

"No, Ceder, I didn't know that. Where in Texas was George Gore from?"

"Oh, no, Rich, he wasn't from Texas. Saccarappa, Maine. Up near Naples. You know, Sebago Lake area. His nickname was 'Piano Legs'! Played for the Giants and the Cubs, 1879 through 1892."

"That's not funny, Ceder. But interesting. Very interesting. Thanks Ceder. Incidentally, it will be an interesting off-season. A lot of free agency activity this coming winter. LaChance looks in to his catcher, Dan Greene. Spits, shakes off the first sign, and the second. He seems ready … the windup and the pitch. It's a well-hit ball to deep centerfield. Ollie Oliver is going back, back, and makes a nice running catch on the edge of the warning track. Wow! That's about the best ball hit off No Chance all afternoon. But it's out number two, with a 400-foot fly ball to Oliver in right-center."

"Attention-n-n-n-n! Pinch hitting-g-g-g-g for shortstop Jose Mokaba-a-a-a-a, number 44, Bartholomew-w-w-w-w Bowers. Bowers batting for Mokaba."

"Well, the Cubbies are down to their final out. Here's Bart Bowers. Bowers was brought up from the Triple-A Iowa Cubs on the first of September and has shown that he's the real deal with five homeruns, thirteen runs batted in, and twenty-three hits for fifty-one at-bats for a .451 average. Bart Bowers was Player of the Year in the rookie league at Mesa, Arizona, last year. This season he started with the Lansing Lugnuts, in Single-A. After hitting fifteen homers, he moved to Pringle's Park in Jackson, Tennessee, where he hit another fifteen homers with the Double-A Diamond Jazz and was brought up to Triple-

A Iowa Cubs in Des Moines. Bart Bowers has hit forty-seven home runs this season. Looks like the Cubs will have trouble keeping him down on the farm next spring. Don't you think so, Ceder? "

"You got that right, Rich. We didn't know if we would see Bowers today after his moving altercation with the left-field scoreboard in the sixth inning of Friday night's game. He missed yesterday's game and was listed as day-to-day by Manager Sherman. I wonder if they'll take the expenses to fix the fence out of his pay."

"That's not funny, Ceder. … LaChance looks in; Greene flashes the sign. The pitch. Strike one. Wow … 93 miles per hour on the gun, 123 pitches, and LaChance is still throwing in the nineties. Bill LaChance is wasting no time with the rookie. Here's the pitch. Strike two; 95 miles per hour is flashing on the center-field pitch-speed display. Bowers still has the bat on his shoulder. LaChance looks in for Greene's sign. Shakes off the first, now the second, and the third. Danny Greene is trotting to the mound. Greene says nothing as Bill LaChance, glove to mouth, tells his catcher what his next, perhaps last, offering will be. Greene heads back to the plate, has a couple of words with home-plate umpire Gerry MacEachern. Another couple of words to Bart Bowers, and we are ready. LaChance stares in, spits for about the fifteenth time this inning. The windup, the pitch … swinging strike three; 97 miles per hour!"

"Well, Rich, twenty-three wins and sixteen complete games for No Chance LaChance. This Chicago crowd is on their feet, giving LaChance the ovation that is due. As the cheers become jeers, Dollar Bill spits one final time while marching to the dugout. Hm-m, maybe LaChance gets a bonus for each time he spits. Perhaps he has a spitting clause in his contract. Interesting, Richie, LaChance doesn't chew tobacco. Never did! They say he consumes about two bags of sunflower seeds every appearance."

"D-o-l-l-a-r …B-i-l-l-l-l! D-o-l-l-a-r …B-i-l-l-l-l!"

"Spitting clause? Disgusting! That's not even remotely funny, Ceder. Sunflower seeds?"

"The final score 5–1 Mets. LaChance with fourteen strikeouts. Wow, the crowd is really giving it to LaChance. They're as loud and enthusiastic as the mob at the Saw Doctors concert I went to the other night."

"The Saw Doctors? Ceder, who or what are the Saw Doctors?"

"Richie, my friend, you really got to get a life. You are so clueless outside the baseball booth. I don't believe it, who are the Saw Doctors? You've got to be kidding me."

"Sorry, Ceder, I didn't intend to insult you or your Saw Doctors. Sorry. Well, listeners, this is Rich Cleary and your WMET sports broadcasting team, wishing you a fine off-season. Hope you'll be joining us on March 2, 2003, when we start our 2003 spring training schedule from Florida. Thanks for listening. Be sure to listen in to our weekly sports talk show, 'Sports Beat,' right here on WMET on weekends starting at 7:00 p.m. That's Saturday and Sunday at seven o'clock in the evening. The tradition continues here at Wrigley Field, the final game of the season and everyone has a bag or two of white confetti. As the cool fall breezes of late September carry the white stuff throughout the stadium, like a blizzard, the 2002 baseball season has ended. Mercifully so, for the New York Mets. What a mess!

I wouldn't want to be on the cleanup crew, would you, Ceder?"

Chapter 2

U.S. Customs Station North Troy, Vermont 26 January 2003

S now the size of white confetti blowing horizontally, -5° wind chill, Super Bowl Sunday. None of these facts brought more traffic past this outpost in the woods as the 4:00 p.m. shift change approached. Agent Bill Atwood would be arriving shortly at the Customs Station with his brother-in-law, Sheriff Franklin Ames, to watch the Super Bowl. Frank Ames, the sheriff for Orleans County, with its 25,400 residents, often visited the Customs Office during his patrols. Ames lives in Newport, population 5005, the largest town in the county.

4:17 p.m. Dusk had arrived, and the chilling effects of the storm were beginning to be felt. The temperature was dropping, and snow was beginning to accumulate. The wind scattered snow in all directions, adding to this Arctic portrait.

Station director Margaret "Peg" McCarthy snapped the top button of her heavy green parka and headed for the rear door. "Well, Bill, the place is all yours. Hope you and Frank enjoy the football game. I'm out of here."

Bill Atwood, in his usual monotone manner, replied, "Okay, Peg, see you later. I.B.B.Y."

Peg McCarthy shook her head, thinking to herself, Why does Bill always say good-bye with I.B.B.Y.? Something about a childhood TV show from the 1960s that closed with the spaceman host exclaiming I.B.B.Y. (I'll Be Blasting You). Why does Bill have to say that every time and to everybody? Whatever.

As soon as Peg shut the driver's door, her instant response was, "Damn! That seat is cold, even with the car parked inside."

North Troy was considered out in the boonies and, therefore, at the bottom of the equipment-replacement ladder. The station had three Jeeps, and at ten years-old, "Bertha," as she was affectionately called, was the matriarch of the fleet. Bertha, ID # 314581, was equipped with the usual assortment of U.S. Customs Service amenities: insignia, seal, and logo on each front door; flashing strobe lights (although one was not working); siren and speaker.

Snow whistled across the hood as the ten-year-old Jeep Cherokee rolled out of the garage onto the now-white parking lot. As Peg was departing, Ames backed his car into one of the vacant bays of the garage that was attached to the Customs Office. Lights on, seat belt secured, a quick wave to Sheriff Ames, and Peg McCarthy was on her way south on U.S. Route 243.

"This is the part of the job that I like best, only four minutes to home, a garage at each end, and no traffic," Peg said aloud.

A lukewarm breeze started to flow from the heater as Peg approached the reverse fork that lead to the U.S. Customs compound on the left. The snow was now blowing wildly from all directions, and the entrance was nearly invisible. "Interesting", Peg thought, "why would someone park along the side of the road, headed north, about 500 feet from the compound driveway? Agent McCarthy to North Troy Customs Station. Come in, Bill."

Silence. Adjustment of the volume knob brought a rapid and deafening response.

"*Go ahead, Peg. Atwood here,*" blared from the radio speaker at nearly 85 decibels.

"Bill, ask Frank if he saw a vehicle parked on the northbound shoulder, lights on, about just south of the compound driveway."

With the snow blowing, the distant car was nearly invisible, except for the bluish glow from the halogen headlights on high beam.

"Negative, Peg. Frank arrived at my house at 3:00 and didn't see any vehicle. When we left for the station at 3:45, neither of us saw anyone parked. What's up?"

"Maybe nothing. Probably a drunk sleeping it off a little before hitting Canadian Customs in Highwater."

"Peg, you want Frank to meet you there?"

"No, if he starts to roll, he'll be heading towards you. I'll let you know what I find. McCarthy out." Peg muttered to herself. "Just what I need. Hopefully, this will be an easy, meaningless situation."

After pulling behind the vehicle, she printed the following on a yellow-lined legal pad in typical Peg McCarthy Customs Agent formality:

Yellow Pad Entry: #1 1-26-2003 4:24 p.m.
Range Rover: year? newer. Color: Black. Lights on. Vehicle running (vapor from exhaust pipe). License Tag # Louisiana K20K.Right front wheel is in the shoulder gully and front wheels are turned sharp right.

Hoping to obtain a response from the occupant, Peg keyed the microphone for the outside speaker. "This is the U.S. Customs Service. Do you need assistance? Repeat: this is the Customs Service. Are you having problems?"

Through the falling snow Peg could see approaching lights. She could only wonder. "For crying out loud, here comes another vehicle. This one is heading south. Is everyone out for a Sunday drive in the snow? Oh, it's Sheriff Ames, following proper police procedure."

With Ames in front of the Range Rover and Peg behind, the scene was starting to resemble the start of the Fourth of July Parade in Newport. With lights flashing, both Ames and McCarthy exited their vehicles and walked toward the big black SUV. Wiping away the snow from the left front-door window revealed a driver slumped over the wheel. Tapping on the window with his flashlight, Ames received no response. Cleaning the snow from the right-side window elicited an immediate response from the right-side occupant. He or she was obviously anxious to see someone—anyone. Cowering and shaking on the floor was one distressed canine.

"Frank, we got a dog on this side, Seems timid. It would probably try to climb into the glove box if it were open."

Frank, knowing Peg's love of animals, retorted, "Be careful. That's all I need is a dog report."

As Peg opened the right door slightly, the dog catapulted past her left ear at Mach 1. Paw prints in the snow might help, yet the dog might be gone forever (perhaps longer). Twenty-five feet of paw prints led to one sorry dog in the process of manufacturing yellow snow. Bodily functions indicated a male. He seemed nervous but nevertheless glad to see Peg. Fortunately, the now-relieved pooch had a collar and long leash. With Peg grabbing the leash, the two of them headed back toward the highway.

"Frank, I got him. Just needed to pee. The dog, not me."

"That's good, Peg. You got the dog but we got problems; the driver doesn't respond. Pulse is very weak and his breathing is shallow. He's got a bump on his forehead where he must have hit the steering wheel." Ames keyed his portable radio. "Sheriff Ames to Newport Fire. Come in."

"Newport Fire. Go ahead, Frank. Dominic Van Order here."

"Hi, Dom. Agent McCarthy, director of North Troy Customs Station, is here with me on Route 243, about a half-mile south of the border. We have a male, about thirty-five years old, unconscious, sitting in running vehicle northbound. We can't seem to rouse him. Weak pulse; shallow respiration. Looks like he went off the road and bumped his head."

"Okay, Frank, we'll head up your way. ETA eight to ten minutes. Van Order out."

As Peg surveyed the accident scene her initial thoughts were, *That's just what I need. Two and a half weeks to retirement and I have an incident and a dog on my hands.*

Technically, a vehicle incident such as this would be under the jurisdiction of the local law enforcement agency. In this case, that would be the Orleans County Sheriff's Department but since 9/11 and the advent of the Department of Homeland Security, any unusual activity or event at or near the U.S. border invited the interest of the U.S. Customs Service and/or the U.S. Border Protection Agency.

"What do you think Frank? Anything look suspicious? Maybe he fell asleep at the wheel and bumped his head when he went off the edge of the road."

Ames walked around the Range Rover and noted damage to the right front fender and bumper. Not serious damage, but pieces of the amber parking-light lens on the ground, protected from the falling snow by the overhanging, slightly bent bumper, indicated fresh damage.

Now dark, the snow flurries had gathered to about two inches, with the wind at 15–20 mph. A meeting outside the vehicles was not a place to discuss proper police protocols. Frank, Peg, and the dog all headed for the warm and toasty confines of the Orleans County Sheriff's Department sedan, with its heated front seats and wire partition between the front and the rear. Safely protected from the humans, the dog quickly rolled into a ball and fell asleep on the rear seat.

"Nothing looks strange inside the car. I turned the ignition off in case it's carbon monoxide. Newport Fire & Rescue should be here before he gets too cold. Who knows? Maybe Orleans County Hospital can jump start him," said Frank as he adjusted the frequency knob of the cruiser radio.

Flashing lights coming from the south announced the arrival of EMT Van Order and the ambulance known locally as the "Meat Wagon."

Chapter 3

Mishap on Route 243?

T he border that divides the United States and Canada has about 140
stations that monitor the vehicular traffic between the two
countries. Stations at major crossings are large, with many agents.
Some are dual complexes with staffs of each nation monitoring traffic
from both directions. They are constructed on either side of the border
and may or may not be at the actual line of demarcation. Some are as
many as five miles away from the actual boundary.

Most days at the North Troy Customs checkpoint are quiet. At this
time of winter—cold and quiet. The North Troy location is officially
known as U.S. Customs Station 72W and is located on an extension of
Quebec Route 243, which connects to Vermont County Highway 105,
seven miles south in beautiful downtown North Troy. "NotRoy," as the
natives pronounce it, is a typical hamlet of God's Northeast Kingdom.
No McDonald's, no pizza shop, no stoplights—just Bud's Bait &
Barber Shop and Eric Burgess's Merit Gas Station (two pumps: diesel
and regular). Only southbound vehicles must stop for a customs check.
Northbound into Canada, vehicles are checked three miles up the road
at Highwater. Between here and Highwater (also known as between
hell and Highwater) there are no roads, paths, or turnoffs. All who pass
the NotRoy Station, headed north, are checked at Canadian Customs in
Highwater. The only contact between U.S. and Canada personnel is
usually via radio.

Peg McCarthy had twenty-two years' experience with the Customs
Service and had been the North Troy station director since her transfer
here three years ago. Twenty-two years of Customs Service, together
with three years seven months in the Peace Corps, and two years as a
public school teacher made Peg's early retirement date February 12,
just two and a half weeks away. Compared to past duty stations (two
nonconsecutive tours of three years each at Mirabel Airport–Montreal,
seven years at JFK in New York, and five at Dulles Airport–
Washington), North Troy could only charitably be described as the
boondocks. Peg compared the boredom of North Troy with that of
living in a small town when she taught French in the mid-'70s. Ah, that

was the key: without the background as an educator of French, Peg might have served in more exciting locations such as Hawaii, California, or Miami. Looking back, Spanish language expertise might have been a brighter idea or at least offered warmer choices of employment.

Seven agents shared the staffing situation, rotating eight-hour shifts. North Troy Customs Station was always open for business. The only closures occurred during heavy snowfall and white-out conditions. Two customs personnel were on duty during the day, from 8:00 a.m. to 4:00 p.m.; while one agent staffed the office from 4:00 p.m. to midnight. The graveyard shift, from midnight to 8:00 a.m., also had one person (usually Ed Hawley) at the helm of this desolate U.S. Customs Agency garrison in the woods.

Just a quarter mile south of the checkpoint was a reverse fork that looks like a road but was actually a driveway to the living quarters compound of the seven agents and their families. Last month several smugglers, to their dismay, used this road (driveway) to avoid Customs, only to wind up in a very small place with a very large trailer truck filled with stolen auto parts headed to Cuba by way of Canada. What action!

The compound had seven modular manufactured homes. All were double-wide units with about 1800 square feet each. There was plenty of room, with too much cleaning for Peg, who was unmarried. But very crowded, even with two baths, for Agent William Atwood, wife Amy, and their four girls. The homes were equally spaced around a circular drive. The center oval had playground equipment and, in summer time, a vegetable patch. This area of cultivation, complete with unusual herbs and flowers was the domain of Agent Atwood, who had deservedly earned the title of "Farmer Bill."

Heading south, the departing ambulance and its flashing red strobe lights quickly faded into the falling snowflakes. Peg scanned the scene once again, observing the SUV with Louisiana tags, the dog, and the unconscious driver now heading to Orleans County Hospital in Newport.

"So, what do you make of it, Frank? Drugs? Booze? Heart? Damage to the vehicle doesn't seem to be that severe. What the heck are we going to do with the dog?"

Frank completed his notes and replied, "We'll have to wait and see what the hospital report looks like. Looks like he just ran off the road, hit the embankment, and struck his head on the steering wheel. I didn't see any bottles or smell any alcohol." Ames keyed his microphone. "Sheriff Ames, Orleans County to Vermont State Police Central, come in please."

"Sheriff Ames, State Police here. Dispatcher Brian Gallagher. How can I help you?"

"Ames here. I need an out-of-state vehicle tag ID check. Louisiana K20K. That's Kilo … Two … Zero … Kilo."

"Okay, Sheriff Ames. I got that. Louisiana K20K. I hope Louisiana is in the national registration data base. The Feds are still missing a few states."

The snow was still falling, and this spot was so isolated there hadn't been another vehicle, other than the Meat Wagon, traveling in either direction since Sheriff Ames and Peg arrived. It was weird how this guy from Louisiana would have wound up here. Really weird.

"Ames, state police here. Okay, on Louisiana K20K. Registered to a William LaChance. Louisiana driver's license: number 234716844. Address: Rural Route 300, Delacroix, Louisiana. 2002 Range Rover. VIN # SALPM16472AF881093. Color: Black. Eight cylinders. Automatic Transmission. Do you want me to fax a copy of this report to your office?"

"Good idea on the fax. Thanks for the info, Gallagher. Ames out."

Both Ames and McCarthy wrote the details of the Vermont State Police radio transmission into their respective notepads. The dog ignored their actions.

"This guy's a long way from home, Peg. I wonder where he's heading."

Yellow Pad Entry: #2 1-26-2003 7:15 p.m.
Range Rover: Louisiana Tag K20K moved to vacant bay in the Customs Station garage. Dog to remain in custody of Agent P. McCarthy. Vehicle secured inside garage, locked, and keys locked in the office safe.

Chapter 4

Peg McCarthy

Peg McCarthy's fiftieth birthday was coming up in March. She was first-generation American, her parents being off the boat from Ireland. She looked stereotypically Irish Catholic—red hair, freckles, fair skin. Peg, a slave to practicalities, kept her fire red hair cut short in a bob, didn't wear makeup, and her wardrobe consisted mainly of khakis, jeans, turtlenecks, T-shirts, and sweaters. Her wardrobe did not do justice to her thin yet curvaceous figure. Had she dressed the part, she would have been a definite "hottie," even for a soon-to-be fifty-year-old. She owned two dresses, one black—for winter and funerals—and one beige; both with short sleeves and blazer to make them year-round outfits. Peg didn't see herself as the "typical" female. She was still single. She dated more in her previous jobs at JFK, Dulles, and Mirabel, but not much in North Troy. *Slim pickings here*, she often thought to herself. She had one serious relationship during her time at JFK, but that left her a bit gun shy. She was not into romance novels; she felt they gave people unrealistic expectations of love and relationships. Peg didn't cry at weddings, and she didn't cry at funerals—until about two years ago when her friend's eighteen-year-old son was killed in a car accident. After that, she seemed to cry at every funeral or wake, whether she knew the person or not. One thing Peg did do was keep a diary. She saw this as a weakness and would never admit it to anyone, especially her male co-workers who saw her as one of the guys. She preferred to call it her journal to make it seem less "femmy."

Peg grew up outside Washington, D.C., in the Maryland suburbs. Her parents still lived in the same house as they did when she was born. The neighborhood had gotten older and was starting its rejuvenation. The older, original owners of these post-WWII homes were starting to either pass away or move into less demanding living arrangements. Younger, energetic couples and families were moving in and doing the renovations and maintenance that were desperately needed to restore character and class to these homes. Peg visited her childhood home about every two months to check in on her parents, who were approaching their mid-seventies, and to do odds and ends around the house and yard. They were from a generation where people married young and had their children in their early twenties. Peg was the oldest of three girls. Her sisters had chosen the more traditional paths of marriage, families, and part-time jobs that didn't interfere with the taxiing of kids to all the various after-school activities. Peg didn't see her sisters very often but talked to them and her nieces and nephews frequently. Her lifestyle hadn't really promoted a lot of bonding time (the Peace Corps, moving every few years, single, no family), but she went out of her way to build a relationship with her nieces and nephews. Peg periodically pondered the very different path she has chosen and was honestly and completely without regret or envy. She would have liked to have found a partner to share holidays and vacations with, and just to snuggle on the couch with and watch a movie, but she had no desire at all to be tied down. She had no qualms with admitting that; in some ways, she was somewhat selfish. After all, the snuggling on the couch thing, up until a few months ago, she could do with her loyal and longtime friend, Fritz, her golden retriever, who'd passed away four months ago. That only left vacations and holidays, and vacations were rare for Peg. Holidays came every year, whether you wanted them or not.

Peg sat on the couch under a thick afghan with her journal and pen in hand. She always read her last few entries prior to writing, in case there were any issues to update.

Journal Entry
Friday, January 24, 2003
I'm off today. Have to work the weekend. Cold, cloudy. Looks like snow, but none is forecasted. Talked to Mom today; went through the normal routine of defending my status of single, approaching-middle-age female. You know what they say—it's easier to be killed in a plane crash than it is to get married over the age of forty. That statistic is *not* true! Why my mother believes some statistic from a 1993 Meg Ryan movie I'll never know! She just pisses me off sometimes with that crap! I haven't been down to see Mom and Dad since Christmas, and they're asking when I'm coming to visit. They want to know what I want to do to celebrate my quickly approaching retirement. To be honest, I haven't even thought about it. I'm not sure why; I'm definitely looking forward to retiring. After all, it is my choice. I've applied for a consulting job back in D.C. that I haven't heard anything from yet. I'm pretty sure I'm a shoe-in; overqualified, if anything. Will

definitely be nice to get back to civilization. We shall see what happens. Well, I have to go run errands. No food in the house. Will get pretty hungry if it really snows! Until next time.

Saturday January 25, 2003
    Worked today. Nothing exciting, as usual. Almost a record though—fifteen cars! Bill and Frank have their annual Super Bowl bets and rivalries going on. I don't even know who's playing! Oh, well, come Monday, one will be $100 poorer and one will be $100 cockier. I talked to Kate and Rich and the kids today. I love being Aunt Peg! The kids still get excited to talk to me, even though they are getting to that pre-teen stage where everything is "fine." I can actually get more than one word answers to my questions! I haven't talked to Mary and Patrick in a while; need to call them and check in. Kate, of course, is also asking me about my retirement party. I think it will be a significant gathering, regardless of what I want. Family alone is eleven people, plus Bill and his family, Frank, etc. Too much to think about, but looking at about thirty people or so. Need to call the motel in town and reserve rooms. I guess I need to start working on this and pick a date if it's going to happen. Still didn't get anything in the mail today about that job in D.C. Not sure if they're going to call or mail something. Well, I'll call on Monday if I don't hear anything.

    As the half-moon crossed the cold winter sky, darting in and out of the condensing mountain clouds, Peg was in a deep sleep with her journal open and pen in hand. She slowly awakened to a barking dog belonging to one of the neighbors and decided to turn in for the night. She resigned herself to the idea that her journal would have to wait, slowly dragged herself from the couch, and retreated to the bedroom. The only sound was the snoring of the dog that was found in LaChance's SUV. Peg found the sound reassuring rather than annoying. It was less lonesome with a dog. She thought of poor old Fritz.
    Looking out the window Peg noticed a few snow flurries. As Peg watched the flakes slowly falling, she drifted to an earlier, less complicated time of her career when she worked at Kennedy Airport and lived in nearby Rockaway Beach.
    Peg was working at JFK in Customs. She was young, only twenty-six and her career was only three years old. She drew the swing shift that night. It was quiet, as usual, with only two or three flights arriving. She was on duty with an old friend, Jim, whom she had

known from Customs training. They spent many hours discussing the state of the union, the state of society, the state of their personal affairs, and just about the state of almost anything. On this particular night, they were discussing the state of Peg's personal affairs. Peg was dating this guy, Kevin, whom Jim very much disapproved of. Everyone Peg dated wasn't good enough, according to Jim. What Jim could not admit to himself, and certainly not to Peg, was that no one was good enough for Peg, except him. He had known Peg for over three years and admired her strong will and determination. These same qualities made her believe she didn't need anyone else. Kevin was there just for the company and the dinner conversation. The thing with Kevin that confused Peg was his apparent indifference towards her. In her previous relationships, she always had the upper hand. She always called the shots, and the other guys always seemed to follow with their tails wagging and tongues drooling. Kevin was different, and this confused Peg. Jim didn't understand why this concerned Peg because she obviously was not interested in keeping Kevin around for an extended period of time. The conversation came to a sudden halt as they heard the announcement of the arrival of the third flight of the night. Jim reluctantly took his post with an unsettled feeling deep in his heart.

Peg finished her shift and drove home to her apartment in Queens. She checked her machine: no messages from Kevin, as expected. Why did she jump when he said "jump"? Especially since he didn't seem to care one way or the other. Intellectually, Peg could identify the nonchalant, hard-to-get game Kevin seemed to be playing, but she couldn't seem to step away. Why couldn't she just call a spade a spade and let go? As she climbed into bed, the phone rang. She jumped up and answered with a hesitant "hello."

"Hi. It's Jim. Sorry to bother you at home." He always apologized whenever he called, which was cute but also annoying.

"It's okay. What's up?"

"Nothing, I … just wanted to make sure you made it home okay."

"Yep, just got home around ten minutes ago. Pretty beat; going to bed now."

"Oh, okay. Well, um. I … um …"

"Are you okay? What's wrong?" Peg asked, a little confused.

"I just wanted to say, don't worry about Kevin. There are better fish in the sea. If Kevin doesn't see how wonderful you are, then forget him."

With her eyes welling up, Peg simply said, "Thank you. Good night, Jim."

Jim spent the next six months in complete awe of Peg but never mustered up the courage to act on his feelings. Peg and Jim continued their late-night talks (at work or by phone on their days off) and continued to debate the state of affairs.

The snow started with a vengeance midway through their shift on this Christmas night. The airport was closed, but Jim and Peg couldn't leave until their replacements arrived. Based on the traffic reports, that could be a while. The drive home would be a bear, even if they were allowed to leave. Jim went to fetch some hot coffee. He returned with two large, black javas, which they sipped in silence. Silence was uncommon between the two. They always had something to talk about. Jim was deep in his own personal debate regarding what to do with these feelings toward his friend and soul mate. He looked up into her eyes and simply said, "Peg, I think I'm in love with you."

The look in her eyes was not that of shock or unknowing but one of sorrow. As the tears rolled down her cheeks, she hugged her dear friend with all her might. It was the answer he feared most. For now, he knew she would do what she needed to do. At the end of January, Peg transferred back to Montreal.

Chapter 5

Monday Morning
Minus-5 Degrees

L eaving the bathroom, wrapped in a large green towel, Peg was greeted by the blinking red light of her answering machine.

"Peg, Frank here. It's 6:45 a.m. LaChance didn't make it. The hospital worked on him for an hour or more with no luck. How's the dog? I have an appointment at the courthouse at ten and will see you at the Customs Station sometime after eleven. We need to look over the Range Rover and inventory the contents. Hey, dress warm. It's five-below out. See you later."

Peg looked over at the old blue blanket to check on her new canine friend and thought, *Doesn't look like he moved all night; I hope he's not dead, too.* This was soon disproved as he slowly roused himself from his slumber, led Peg to the door, and effectively communicated his needs. The short walk from the porch to the garage proved Frank's point about *cold*. With four inches of fresh snow, the sound produced by walking was a unique crunching that only exaggerated the extreme temperature. Peg noticed how quickly the dog took care of his morning business and considered the Louisiana tags on the Range Rover. *He's a warm-weather dog*, she thought to herself. *He obviously loves to ride*, Peg thought as she watched him eagerly jump into the back seat of the Jeep for the short drive to the Customs Office.

Ed Hawley, dubbed the "Night Owl," enjoyed the night as the graveyard shift master of the Customs Station at North Troy.

"Mornin', Peg ... Mornin', Peg" blared out of the outside speaker. The silence of a dark, 7:20 a.m., -5° Monday morning was shattered. Even the dog jumped at Hawley's verbal intrusion.

Peg entered the inner office after wiping the snow off of her boots. "Hi, Ed. How many last night?"

"One and a half. Hey, where'd you get the mutt? Come here, buddy. Want a biscuit?"

Ed often ran sentences and questions into a long stream of conversation which, at times, often seemed to be one-sided banter.

Everyone agreed that being on duty alone all night for nearly three years would do that to you.

"Ed, how did you get 1½ vehicles last night? The dog was in that Range Rover that's in the garage. I'm going to inventory it this morning. Did you make coffee?" Giving Ed some of his own dialect was often fun.

"Coffee's fresh, Peg. What's the story with the Range Rover? You going to keep the dog? What's his name? I had a furniture truck at 1:15 and a doctor doing an emergency house call in Bolton Center at 3:30. He should have gone left in South Bolton. Instead he went right and continued on until he got here. They must have doctors in Canada that still do house calls. We should remember that in case anyone gets sick around here. You know what I mean?"

"The Range Rover was a stone's throw from our compound driveway when I was on my way home after 4:00 yesterday. The driver was slumped over the steering wheel. Frank and I investigated. Newport F&R took the driver to Orleans County, but they couldn't revive him. According to the papers and registration the vehicle is owned by a William LaChance from Louisiana. I'm guessing that was him driving."

Ed and the dog were now chasing each other around the office, and Ed had a dog biscuit in his mouth. Ed tossed the biscuit to the smiling pooch. "So, Peg, what's your new dog's name?"

Peg had to laugh while she watched this dancing duo do Ed's biscuit ballet. "His name is Sarek."

"I didn't know you were a Trekkie, Peg." Ed reached for another biscuit. "You know what I mean. From Star Trek. He was Spock's father."

Not being a Star Trek fan Peg explained, "I had no idea! His name's on his collar along with a phone number and a Massachusetts license number."

"Hey, Peg, the guy in the Rover, it wasn't No Chance LaChance? The baseball pitcher for the Mets? Well, he was with the New York Mets. All the papers said he was going to the Red Sox. But now he's going to Canada".

Peg was not a baseball fan. However, she had heard of Bill LaChance. Most everyone had heard of LaChance. Mean to kids, lousy to fans, antagonistic to the press, and above all *Mr. Money*; at least, that's what's reported. All of these attributes gave Mr. William No Chance LaChance the less than flattering nickname, Dollar Bill.

As Ed stepped into his insulated green winter jumpsuit, he bid good-bye to Peg with one of his annoying departures. "I'll see you later, Peg. Time for the Night Owl to get some sleep. There are more dog biscuits in the right third drawer down, in my desk. Let me know if that's LaChance's car. I'll come back and take some photos."

Peg inquired, "Photos? Why Photos?"

"If it is LaChance, the press will be hounding us for pictures. We can make a few bucks. You know what I mean? Maybe even sell them on eBay." Ed was still muttering even after the outside storm door closed behind him.

EBay! *Weird*, thought Peg. Although getting pictures of the exterior and interior of the Range Rover prior to the inventory was a prudent idea. If this was No Chance LaChance, all aspects of this incident should be documented. Also, get a couple of shots of the now sleeping dog.

Chapter 6

The K-9

Yellow Pad Entry-- #3 1-27-2003 8:30 a.m.
The Dog—Approximately sixty-five pounds. Black. Male. Has a license #87 from Norton, Mass. Additionally, there is a rabies tag from the Ashodod Animal Hospital in Easton, Mass., dated 12-2000 & a blue metal tag stating: "My Name is SAREK; if Found Call: (857) 737-2020." All tags are on a hunter green LAND ROVER dog collar.

After receiving no answer and getting a number in Norton, Massachusetts, for the Norton Emergency Headquarters from information, Peg dialed once more.

"Hello, Norton Emergency Headquarters. Dispatcher Kelly Jennings speaking. This conversation is being recorded. How can I help you?"

"Hi there, this is United States Customs Office in North Troy, Vermont. Agent Peg McCarthy speaking. We had an incident near the U.S./Canada border late yesterday afternoon, where a vehicle left the road and the driver was DOA at the local hospital. The reason I'm calling is that a dog was in the vehicle, and he has a Norton Massachusetts dog license. What local agency could run an ID on the dog tag?"

"Ma'am, the town of Norton has a shared animal control officer with two other communities, and he is at one of the other offices today. The Norton Town Clerk's Office issues dog licenses, and they should have the list of license numbers. Wait a second; I'll look up that number. Okay, here it is: (508) 287-0011. That office should be open in about ten minutes."

"Thank you so much for your help. And your name again?"

"Kelly Jennings. J-E-N-N-I-N-G-S."

"Thanks again. I'll call in a few minutes."

"No problem. Call us back if you need anything else. Have a great day," she said nicely enough, but kind of flat, which made Peg wonder if she really wanted her to have a great day or if she was required to tell everyone to have a great day.

Well, a competent government employee first thing on Monday morning. Maybe this is going to be a good week, thought Peg as she dialed the number of the Town Clerk's Office in Norton.

"Good Morning. Esther Brackett, assistant town clerk, Norton, Massachusetts."

The phone hadn't completed one complete ring before pickup. Peg could imagine that Esther Brackett had been assistant town clerk for over thirty-five years and probably would be for thirty-five more.

"Yes, I was wondering if you could look up a dog if I gave you the license number? My name is—"

"Just give me the number; I don't need anything else but the number," Esther interjected curtly.

"Typical small-town bureaucrat," Peg muttered under her breath as she reached for her yellow notepad. "Yes, the number is 87."

"You did say 87? Well, I'm going to put you on hold. I'm all alone here this morning and I'll have to unlock the files. Give me a moment."

Obviously Esther was beginning to feel the pressure of another strenuous day at the Norton Town Hall. "Hello, Brackett here. Do you have the dog at your location?"

Smiling, Peg replied, "Yes, the dog is with me. I'd like the name and address of the owner."

"I'm sorry, I'll have to put you on hold again." Esther was well into the initial stages of a difficult day. "Hello, Brackett here. That license is expired and the rabies tag is probably out of date as well. If you give me your address, I'll send the animal control officer to pick up the animal. Is the dog acting oddly?"

Rather than being annoyed, Peg decided to play along with this bureaucratic formality. "Okay, my name is Peg McCarthy. That's McCarthy, M-C-C-A-R-T-H-Y. My address is United States Customs Service, North Troy, Vermont. On route 243, about a half-mile from the Canadian border."

"This is Esther Brackett, assistant town clerk of Norton, Massachusetts. Is this some type of joke?"

"No, this is Station Director Peg McCarthy of the U.S. Customs Service. I have a dog that was in a vehicle that had an accident near our Customs Office here in northern Vermont. Could you please give me the name and address of the owner? Thank you."

"I'm awful sorry, Agent McCarthy. I'm all alone in the office this morning. Dog license #87 is issued to a William LaChance, 14 Toad

Island Road, Unit # 149, here in Norton. The listed phone number is (508) 206-3791. That's a new, extravagant townhouse development over near Route I-495 at the Bay Road exit. Mr. LaChance is a fancy baseball player or something. His name is in the papers all the time. But I guess you don't need all that information." Esther quickly realized she had probably given too much information without proper confirmation. "If you send me an e-mail or fax on your official stationary, I'll be glad to fax you this information for your records. Of course, there will be no charge for this inter- governmental exchange."

"Thanks, Mrs. Brackett," although Peg assumed it was Ms. or Miss. "The information will be very useful. I'll fax you an official request. Thank you."

Yellow Pad Entry: #4 1-27-2003 9:14 a.m.
Norton, Massachusetts Emergency Dispatcher K. Jennings referred me to Norton Town Clerk's Office; opens at 9:00 a.m. Assistant Town Clerk Esther Brackett states that Norton Dog License #87 is expired and owner is William LaChance – 14 Toad Island Road – Unit # 149 – Norton, Mass. Phone Number (508) 206-3791. Brackett was hesitant when she realized she released information without proper authorization. Note: Phone numbers on the Norton dog license application and metallic blue nametag on the dog do not match.
Ms. Brackett also states that Mr. LaChance is a baseball player.
Fax to follow.

The fax machine in the corner started its whining warm-up as the official U.S. Customs Service information request was sent to Esther Brackett.

All that could be said of the Night Owl's coffee was that it is always very strong and very hot. This potion, black with no sugar, commanded your attention, especially first thing in the morning.

As Peg surveyed the cold winter landscape outside the wide bay windows of the North Troy Customs Station, the Crown Victoria of Orleans County Sheriff Franklin Ames pulled into the snow-covered parking lot.

The fax machine in the corner hummed once again as the return facsimile from Esther Brackett found its way to North Troy.

Facsimile transmittal Fax Page 1of 2

Town Clerk's Office
374 Main Street
Norton, MA 02766
(508) 287-0011
(508) 287-1818 fax

To:	Agent Peg McCarthy, U.S. Customs Service North Troy, VT 05859	Fax:	(802) 711-3007

From:	Esther Brackett, Assistant Town Clerk Norton, MA 02766	Date:	1/27/03

Re:	Dog License Information	Pages:	2 including cover
CC:	[Click here and type name]		

☐ Urgent	☐For Review	☐Please Comment	☐Please Reply	☐ Please Recycle

Fax Page 2 of 2

In regard to our phone conversation of this morning, included you will find all the information concerning 2001 Town of Norton dog license # 87.

Please note: This license was due for renewal on or before April 20, 2001. If I can be of further assistance, please contact this office via phone or fax.

E.B., Town Clerk's Office, Norton, Massachusetts
TOWN OF NORTON
TOWN CLERK'S OFFICE
NORTON, MASSACHUSETTS
Animal Control Data Base
License # 87
Owner William LaChance
Address 14 Toad Island Road, Unit # 149
Phone (508) 206-3791

Dog Name: Sarek
Age: 3
Breed: Mixed
Color: Black   Gender: M   Spayed or Neutered: yes
Weight: 65   Rabies Vaccine: 12-30-2000

Chapter 7

Cold Nose

A s she read the fax from Norton, Massachusetts, a second time, Peg wondered about the dog. *What the heck am I going to do with this dog? Can I just keep him? I don't think so. Do I try to find the next of kin? He is a sweetheart! And I miss Fritz so much. It would be nice to have him around. I've thought about getting another dog, but puppies are so much work and adult dogs can have such bad, unbreakable habits. This ol' boy is well trained and so affectionate. He's perfect. Well, I'll have to start looking for any of LaChance's relatives.*

Peg looked over at Sarek sleeping on a blanket under Hawley's desk as she found herself day dreaming. She thought about Fritz and their last visit to D.C. They were taking a walk around her parents' neighborhood and stopped to talk to a family who wanted to pet Fritz. The two little girls giggled as they showered Fritz with attention; he gobbled it up and showed his appreciation through wet, sloppy kisses. Peg spoke to the parents of the adorable girls. What impressed her and now nagged at her was the pride in the parents' voices and in their eyes as they spoke about their daughters. "Do I feel the same way about my professional accomplishments as they feel about their daughters? Do I feel that same kind of pride?"

Peg recited to herself select parts of her favorite poem, Robert Frost's "The Road Not Taken."

> *Two roads diverge in a yellow wood,*
> *And sorry I could not travel both...*
>
> *And both that morning equally lay*
> *In leaves no step had trodden black.*
> *Oh, I kept the first for another day!*
> *I doubted if I should ever come back.*

Peg admitted to herself that she had been thinking about Jim lately. She still didn't feel any regret regarding her decisions. She just wondered sometimes. She had no desire for the housewife lifestyles that her sisters had chosen, but was there a happy medium? Maybe it wasn't the relationship road she didn't choose; maybe it was the "Jim" road. Maybe he wasn't the right one; maybe there was someone else out there. Someone Peg could talk to late into the night about anything. Someone to snuggle with under a blanket. Watch a movie. He wouldn't complain about watching some "chick flick" but just enjoy being close. Maybe he was really out there. Peg could do all those things with Jim, but something was missing—or at least she thought something was missing. Peg contemplated all the uncertainties in her life. Her retirement, the possible postponement of her retirement, the dog, this case, her love life (or lack of one).

Oops, Sarek needed to go out. Peg just then realized what that nudging was on her arm, his wet nose asking—no, pleading—for her to let him out.

Chapter 8

$$$$$ Bill

"You have reached (555) 206-3791. Please leave a message." The robotic voice of an answering machine at the number that Esther Brackett provided droned in Peg's ear.

Not getting a response, Peg called the other number, the number that was on the blue tag on the dog's collar, for a second time.

"Hey, Peg, there's a phone or something ringing inside that Range Rover in the garage," Sheriff Ames remarked as he entered the office.

Looking up from her desk, Peg quickly assessed the situation. "Hi, Frank. That must be who I'm calling with this number on the dog tag; LaChance's cell phone inside the car."

"Peg, you ready to inventory LaChance's Range Rover?"

"Okay. You're back early, Frank. It's only 10:30. Short meeting?" Peg reached into the second drawer of the file cabinet and removed a yellow legal pad.

"No, Judge Adams has a touch of the flu so we postponed to another day. Wasn't all that important anyway."

Armed with her yellow legal pad and clipboard, laptop, latex gloves, and the keys to the Range Rover, Frank and Peg entered the cool confines of the North Troy Customs Services garage to check the contents of the big black SUV with the Louisiana tags. As Orleans County sheriff, Frank was in charge of this accident investigation, and the U.S. Customs Service was only assisting.

Peg noted to herself, *I'm not sure why. I just can't give up my old yellow legal pad. I've been using one since my early days at Bard College. So archaic.*

Yellow Pad Entry: #5 1-27-2003 10:38 a.m.

Franklin Ames, Orleans County Sheriff assisted by North Troy U.S. Customs Station Director M. McCarthy inventoried the Range Rover that was involved in the accident near the U.S. Customs Service housing access road on 1-26-03.

Using Customs Form 3499 as a format.

Placing the laptop on the bench along the side wall of the garage, Peg keyed the Custom Service index and entered 3-4-9-9. Although not an official inspection, Form 3499 was often used for inventories. Frank called out the contents as Peg entered the data into the computer via Form 3499.

Customs Form 3499 (102695)(Back)

The estimated average burden associated with this collection of information is six minutes per respondent or record keeper, depending on individual circumstances. Comments concerning the accuracy of this burden estimate and suggestions for reducing this burden should be directed to U.S. Customs Service, Paperwork Management Branch, Washington D.C. 20229. DO NOT send completed form(s) to this office.

CUSTOMS OFFICER'S REPORT

Date: 1-27-2003

MANIPULATION COMPLETED AS REQUESTED: When goods are repacked the customs (warehouse) officer will report hereon the marks and numbers of packages repacked and the marks and numbers of packages and the weights or gauge of same after repacking.

Inventory of 2002 Range Rover

Location & Contents:

Glove box (note: not locked)

Item # 1: Vehicle registration; Item # 2: Owners Manual; Item# 3: Empty bottle of Tylenol; Item # 4: Quantity two – small plastic bottles (similar size to a liquor nip bottle); bottles marked "No Chance" LaChance Hi-Heat Hot Sauce; 1.7 fl. oz. (50ml)

Front Seat

Item # 1: Sealed box of Happy Pup Dog Chews; Pueblo, Colorado; Item # 2: Nokia Model 5165 cell phone – unit turned on; Item # 3: White three-ring binder w/ 'Newspaper Articles' embossed on cover

Back Seat

Item #1: Maroon garment bag, contents four pants various colors, five shirts various colors, one suit – tan, one dress shirt white, three ties, one baseball uniform-style shirt.

Item #2: Zippered leather shaving/travel bag, marked with NY Mets logo. Contents (one each): razor, shaving cream, aftershave, toothbrush and toothpaste, stick deodorant (still in factory-sealed package)

Rear Cargo Area

Item #1: Quantity three, open cartons 12 in. by 9.25 in by 4.25 in

Printed on two sides: 'Pro*Star Sports Cards; Plano, Texas – All boxes contain baseball cards, Pro*Star, #71, William "No Chance" LaChance. Two of the three boxes have cards with a signature on the face side of the card. The third box has unsigned cards plus a box of pens marked 'orange wide stroke.' Total number of cards unknown. Signature on signed cards appears to be "No Chance"

Item #2 -- Quantity two, sealed cartons;10 in. by 14.5 in by 8 in

Marked: "No Chance" LaChance Hi-Heat Hot Sauce; prepared by Cajun Food Specialties; Ponchatoula, LA 70454; 48 1.7fl.oz. (50 ml) bottles; net wt. 8.5 lbs.

Item #3: Quantity four, Sealed cartons, 10 in. by 14.5 in by 8 in – Marked: "No Chance" LaChance Hi-Heat Hot Sauce; prepared by Cajun Food Specialties; Ponchatoula, LA 70454; six 48 fl. oz. (1.36 kg) bottles; net wt. 19.0 lbs.

Item #4: Quantity one, opened carton; sized marked as item above. Contents: four glass bottles of sauce described on box exterior. Appears two bottles missing from carton. Remaining bottles marked: "No Chance" LaChance Hi-Heat Hot Sauce; prepared by Cajun Food Specialties; Ponchatoula, LA 70454; 48 fl. oz. (1.36 kg).

Item #5: Quantity one, opened cardboard carton 12 in. by 9.25 in. by 4.25 in.; Contents: ten cans – Calo Dog Food; Beantown, Maryland

(Customs Officer and Title)

Forty-five minutes in the cold confines of the Customs Station's unheated garage made Ed Hawley's six-hour-old coffee, in its unclean pot, a welcome reprieve.

Chip Randall was the other agent on duty that cold Monday morning. Agent Randall lived in Unit #3 at the compound, a home that he shared with his brother Jim. Jim Randall, a.k.a. the Birdman, was an ornithologist with the University of Maine at Orono. He'd been surveying the owl population in the Orleans County area for the past six months.

"Where's the dog, Chip?"

"He's under Ed's desk, Peg, guarding Hawley's dog biscuits, I suspect. You and Frank had several phone calls while you were in the garage. Frank's info is on your desk. Peg, I sent your call to your voicemail. Anything unusual in the Range Rover?"

Peg rolled her chair from her desk. "Nothing exciting with the Rover. I'm going to look through this binder that was on the front seat to see if I can get any ideas about this LaChance guy. Looks like it is that pitcher for the New York Mets. Wonder what he was doing around these parts."

Picking up his latest copy of *Baseball Weekly*, Chip remarked, "He signed with the Montreal Expos a month or so ago; he probably was heading for Canadian Route 10 into Montreal. He probably wanted to avoid the long customs line on the interstate so he came this way. Frank, your second call was from Muriel, the lady in your office. She says to call her back first."

PHONE MESSAGE
For: Sheriff Frank, date: 1-27-03
From: Dr. Edward Freccero, Orleans County Hospital in Newport time: 10:17 a.m.
Message: Returning your call of earlier this a.m. Will be at 802-343-1010 ext.356 until 1:00 p.m.

PHONE MESSAGE
For: Sheriff Frank, date: 1-27-03
From: Muriel, Orleans County Sheriff's Office, time: 10:19 a.m.
Message: Call office when you're available. Please call office before returning other calls.

"Hi, Muriel, Frank here. What's up?"

"Frank, you've had several calls concerning that accident last night up near the Customs Station. The first was from that new doctor at Orleans County Hospital, Edward Freccero. I told him you were examining the vehicle at the Customs Station. The second call was from a Mr. Buckley Roberts, sports attorney. He said there was a message on his machine this morning asking him to contact the Orleans County Sheriff's Department in Newport, Vermont. He can be reached at—"

"Hold on a second, Muriel. Let me write the number down." Using a blank phone message slip he recorded the information.

PHONE MESSAGE
For:_____, date: 1-27-03
From: Mr. Buckley Roberts, sports attorney time: 10:45 a.m.
Message:Can be called at
617-282-5660.

"Okay, Muriel, got it. Please hold all calls that come in on this situation. Only let official calls reach me. Yes, okay on any local calls. Okay, on Dr. Freccero; he's probably the doc that signed the death certificate and might have more info. I think we will be getting very busy very soon concerning this matter. Thanks. Ames out."

Frank rapidly punched numbers into his new communicator phone.

"Hello. You have reached the non-emergency number for Orleans Country Hospital. If you know your party's three-digit extension number, you may enter it at any time." Ames added 356 and the phone in room 356 started to ring with two sharp buzzes. On the second set, "Hello. Ed Freccero here."

"Doctor Ed, Sheriff Ames here. What's cooking?"

"Good morning, Sheriff. I was the attending physician on the accident victim that was transported in last night. I was called when the ambulance was on its way. He was DOA, but we spent an hour trying to restart his heart."

"Understand that, Doc. Any clues to the actual cause of death?"

"Well, Sheriff, I was calling you to ask the same question. Unusual for someone that young, with what appeared to be relatively minor injuries, to succumb to the result of an accident. We'll know more after the autopsy, but the medical examiner won't be here until tomorrow morning. I'm going to assist him; this will be my first official autopsy. I understand they are calling in some hot shot from Boston as well. Should be interesting. How did the vehicle look? Did the airbag strike him, without a seatbelt?"

"Nothing like that, Doc. No airbag deployment. The vehicle is drivable. Agent McCarthy was the one who spotted the SUV along the side of Route 243, and we moved it to the Customs Service garage to get it out of last night's snow. McCarthy and I just inventoried the vehicle. Did you find any information in LaChance's personal effects?"

"Not much, Sheriff. Just the usual stuff: wallet, credit cards, and a small amount of cash. He did have an accident notification card in his wallet. You know, the one that comes with a new wallet and nobody bothers to fill out. LaChance's card was filled out. I called the number of the person listed to call in case of an emergency. No answer. A Buckley Roberts with a 617 number. That's Boston area, I think. I left a message to call your office, Sheriff. I might be more difficult to reach."

"That's good, Doc. Buckley Roberts called my office about a half an hour ago. He's next on my to-call list. Let me know what you find with the autopsy. Talk to you soon. Ames out."

Rather amusing, Peg thought to herself. *Every conversation that Sheriff Ames has, it's as if he's still using an old police radio—Ames out.*

Ames has been at this job for the past twenty-five years and didn't like to talk retirement.

617-282-5660. "Hello, you have reached the law offices of Maye & Associates. If you know your party's extension, please enter it at any time, followed by the # sign. To forward your call to Monique Maye, please enter 23 followed by the # sign. To forward your call to Buckley Roberts, please enter 54 followed by the # sign. All other calls, please remain on the line while you are transferred to the receptionist. Thank you."

54 # … "Good morning. Mr. Roberts' office. Susan Mason speaking."

"Yes, this is Sheriff Franklin Ames of Orleans County in upstate Vermont. I'm returning Mr. Roberts' call to my office earlier this morning."

"Yes, Sheriff Ames, Mr. Roberts will be right with you."

"Hello, Sheriff Ames, Buck Roberts here. How may I help you?"

"Well, Mr. Roberts, we had a vehicle accident here in North Troy, Vermont, late yesterday afternoon. The driver had an emergency notification card in his wallet and you were listed as the person to be notified. Dr. Edward Freccero, from Orleans County Hospital, called you last evening. When he didn't receive an answer, he left a message for you to call me."

"Sheriff, I'm intrigued. Who would have me listed on an emergency card?"

"Well, Mr. Roberts, the paperwork in the vehicle and in the driver's wallet indicate the person involved is one Mr. William LaChance."

"Bill LaChance? Is he okay? What exactly happened, Sheriff?" Mr. Roberts' voice suddenly changed, and he came down from his legal pedestal and became a concerned counselor.

"Well, Mr. Roberts, I'm sorry to report that Mr. LaChance was taken from the accident scene to Orleans County Hospital, where he died shortly after arrival. Details of the incident are under investigation, and an autopsy will be conducted tomorrow morning. Do you know who the next of kin might be?"

Silence. "Sheriff, we can handle all the particulars concerning the next of kin, transportation of the body, as soon as you let us know when it is released. I must say I'm shocked. Mr. LaChance has been a client of this firm since he was drafted by the Astros in 1986. Any other parties involved in the accident, Sheriff?"

"It wasn't much of an accident. Only minor damage to Mr. LaChance's Range Rover. The vehicle is drivable; his dog was in the car and was unhurt. The SUV and the dog are at the North Troy Customs Office, which is about a quarter of a mile from where the vehicle was noticed by the U.S. Customs Service yesterday afternoon."

"Sheriff Ames, as soon as you have more information concerning the autopsy and release of the Mr. LaChance's remains and the vehicle, could you please contact this office and leave the details with my secretary if I'm not available?" Mr. Buckley Roberts had regained his composure and was once again the compulsive attorney who represented some of the leading names in professional sports. "Sheriff Ames, your office will probably become very busy when the news of Mr. LaChance's death is released to the media. Please feel free to direct any questions that don't seem pertinent to your investigation to this office, as we are very well equipped to handle the press. Thank you."

"Affirmative, Mr. Roberts. I will call you with additional info. Ames out." Sheriff Ames smiled as he hung up the phone. "Hey, Peg, interesting that a money-hungry baseball player with a nickname of Dollar Bill would have an agent by the name of Buck Roberts. Almost deserving."

Chapter 9

The Scrapbook

As Peg listened to her voicemail, she jotted down the message:

Yellow Pad Entry: #6 1-27-2003 11:11 a.m.
From Voicemail – Paul DeBillare – Apex International – 888-398-2211
Please call to set up appointment for interview.

888-398-2211 … "Apex International. Bonnie speaking. How may I direct your call?"

"This is Peg McCarthy. That's M-c-C-a-r-t-h-y, returning the call of Mr. DeBillare concerning an appointment for a interview."

"Yes, Ms. McCarthy, Mr. DeBillare was wondering if you could come to our Boston office in the next ten days or so. He will adjust his schedule to meet you there. He and our Boston office director, Mr. David Lindahl, would like to discuss the aspects of your possible employment with Apex."

"Okay, Bonnie, a Boston interview will be all right. I thought a D.C. interview might be arranged."

"Ms. McCarthy, I believe they wanted a Boston interview because the open position with Apex is in our Boston office. I'll check on that for you to be sure."

"No, Bonnie, a Boston interview might be just as convenient. I have a few vacation days that need to be used. Let me iron out the details on travel and get back to you by Thursday the 30th."

"Thanks, Ms. McCarthy. I'll pass the information to Mr. D. Have a good day."

Looking out the window at the empty parking area, Peg hung up the phone. "Damn! I thought the job was going to be in Washington. This will change my whole outlook on working with Apex. Living in D.C. would let me commute from my parents' house with the major advantage of no rent. But could I really live with my parents? I could help take care of them, but I just don't know. On the other hand, living in Boston is ultra-expensive. Just have to wait and see. A Boston interview would be closer, and I could express my desire for

Washington at that time. If this doesn't work out, there should be plenty of other opportunities. Look at my experience and record. I will have to give Boston some serious consideration. It is a very cool city, and I love the metropolitan atmosphere."

The door closing quickly snapped Peg back to the reality of another completed shift as Customs Agent Scott Robertson arrived for his 4:00-to-midnight tour. Because he was the youngest at age twenty-four, Scott, was affectionately called Rookie Robertson.

"Hi, Chip. Hi, Peg. Has it been another busy day here at NotRoy?" With his North Texas accent and wide-brimmed Customs Agent hat, Rookie looked and sounded very much out of place in cold Vermont. "Hey, Peg, you counting days? How many more get-ups? Less than three weeks, Peg. Lucky you. Hey, Chip, got time for a quick game of chess?"

"Okay, Rookie, set 'em up. What's the score? 54 to 3?"

Chip, a quiet gentleman from the Pittsburgh area, had been with the Customs Service for nearly eighteen years. For the last two years, he had been teaching Rookie the rules of chess with limited success.

"No, Chip. It ain't that bad. The tally is 47–5 since we started keeping score. I've won three out of the last twenty-one. I'm getting better."

"I'll see you two later. I've got reading to do." Peg lifted the scrapbook that was on the front seat of LaChance's vehicle. "Going to see what I can learn about baseball. Let's go, Sarek, almost time for supper."

Sitting on the couch after supper with Sarek at her feet, Peg opened the white three-ringed binder titled "Newspaper Articles," and entered No Chance LaChance's world of baseball.

SPORTING NEWS
Sept. 30, 2002

In his final pitching start of the 2002 baseball season, and perhaps his last appearance as a New York Met, Bill "No Chance" LaChance picked up his twenty-third win against five losses, in a 5–1, fourteen-strikeout performance versus the Chicago Cubs. LaChance pitched the ninth inning to notch his sixteenth complete game of the season and continues to be the leading candidate for another Cy Young Award. Despite a standing ovation, LaChance stoically marched off the mound without acknowledging the enthusiastic crowd.

The Norton Weekly Mariner
October 6, 2002
Students of Nourse Elementary School Have Special Guest Speake

A simple writing assignment in the fifth-grade class of Ms. Karen Lewinnek last March turned into an exciting event last Friday when the school received a visit from renowned baseball player Mr. William LaChance. Ms. Lewinnek asked her students to write a letter to anyone of their choosing with the question: What is your favorite genre of reading? The replies included many different types of writing: historical novels, mystery, science fiction, the Bible, biographies, and romance novels.

Kenny Nichols, a student in Ms. Lewinnek's cluster and an avid baseball fan, wrote to Mr. LaChance. Mr. LaChance, called "No Chance" because of his pitching talents with the New York Mets, replied to Kenny's letter that one of his favorite styles of reading is poetry. He also stated that he might try to visit the school after the baseball season.

LaChance and his faithful canine companion, Sarek, visited Nourse Elementary on October 4. He presented several poetry books to the school library and then LaChance recited his rendition of "Mighty Casey."

With a battered, three-fingered baseball glove on his left hand and wearing an old-style baseball cap with a large "M" on the peak, Bill "No Chance" LaChance concluded his visit to Nourse Elementary with these words:

"Somewhere, the sun shines. Somewhere, a band plays.
Somewhere, people laugh, and children shout.
But not in Mudville. There's no joy in Mudville.
Mighty Casey has struck out."

The St. Bernard & Plaquemines Weekly Banner
Week of October 27, 2002

A new state-of-the-art X-ray facility for the Delacroix Health Clinic was dedicated on October 28, 2002. In the photo below (left to right) are Plaquemines Parish Commissioner Mr. Leon T. Beauregard and St. Bernard Parish Commissioner Mr. Rudolph (Rudy) P. Weekes, Drs. Michael Fifer and Cary Akins, New York Mets pitcher Mr. William LaChance, and nurses Edna T. Washington, J. D. Hamblin, and Annmarie Gagnon.

The new X-ray equipment will bring much needed health care to the area. Previously, the nearest X-ray machine was at the Bayou Hospital in Violet, La., some twenty-three miles away.

The Boston Post
November 2, 2002
Buckley Roberts, agent and spokesman for ace starting pitcher of the New York Mets, Bill LaChance, announced late yesterday that his client has signed with the Montreal Expos of the National League. LaChance, a free agent, was unavailable for comment. This concludes a stormy eight-year relationship in New York with the Yankees and later the Mets, during which LaChance was the National League Cy Young Award Winner on three occasions, All-Star pitcher each of the eight years, starting three of those years, and MVP during this last year of his contract.

The New York Daily Sports Reporter
November 3, 2002
The whole town is abuzz over last night's audio confrontation between New York radio station WMET baseball announcer Rich Cleary and pitching ace William "No Chance" LaChance, formerly of the New York Mets. Fortunately for all parties, the verbal fisticuffs were by telephone. Cleary's weekly broadcast "Sports Beat" asked LaChance to discuss his departure from New York, but it didn't take Cleary long to shift the topic to outrageous salaries. Credit must be given to LaChance, who did not lose his composure as he explained that people only consider wages greater than their own to be outrageous. To quote LaChance; "Outrageous is in the eye of the beholder."

The St. Bernard & Plaquemines Weekly Banner
Week of Nov. 3, 2002
OPEN HOUSE ON SATURDAY NOV. 9, 2002
The newly opened St. Bernard County Animal Shelter was dedicated on Tuesday (Nov. 5, 2002). The building, which is located on Bayou Road just northeast of Reggio Center, has air-conditioned accommodations for twelve dogs and thirty smaller animals. There is a veterinary examination room and an adoption center. The complex has been officially called Sarek's Spot. It is named after the pet of an anonymous benefactor. The animal shelter will have an open house this

Saturday, Nov. 9, 2002, from 9:00 a.m. to 3:00 p.m. A rabies shot clinic will be available, at no cost, from 1:00 to 3:00 p.m.

The Enterprise
November 11, 2002
Letter to the Editor:

The utter audacity of a professional athlete was demonstrated this past Saturday at the Southeastern All Sports Card Show, which was held at the Taunton Green VFW Hall. Show promoters stated that the autograph fee, for the signature of former New York Mets pitching ace Bill "No Chance" LaChance, was not set by the show organizers. One can quickly deduce that the $75 charge for a photo and $100 fleecing for a signed baseball was dictated by Mr. LaChance and/or his agent.

To force youngsters and their parents to pay up to $100 for the autograph of a future Hall of Fame player is most disturbing. Especially when it is reported that Mr. LaChance just signed with the Montreal Expos for a reported $9.5 million a year for each of the next three years.

Shame on you, Mr. LaChance. Your nickname, Dollar Bill, is well deserved.

Dejectedly yours,
Sebastian Santagati
Marshfield, MA 02050

LaChance had added a hand-written notation to this letter to the editor that stated:

"Copy to B. Roberts. Please notify future personal appearance promoters to indicate all autograph fees are a contribution to the Take a Chance Foundation. Have charitable contribution tax forms printed for future events."

Sarek's loud snoring reminded Peg that it has been a long day and she had the early shift in the morning.

Chapter 10

Tuesday, the 28th

S arek and Peg arrived at work at 7:20 a.m. Chip Randall was already hanging up his heavy green parka as they entered the office. Ed Hawley couldn't contain himself after another long night of solo duty at the Station. "Morning, Peg. How's the dog adjusting? Did you hear any news about LaChance?"

"Good Morning, Ed. Quiet night?"

"Yes, Peg, quiet night, but you've had two phone calls already since 7 a.m. Neither party wanted to leave a message on your voicemail. Some people really hate them, Peg. *Hate.* Hate! You know what I mean?"

"Hate what, Ed?"

Poor Ed was really hyper this morning. *Being alone all those hours at night will do that to you*, Peg guessed.

"Answering machines, Peg. They hate them. Hate them. Too impersonal."

"I know what you mean, Ed." Peg realized she sounded almost patronizing to poor Ed. But Ed didn't seem to notice as he and Sarek were in warp-speed biscuit mode.

"Peg, you going to keep the dog? You can, you know?"

"Ed, I just can't just keep the dog. He belongs to someone; well, actually, he belongs to the estate of someone."

"I'm telling you, Peg, you can adopt Sarek. You found him; you're taking care of him. There's a legal procedure to adopt an animal that is lost or, more likely in Sarek's case, abandoned. After three weeks, you have to put a notice in the newspaper and see if anyone claims him. Meanwhile, keep track of all the expenses, and, if someone wants him shipped back to Louisiana, then, at least, they have to reimburse you for your expenses."

"Good morning, U.S. Customs, North Troy, Vermont. Agent Randall speaking. Yes … okay, I'll transfer you to the director's office. Hold on a second … Peg, phone call on line one. Something about the LaChance incident."

"Station Director McCarthy. Good morning."

Peg was greeted by a pronounced French-Canadian accent. "Good day, Director McCarthy. My name is Jean Paul Bellevue, and I'm Director of Player Personnel for the Montreal Expos. I talked earlier with Sheriff Ames, and he suggested I call you. I was wondering if I might make an appointment to meet with you about the unfortunate death of William LaChance. I understand that you discovered the vehicle and may be able to answer some questions about the details of Mr. LaChance's accident."

As Peg wrote down the particulars of the caller, she asked herself, *Meet with me? What is this about? There was nothing of significance, other than Sarek in the vehicle. What reason, other than the dog, would prompt someone to drive the ninety miles from Montreal to North Troy?*

"Mr. Bellevue, any legal aspects of this accident will have to be through Sheriff Ames and the Orleans County Sheriff's Department. I'll check to see if he's available."

"Please, Ms. McCarthy, call me J.P. I don't want to seem mysterious, but there are some things concerning this matter that I would rather not discuss over the phone. Is tomorrow morning too soon?"

"I can meet you here at the Customs Station."

"What would be the best time for you?"

"Well, Mr. Bellevue, the earlier the better. Is 8:00 a.m. too early?"

"No. No, 8:00 a.m. will be fine. I'll leave St. Laurent at 6:00. How many agents in the office at that time? If you make the coffee, I'll bring some of our famous Montreal croissants and palmiers," offered Bellevue.

"There will be four of us in the office at 8:00. See you tomorrow morning."

Peg thought back to her days at Mirabel Airport. *I haven't had fresh palmiers in nearly fifteen, maybe sixteen years. Wow! Elephant ears! I can smell them cooking at that little bakery on the way home from work. Has it been that long? I haven't seen Jim in almost ten years.*

Peg should have told Bellevue to bring a couple dozen—one dozen alone for Ed and Sarek.

Peg turned to the Night Owl, Ed Hawley. "Well, Ed, looks like someone is coming down from Montreal tomorrow morning to discuss the dog issue."

"Peg, did you tell them they owe you for care and maintenance of the dog? Give them a bill for taking care of the dog. Give them a bill. You know what I mean?"

Sarek was sleeping under Ed's desk, and Ed was crossing the parking lot toward his car, still muttering, "Give them a bill. Give them a bill, Peg."

"Good morning. U.S. Customs, North Troy, Vermont. Agent Randall speaking. Yes. Okay, I'll transfer you to the director of this office. Hold on a second. ... Peg, phone call on line one. Something about the LaChance incident. Am I repeating myself?"

"Station Director McCarthy here. Good morning."

"Hi, Agent McCarthy. Dr. Stu Mirkin here at the hospital. I just talked with Sheriff Ames, and he suggested I call you."

With a smile, Peg wouldn't let Dr. Mirkin's last statement pass. "Lately, Sheriff Ames suggests everyone call me. How can I help you, Dr. Mirkin?"

"I've been called in from Boston to work on the LaChance case. We just finished the autopsy on LaChance. After lunch, the local medical examiner, Dr. Martin; the state of Vermont's chief of pathology, Dr. Edwards; and I would like to come by to look at LaChance's car. Ames is meeting us for lunch at the East Side Restaurant in Newport. Can you join us?"

"Sorry, Dr. Mirkin, I'm here until 4:00 p.m. I'll be here when you arrive. What time approximately?"

"We are meeting Ames at 12:30. Should arrive at the Customs Station no later than 2 p.m. See you then."

Peg felt as if she knew this doctor. Interesting phone call.

Chapter 11

A. Coronet Edwards

At 1:58 p.m., as Peg looked out the bay window of the station, the dingy Crown Victoria of Sheriff Ames pulled into the parking area. Close behind was a dark green Chevrolet Suburban with official Vermont state license tags and the Seal of the State of Vermont on the side, with bold letters announcing "State Medical Examiner's Office." The ultra-dark tinting to all windows, except the front windshield, gave ample warning as to the designated use of this vehicle; namely, the transportation of the recently (more often than not traumatically) deceased.

Sheriff Ames, usually jovial, was all business, especially with the chief of forensic pathology for the state of Vermont in attendance. "Ms. McCarthy, this is Dr. A. Coronet Edwards, the chief of forensic pathology, State Medical Examiner's Office. Dr. Edwards, Peg McCarthy, Director of the U.S. Customs Station here at North Troy."

Dr. Edward's appearance fit his name and position: sixtyish, black overcoat, black suit, black tie, white gloves, black cane with a gold knob, black hat and white shirt—the Grim Reaper in person. However, appearances can be deceiving.

"Hi, Peg McCarthy. Just call me "Ace"—the world calls me Ace. I was named after two relatives, Uncle Arthur and Grandfather Coronet. Combine that with my surname Edwards and you can become Artie, Connie, or Eddie. I choose to take the first letter of each and now I'm known—affectionately, I hope—as Ace Edwards." The disarming chief of forensics said this with a wink and a smile.

Sheriff Ames continued. "Ms. McCarthy, this is Dr. Paul Martin, District Medical Examiner. Dr. Martin, Peg McCarthy."

Before Sheriff Ames could finish his introductions, the last of this medical triad stuck out his hand: "Hi there. We talked on the phone. I'm Stu Mirkin."

Reaching inside the already unlocked pull drawer of the office safe, Peg grabbed the Range Rover keys and led Sheriff Ames and his medical entourage toward the cool confines of the garage.

"Here it is. Anyone need latex gloves?"

"Perhaps in a minute, Peg. Did you find anything interesting inside the vehicle, Sheriff?" Doctor Edwards asked while slowly circling the Range Rover. His cane clicked sharply on the shiny painted garage floor. Because of the cold, the fluorescent lights in bay number three pulsated rapidly, giving the entire interior of the garage and the black SUV with the Louisiana plates an eerie glow.

With typical Peg McCarthy efficiency, she said, "Doctors, here is a copy of the inventory that was compiled yesterday. Everything in the vehicle is on the list, except the dog."

Looking at the damage of the right front, the doctors nodded to each other. Dr. Martin sketched a drawing in his folder and indicated the location of the minor dent. Mirkin and Edwards both accepted Peg's offer of latex gloves. Mirkin opened all the doors, front and rear.

Ace removed his black hat, black cane, and white gloves. After several long seconds, he spoke. "Dr. Martin, I need a few sterile evidence bags. There are several items I want to take back to Burlington to be tested. Sheriff Ames, could you take one of the inventory lists and indicate that the following items will be removed from the car?"

As Ace slowly examined the contents of the Range Rover, he announced precisely the item, the location, and its designation. The pathologist picked up each item with a pair of rubber-tipped tongs, which he had pulled from his inside coat pocket.

"Okay let's start with the glove box—one empty Tylenol bottle. Evidence Bag #1 from the glove box—two small plastic bottles marked "No Chance" LaChance Hi-Heat Hot Sauce; 1.75 fl. oz. (50 ml). Evidence Bags #2 and #3 from the back seat—toothbrush and toothpaste from Shaving Kit. Evidence Bags #4 and #5 from rear cargo area—quantity one. Carton, 10 inch by 14.5 inch by 8 inch, marked "No Chance" LaChance Hi-Heat Hot Sauce; Prepared by Cajun Food Specialties, Ponchatoula, LA 70454; six 48 fl. oz. (1.36 kg) bottles; net wt. 19.0 lbs. Contents: four glass bottles of sauce described on box exterior. Appears two bottles missing from carton. Remaining bottles marked: "No Chance" LaChance Hi-Heat Hot Sauce, prepared by Cajun Food Specialties, Ponchatoula, LA 70454; six 48 fl. oz. (1.36 kg). Wrapped with evidence tape and tagged Evidence Item #6. Nokia Model 5165 – cell phone."

As Peg watched Edwards pick up each item with his rubber-tipped tongs, she suddenly realized that she might have compromised some of the evidence by removing and later reading the LaChance scrapbook. She sheepishly admitted this faux pas to Edwards and Mirkin.

Edwards never flinched. He looked up from the gathering collection of evidence bags. "Don't worry about it, Peg. It happens. We'll include the scrapbook in the evidence list. The lab will look through it. You never know what might be found. You mentioned earlier that the dog seems to be in good spirits. I think we can safely conclude, at least for now, that the unopened dog food and biscuits in the vehicle are not contaminated."

Edwards paused for a moment before continuing. "Our official autopsy report won't be complete for several days, but I'll give you our initial findings. Other than two recent tooth extractions, the autopsy of Mr. William LaChance can be best described with one word that is found in many autopsy reports. That word is 'unremarkable.' The three of us conclude that the accident associated with this motor vehicle did not cause the death of Mr. LaChance. All initial results of lab tests are normal with the exception of the preliminary toxicology report. The cause of death seems to be complications caused by an excessive concentration of the drug Oxycontin. This leads us to conclude that the cause of death of Mr. LaChance was either overdose, suicide, or homicide.

"Please keep this information confidential. I'll release the information to the media through my office in Burlington. If there is, and I'm sure there will be, pressure from the press, just direct their queries to the Medical Examiner's Headquarters in Burlington. Has anyone any questions? Any comments?"

"I have a question," Doctor Mirkin said as he snapped off the latex gloves. "How far to Jay Peake? If I'm in northern Vermont during the winter I want to ski for at least half a day."

"It's right off of Route 242, about twelve miles from here. I ski there occasionally myself. You can rent equipment at the lodge. Use the phone on my desk if you want to reserve a room. It's a nice spot," Peg offered.

"Great, can you drop me off, Ace? I'll hitch a ride back to your office in Burlington tomorrow afternoon and catch a flight back to Boston on Thursday. Perhaps by then the lab work will be finished on the stuff from the SUV."

Doctor Mirkin dialed to make his arrangements with the Lodge at Jay Peake. "I'm on hold. Hey, Peg McCarthy, want to join me for skiing tomorrow morning? I'll buy lunch."

"Sorry, I have an early morning appointment with someone from the Montreal Expos. Oh, Frank, I was wondering if you might be around when this guy arrives in the morning. I told him any aspects of the investigation would be handled through your office."

"Okay, Peg, I'll be here at around 8. I talked to Mr. Bellevue, and he wants to talk to me in person as well."

As Dr. Mirkin hung up the phone. "All set. Well, Peg McCarthy, I hate to ski alone. How about after your appointment? You said tomorrow's your day off. It's only twelve miles. What do you say?"

"Okay. Okay. I've only skied twice this season so don't expect Picabo Street. I'll see you at the bottom. I'll wait there at the lift line. See you then."

The three forensic doctors headed south in the Suburban. Peg rued the early January sunset and wondered why she accepted a skiing invitation from an unknown doctor from Boston whom she had just met.

Peg thought, *What the hey? Skiing with the doc could be fun. It's so close and I'm driving up by myself, so I can always leave whenever I want. What's the worst that can happen? He's a jerk, and I leave after a few runs.*

Upon reaching home, Peg entered the storage shed behind the garage and picked her way through all the junk to her good ol' Rossies. It was like a reunion with an old best friend every time she went skiing. They weren't the newfangled-shaped skis, but they were her old faithfuls! She strapped the skis on top of Bertha and went inside to gather the paraphernalia required for tomorrow's outing.

Chapter 12

The Good Doctor

S tuart Alan Mirkin, Jr.
Born: Independence Day, 1953 (49 years old)
Hometown: Sturbridge, Massachusetts.
Parents: Mary Alice Weich and Stuart Alan Mirkin, Sr. (Deceased)
Siblings: None

Stuart, nicknamed "Stu," grew up in a very middle-class neighborhood, the son of a plumber. Being an only child, however, he grew up wanting for very little. As a youth, he played Little League baseball in the spring, Boys Club football in the fall, and basketball in the winter. His athletic prowess resulted in his achieving All-State recognition in baseball and football as a senior at Tantasqua Regional High School. His parents never missed a game and logged many of them for history with a then state-of-the-art 8mm camera. Mr. and Mrs. Stu Mirkin, Sr., spared no expense when it came to Stu, Jr. On the other hand, they were determined not to raise the stereotypical spoiled brat only child. Stu, Jr., started volunteering for church projects when he was nine years old, including food drives, clothes closets, home repairs and landscaping for the needy, inner-city park rejuvenation projects, to name a few. When he was fifteen, he took an advanced first-aid course and volunteered for the Red Cross safety team. He had the distinct privilege of working a first-aid station at the Boston Marathon for four years in a row. Stu attributed his interest in medicine to the service mind-set instilled by volunteering and by his experience with the Red Cross.

After graduating from Tantasqua Regional with a respectable 3.75 GPA, he enrolled as an undergraduate at Northeastern University in Boston. It was here that he decided to become a doctor and, after graduating from Northeastern, moved on to Tufts University Medical School, just north of Boston, in the city of Medford. Stu did his residency at Massachusetts General in pediatrics. He was Boston's very own "Patch Adams." He loved to make the children laugh, using it as the best remedy for what ailed a specific child. But losing a patient was like losing his very own child. He told himself that he would learn to deal with it, but his heart continued to break each time. He had many more successes than failures, but he never could forget the failures. He knew that his attachment for each child made him the doctor he was, but the emotional toll became too much.

While at Northeastern, a cooperative university, there was a provision alternating between working a semester, then going back to school for a semester. With an early major of criminal justice and an idea of joining the Massachusetts State Police, Stu Mirkin had spent his co-op time as an assistant in the Suffolk County Medical Examiner's Office. Needing to make a dramatic career shift, Dr. Mirkin used this previous experience to land a job in forensic medicine. He tried to do volunteer work at the Children's Hospital in Boston when his travel schedule permitted, which wasn't very often. Now, when he lost one of his friends, he did not see it as his own personal inadequacy or failure. He was able to give the children the gift of laughter and help them forget for a while, but he wasn't responsible for healing them medically. He didn't have to watch them take their last breath or face the parents with the dreaded news. He would leave the medical care to the very capable men and women doctors who were better able to deal with it.

In his new field of forensics, he had a very different reputation. For the past ten years, he had built his reputation as the best in the field but also as someone who was impossible to work with. He was arrogant, demanding, and downright rude. He had no regard for bedside manner because, after all, they were dead! But he had disregarded the feelings of the subjects' families and his staff. (He now had subjects, not patients.) When people who knew both Stus asked him about his very different mannerisms, he seemed almost oblivious to what they were talking about. He was like a cross between the absent-minded professor and the mad scientist—almost. He was there to do a job and to do it to perfection, and if the people around him didn't share his same determination and unyielding focus, then they were in the wrong place. He saw nothing wrong with his behavior in his current setting and agreed that he would never treat the children with his forensic mind-set.

Stu had read about the mysterious death of LaChance in the papers and was immediately intrigued. Mirkin tried to piece together the meager details that were in the media. He was in between cases right now, and, after all, he was "the" Dr. Mirkin. So, he decided to call in a favor or two and see what he could find out. When his buddies Edwards and Martin asked him to work on the case, he couldn't hide his excitement! He hopped the first plane out of Boston the next morning.

Chapter 13

Journal Entry
Tuesday, January 28, 2002

Jeez! When it rains, it pours! Retirement, the interview in Boston, the LaChance case, all these people coming to see me, the arrival of the dog! My head is spinning! I wish Frank would stop telling people to call me! I can't get anything done! I have to say, I am intrigued by the visits with the doctors and the bilingual phone conversation with Mr. Bellevue of the Expos. I hope Frank remembers to be around to screen the questions with Bellevue tomorrow morning. After all, this is his case. I like what Ed says about adopting the dog. Do you really think Bellevue is coming about some mutt? What other contents would be of interest in the Range Rover? The info from scrapbook articles is all public knowledge. Nothing particularly impressive there except for the ID of the "anonymous benefactor" of the St. Bernard County Animal Shelter. Hm-m, I wonder how anonymous the donation really was. I'll have to look into that. He sure did like hot sauce, though!

Boy, was Jim floored to hear from me! He's still at JFK but moving up the bureaucratic ladder. He'd read about LaChance in the papers and was shocked to hear that I was the one who'd found him. I think he's a little envious that he's in the big city, and I'm up here in the sticks with a nationally covered case. He sounds exactly the same, almost. The same Jim; just maybe a touch of doubt in his voice that I never detected before. He says we should get together sometime, but I doubt it will ever be arranged. Although, I did invite him to my retirement party, whenever that ends up being. Who knows when that will come to fruition with this case. I have to remember to mention to Apex that I may need to stay until this case gets taken care of—at least, all the immediate stuff.

Chapter 14

Cardmn

While walking across the snow at the compound and wondering if this would be Sarek's last ride to work, Peg called out to the now relieved canine, "Sarek, let's go. Time to go to work—biscuit time. Damn, who the hell is out on this road at 7:15 a.m. and going about 80?"

A grimy Caravan passed Bertha and continued toward Canada as Peg and Sarek signaled left into the Customs Station.

"Ed, did you see that fool heading north? What can be that important?"

"Did you get that bill ready for the dog catcher? Yeah, I saw him. Going to see him again; this looks like the same Caravan pulling into the lot. The jerk must be lost. Get the bill ready, Peg." Ed Hawley was wired again.

Peg jotted down the license number of the incoming Caravan and remarked to Ed, "Rhode Island vanity plate: CARDMN. I hate vanity plates, especially ones that try to spell something with missing letters. I wonder what this is all about."

Sarek was working on getting Ed to release biscuit number two. The door opened, and the driver of CARDMN entered the station. Looking at the stranger in the doorway, the biscuit dance was suddenly over when Sarek retreated to the dark underside of Ed Hawley's desk. Sarek obviously knew the CARDMN, and he wasn't one of Sarek's favorites.

"Yes, sir. Welcome to the United States. Do you have anything to declare?" asked Agent Ed Hawley in his deep official U.S. Customs voice.

Thrown off stride by Ed's welcome, the stranger suddenly appeared nervous. "Oh, I didn't come from Canada. I just went by coming from the south. Didn't you see me?"

"Oh," retorted Ed, "that burgundy blur—was that you?"

"Yes, I'm here about the Bill LaChance accident. I've talked with the Sheriff's Office. They told me his Range Rover is here. My name is Walter Qaqish, that's Q-A-Q-I-S-H. I'm a business associate of Mr. LaChance. I'm here to retrieve some items that belong to me from the car. I have a receipt."

Only the end of Sarek's nose could be seen from under Ed Hawley's desk.

Looking up from her legal pad, Peg asked, "You drove all the way from Rhode Island to pick up some items from Mr. LaChance's vehicle? Must be important."

Qaqish could not hide his anxiety. "Oh, no! Oh, no! I didn't drive up from Rhode Island. Mr. LaChance and I did a card show together in Brattleboro on Sunday. I stayed over and was getting ready to drive home when I heard the terrible news. Terrible … just terrible."

Pulling a folded receipt from a shirt that looked as if it had been slept in, Qaqish added, "If I could just pick up my three cartons I'll be on my way. I have an eight-hour drive ahead. Longer if I run into traffic. That's why I got here so early." Pulling out a handkerchief that was dirtier than the van and had more wrinkles than his shirt, Walter Qaqish blew his nose, *loudly*, and then again.

Sarek's snout disappeared completely as he retreated deeper into the darkness under Ed's desk.

Waiting for the foghorn sound of Qaqish's nose to cease, Peg remarked, "I'm sorry Mr. Qaqish, the vehicle is basically impounded until the conclusion of the investigation of Mr. LaChance's death. Perhaps you should talk to Sheriff Ames about this matter. I'm not sure when or to whom the Range Rover will be released."

As he handed the folded paper to Peg, he pleaded, "But …"—he read her name from her nametag—"Agent McCarthy, I have a receipt."

HUMAROCK SPORTS CARDS
571 North Union Street
Rockland, MA 02370
Date 1-18-2003
Sold to: Walter Qaqish
443 Warren St.
W. Warwick, R.I. 02889
Three cases: assorted baseball cards
2002 Pro * Star #71 Bill "No Chance" LaChance
Approximately 750 per box—2250 total count

Peg offered, "The best I can do is make copies of your receipt. I'll give one copy to the sheriff and put the other in the vehicle with what you say are your items. This may expedite the return of your cards."

Returning the receipt, Peg continued, "I'm sorry, Mr. Qaqish, this is not a U.S. Customs issue. You really need to discuss this matter with Sheriff Ames. Beyond that, I don't have any other information."

"I understand, Agent McCarthy. Where is the sheriff's office located?" Qaqish relented when he saw that he was not going to solve his dilemma through a discussion with Customs Agent McCarthy.

Looking at the clock, Peg offered the fact the Sheriff Ames' office was in downtown Newport, only seven miles southeast.

"Well, I need to get something to eat. Where's the closest place to grab a bite?" Qaqish looked at the clock and blew his nose again.

Ed Hawley wanted Qaqish out of the office. "Just follow this road south five miles, then turn left and go straight into Newport. In fact, the Eatery is right across the street from the sheriff's office. If he's there, his car will be parked out front."

Folded receipt and raunchy snot rag in one hand, Walter Qaqish, in the vehicle tagged CARDMN, departed south for downtown Newport, Vermont.

"Damn. Did you smell that guy, Peg? Wow! Business associate of LaChance? Fat chance I'd say. Fat chance. Wonder what kind of business he's in. I didn't want to look in that ratty old Caravan anyway. Who knows what you could catch? Besides, Sarek didn't like him. That's enough for me. Dogs got better instincts than us."

"You got that right, Ed. The dog hid as soon as that louse came through the door. I figured he was here to pick up Sarek. Don't even think he saw him hiding under your desk," said Peg as she noted the following:

Yellow Pad Entry: #7 1-29-2003 7:35 a.m.

Person identifying himself as Walter Qaqish arrived North Troy Customs Station at 7:20 a.m. Wants three cases of baseball cards from rear of LaChance's Range Rover. Claims they are his. Has receipt. Copies of receipt made. Stated that he and LaChance were at card show in Brattleboro, Vermont on Sunday.

Qaqish driving a Dodge Caravan (1995-ish) Rhode Island Tag # CARDMN.

Walter Qaqish: Approx. 5'7", 225 lbs., age 40-50, graying hair, bald on top.

Ed made a quick call to Sheriff Ames, providing him a heads-up on the impending visit from Walter Qaqish.

Chapter 15

Fresh Croissants

T he exhaust of the Caravan was still drifting across the parking lot as another car pulled in. This vehicle, a newer Cadillac, had Quebec tags. Looking out the window, Peg proclaimed, "Ed, the croissants and palmiers have arrived."

Two large green-and-white pastry boxes announced the arrival of Jean Paul Bellevue, Director of Player Personnel for the Montreal Expos. First to greet Mr. Bellevue was Sarek, returning from hiding and heading for Bellevue at warp speed.

"Wow," said a very proper French-Canadian accent, "a croissant-sniffing dog, eh? Is this one of those doughnut-enforcement canines?"

After official introductions had been completed, coffee distributed, and palmiers and croissants devoured by all, Mr. Bellevue asked, "I suppose you wonder why I drove all the way from Montreal this early in the morning, Ms. McCarthy. Could we chat privately for a minute?"

Looking at the clock, Peg was anxious. Sheriff Ames was running late. "I really think Sheriff Ames should be here to answer questions concerning the accident."

"Oh, no, this has nothing to do with the accident, not directly anyway."

As Peg opened the door to her office, she thought to herself, *Well if it's not about the accident, then it must be about the dog.*

Bellevue and Peg entered the office, and she offered the well-attired Canadian a chair. It was apparent that the garage portion of the Customs Station was a recent add-on. A window that once gave visual access to the rear parking area now gave a view of the interior of the garage and the eerie glow from the cold lighting that was cast upon Bill LaChance's Range Rover.

Mr. Bellevue began, "I'll get to the point, Ms. McCarthy. I talked with the sheriff on the phone the day before yesterday, and we discussed the pending media blitz that will soon be headed toward North Troy. The Montreal Expos would like to offer our assistance in this matter while the LaChance issue is in the spotlight. The papers are already selling stories about the demise of Mr. LaChance. I don't know all of the details, but the possibility of foul play is going to receive attention by many. It will soon become public knowledge that the Expos obtained a ten-million-dollar life insurance policy on Bill LaChance. This is a common investment protection, but the sports tabloids will have a field day with that news. Especially with the reported financial difficulties of the Expos. Perhaps I'm speculating, but I think you'll bear the brunt of media investigation for the next several months until this LaChance situation gets resolved."

As Peg was about to thank Bellevue for the offer of assistance, Sheriff Frank Ames entered the station through the rear door.

"Good Morning, Sheriff," said Peg. "This is Mr. Bellevue of the Expos. He says we are in for a heavy media onslaught regarding the LaChance affair. He says it might go on for months. Lucky you, Frank."

"No, you're the lucky one, Peg. How many days to go?"

Looking at the scenic calendar on the wall behind her desk, Peg proclaimed, "Less than three weeks!"

"Are you being transferred, Ms. McCarthy?" queried Bellevue.

"Retired."

"Retirement? You look much too young for retirement." Bellevue's French accent lingered on the word "retirement."

It sounds so permanent, Peg thought.

Peg left the inner office while Sheriff Ames and Bellevue discussed the LaChance situation. In fewer than five minutes, Bellevue was departing Peg's office, bidding his good-byes, and briskly walking towards his Caddy.

"He didn't even mention the dog," Peg mused as Ames began to sample one of the Canadian pastries.

Bellevue sat in his DeVille, apparently on his cell phone, for nearly ten minutes.

"Maybe he wants the remainder of his croissants," quipped Ed. "He's on his way back."

Bellevue wiped his expensive alligator dress boots on the mat as he reentered the Customs Station. "Oh, Ms. McCarthy, could I ask you one or two more questions—privately?"

Peg motioned Bellevue toward her office.

"Ms. McCarthy, I consider myself an astute judge of character, and I often make rapid business decisions. You said you were retiring in a couple of weeks. I was wondering if you might be seeking employment after retirement? On behalf of the Expos, would you consider working for our organization? I don't need your answer today. Could you please think about it?"

"You're kidding," said a startled Peg. "Why not hire someone with a police or investigatory background?"

Looking over the top of his Armani glasses, Bellevue smiled and replied, "I'm figuring that you have about twenty to twenty-five years in the Customs Service. During that time you were, as an agent of the U.S. government, someone who had to quickly size up people and situations. What better experience for an investigator? Besides, I think it would be better for the Expos to hire an individual, rather than solicit an outside company. We may do that also, but I think I'd like someone working directly for me. Plus, your French language expertise will be very useful to the Expos."

Taken aback by Mr. Bellevue's offer, Peg, pensive for a minute, finally replied, "I am retiring. In about two and a-half weeks. I do have an interview in Boston next week, on the sixth." With this said, Peg remembered that, as yet, she hadn't returned a call to DeBillare to set up the interview in Boston. *So damn busy. Too many things on my mind. Maybe I should cancel skiing with Doc Mirkin. I have so much stuff to do*, Peg thought to herself.

Mr. Bellevue looked through the window at the rear of Peg's office. LaChance's Range Rover was barely visible in the now dark interior of the garage. After about a minute, Bellevue asked again, "What do you think, Agent McCarthy? We are willing to pay $7,000 per month, U.S. funds, of course, with a minimum of four months. Your expenses for travel and lodging would be reimbursed as well. Is tomorrow too soon to decide? As far as your interview in Boston, please don't cancel, even if you accept our offer. There are some loose ends in Boston that we have questions about. You could check on them while you are there."

"Well, Mr. Bellevue, I will think about your offer. I actually thought you were here about the dog."

"What? Your drug dog?" Bellevue was confused.

"The dog belonged to Bill LaChance, and he was in the SUV. I assumed you were here to pick him up for return to LaChance's family."

Shaking his head, Bellevue said, "I'm sorry, Ms. McCarthy, I did talk with the family, and no one mentioned any dog. The next of kin are an uncle and aunt in Louisiana. LaChance was divorced about seven years ago—no children, I was told. Seems like a great dog. I thought he was yours." Bellevue headed back into the main office. "Can I call you tomorrow, Agent McCarthy?"

More questions raced through Peg's crowded mind. "Yes, tomorrow morning—here at the office. I have a question for you, Mr. Bellevue. Do you know or have you heard of a Walter Qaqish? Q-A-Q-I-S-H."

"Qaqish? Unusual name. No U after the Q's? That name doesn't mean anything to me. Is he related to Bill LaChance? No, never heard of Qaqish, but you must remember LaChance was only with the Expos for two months. I only talked with him in person once and on the phone maybe three or four times. I can't tell you much about him. That will be your job." Bellevue smiled. "If you accept our offer."

Peg reached for her yellow legal pad. "Right, Mr. Bellevue, that would be my job to find out. If I take your offer, which I find very interesting. Thank you again for the croissants and palmiers. Sarek thanks you, especially."

Sarek greeted Mr. Bellevue with his right paw. "Great dog, Peg. You going to keep him if nobody wants him?"

"We'll see, Mr. Bellevue, we'll see."

"Please, Peg, call me JP. I'll call you in the morning. Eight a.m. okay?"

"Eight o'clock will be fine," said Peg as she wrote her next yellow pad entry.

Yellow Pad Entry: #7 1-29-2003 8:30 a.m.

Mr. J.P. Bellevue, Player Personnel Director for the Montreal Expos baseball team, arrived at 7:58 a.m. Discussed issues concerning the death of Mr. William LaChance. He has contacted LaChance's aunt and uncle in Louisiana. They were listed as the next of kin for Mr. LaChance.

Mr. Bellevue (J. P.) did not know that LaChance had a dog with him.

Expos have offered me employment after retiring.

Bellevue is unfamiliar with Walter Qaqish.

Chapter 16

Jay Peake

As Peg drove the twelve miles to Jay Peake, she wondered about her unusual visitors that morning. She was still trying to figure out what that creepy character from Rhode Island really wanted! And boy, those croissants and palmiers were incredible! She could get used to those! The job offer from one Mr. J.P. Bellevue gave Peg an uneasy feeling. Something just felt odd about his proposal. Were the Expos really making a job offer or just seeking inside information?

As Peg saw the first views of Jay Peake, her thoughts quickly turned to what the heck she was actually doing! "I'm meeting a doctor from Boston, whom I've talked to by phone once and met once, for perhaps thirty minutes. Am I crazy?"

After finding a coveted parking spot, Peg sat for a minute, thinking. "I'm a grown, independent woman and a very good judge of character. What am I so worried about? I'm going skiing! I love to ski! That's that!"

With marked determination, she put on her ski boots, grabbed her skis and poles, and was off. After getting her lift ticket, she trekked through the snow to the rendezvous point. It was only a few minutes after she did her stretching that the "good doctor" swooshed up beside her and sprayed snow all over Peg's skis and boots. He was very amused and proud of himself.

"Well, good morning to you, too, and thank you very much!" Peg said as she glared at the fresh snow sprayed over the front of her skis.

"Glad you came! The snow's great! I've only done two runs, so you're not too far behind."

"Let's go! I need a warm-up run first. You pick."

"Okay, let's start on Northway to Ullr's Dream. You pick the next run, Peg."

They headed for the aerial tramway and to the 3,968-foot summit. It was an absolutely gorgeous day! Blue sky, no wind, about 30 degrees. Perfect skiing weather. The slopes looked so incredibly inviting from the tram. Peg couldn't wait to get to the top! The tram ride was a nonstop monologue by the good doctor. *Boy, can he talk!* Peg thought. And later, the questions started. It would have almost been unnerving how he was so comfortable asking just about anything, yet he was so easy to be with that Peg was completely at ease. No emotional wall was up as she answered all the questions he asked. And the questions didn't stop after the first run. Oh no! She ended up telling him her whole life story. The funny thing was that he seemed genuinely interested. After about a dozen or so runs, they called it a day.

"How about some hot chocolate to warm up before you go?" offered Stu. "My treat."

"Sounds nice. And more questions?" joked Peg. They sat in the lodge and sipped their cocoa and, not surprisingly, there was no lapse in conversation.

"So, you're from Maryland, you have two sisters. Mom and Dad still live where you grew up. University of Maryland. Peace Corps. French teacher and now working for Customs for a long, long time. Ever been married?" inquired Stu.

"Boy, do you ever stop? Is there even an ounce of inhibition in you anywhere?"

"Nope. So, married? Divorced? Single? Significant other of any sort?"

"Single. No significant other male, female, or otherwise. And you? I have a new rule. Any question you ask me, you have to answer first."

"Okay. Single also. Married to my work. I'm guessing the same about you—a type A hopeless workaholic," teased Stu.

"No! I'm not a workaholic. At least not much of one!" joked Peg. "So, my turn. You're an only child from Massachusetts, the apple of your parents' eye, played every sport out there, undergrad at Northeastern, med school at Tufts, went into peds but couldn't stay emotionally unattached, so moved on to dead people. How'd I do?"

"Not bad. Not bad at all. Kids? Me, none. You?"

"Yes, *five!*" joked Peg, giving an "if looks could kill" stare, piercing the good doctor right between the eyes. "Just my dogs, the only children I've ever had."

"Okay, favorite new band. What do you listen to when you think no one else is around? Mine is Linkin Park. It helps me when I'm working on a hard case. Helps get me into the zone."

"I'm not much of a new music kind of person. I'm kind of stuck in the past. A big Parrot Head, I have to admit."

"*Really?*" shouted Stu, almost on the verge of hysterics. "I'd never have guessed! Oh, my!"

"What's so funny? Why do you find that so hard to believe? Tell me! What's so funny?"

"Well, you're just not the stereotypical Parrot Head, that's all. Buffet's cool. No problem."

"Okay, one more. Then I gotta go. I'm almost done with my hot chocolate. My pick."

"Okay, shoot," said Stu.

"Have you ever had your heart broken or broken someone else's?" Peg asked quietly.

"Sadly, no. I've never allowed anyone to get that close or allowed myself to get close to anyone. Like I said, a hopeless workaholic. I've been so focused on work for so long, I'm not sure I'd know how to do anything else. It's actually kind of a rarity that I'm here today skiing—a whole day without work. Kind of unusual," admitted Stu. "And you?"

"Yes."

"Yes to which one? Brokenhearted or heart breaker?"

"Heart breaker," Peg said, looking down into her now empty cup. "Well, I gotta go now. I guess I'll be talking to you about the case in the not too distant future. Thanks for the skiing. That was fun. I needed that!"

"Me, too. I really enjoyed it. And I really enjoyed just sitting here talking too. Maybe we can do it again sometime. Have a safe trip home."

"You, too. See ya."

"Bye." Stu gave Peg a slight wave as he watched her walk away.

Peg drove home completely confused about how this doctor got her to talk so openly about herself. Personal stuff too! Hm-m, interesting.

Chapter 17

Oxycodone & No. 28 or No. 29 Needle

"**G**ood morning. U.S. Customs, North Troy, Vermont. Agent Randall speaking. Yes, Doc, okay, I'll transfer you to her phone. … Peg, phone call on line one. It's Dr. Mirkin."

"Good morning, Doctor. How are things in Burlington this morning?"

"Hi, Peg. I thought we had that doctor crap settled yesterday. Please, Stu or Mirkin or even Doc, but no Doctor. I'm a bit sore from the skiing yesterday, but actually I called to see if you made a decision on the Expos' job offer. It might be interesting."

"Well, Stu," Peg said as she tried to determine if she should call the famous forensic physician Stu or Doc, "I expected a call from Bellevue early this morning, but his secretary called to say he was in conference and would call later. Maybe they are deciding to forget the whole issue and will withdraw their offer. This LaChance matter could be a simple accidental overdose, and the case will be closed. Good-bye fancy private investigator job."

"I'm not so sure about that, Peg. Ace left a phone message at the lodge hotel desk, and we have an important lunch meeting at noon. That's all he said; Edwards can be very cryptic on the telephone." After small talk about Sarek, yesterday's skiing and afternoon lunch, Doc Mirkin got to his real reason for calling. "I was wondering if we might do dinner and a possible show when you come to Boston for your interview on the sixth. How long will you be in Boston?"

"I'm taking three vacation days," blurted Peg, trying to conceal her excitement at the invitation. "I leave here early Wednesday morning to catch the 10:30 train at Montpelier, arrive in Boston late in the afternoon. My interview is at 9 a.m. on Thursday. I'm going to stay over and catch the first train out at 8:15 Friday morning. Dinner sounds like fun. What's playing in the Theatre District?"

"I'm not sure. I'll check. Sorry to say I won't be able to meet you when you arrive on Wednesday. I'm speaking at a conference in New York City, exactly the same time as your interview. I'm returning on the noon Acela Express. Can you meet me at South Station at around three o'clock in the afternoon? We'll go to dinner then."

"That sounds great. Give me your cell phone number, and I'll call you if there are any changes. Wish me luck in my interview."

"Good luck! Break a leg!" Stu exclaimed as he hung up the phone.

Peg's thoughts were reflected by her smile. *Cloud nine—absolutely cloud nine is how I feel. I'm just so comfortable with Stu Mirkin. Not romantically, not yet anyway, but just so damn comfy with him. It's as if I've known him for years.*

The ringing phone brought Peg back to the office.

"Hi, Peg. J.P. Bellevue. Sorry I'm so late. Do you have a decision for me?"

"Yes, Mr. Bellevue, I've decided to consider your generous offer. If I accept, when would you need me to start?"

J.P. Bellevue, now relieved, in a more relaxed tone replied, "As soon as possible. You're going to Boston for your interview on the sixth, correct? Can you fly to New Orleans on Friday morning? Tentatively, LaChance's wake will be Thursday and Friday evening, and the funeral will be Saturday morning. The Expos would like a representative from the team at the services. We will make you some business cards and an ID with the team information. Perhaps you can get some additional family information about LaChance while in Louisiana. There's all kinds of scuttlebutt about the cause of death. Any ideas?"

Peg was taken aback by the events that were unfolding so rapidly. "I haven't heard any more than what I read in the paper and hear on the news." Knowing that she could easily be crossing the fine line of possible unethical conversation, Peg kept her knowledge and ideas concerning LaChance's death to herself. After all, she was still an employee of the U.S. Customs Service and not able to work for the Expos concurrently. She thought to herself, *Be careful. Be careful!*

"Okay, Peg. If you don't have a laptop, you'll need to get one. Don't get a cheap one. All the bells and whistles and save the receipt. You may want to set up a separate bank account for this venture. Get me the account number, and we will wire you an advance so you will be using our funds from the get-go. Do you have an official retirement date?"

So much so fast. "My last day is the 14th of February. I can travel to New Orleans for the Expos over the weekend, but I can't really assume any official duties until after my last day with the agency."

Peg needed a day just to sort all this stuff out. No time to think since last Saturday. The accident, the dog, retirement, new job offer, interview in Boston. Now to New Orleans for a funeral for a major league baseball pitcher that she'd hardly heard of. Peg muttered under her breath, "I don't even like baseball."

All these ideas raced through Peg's mind as she was trying to converse with J.P. Bellevue on the other end of the line. "Mr. Bellevue, we'll have to discuss the details next week."

"Peg, you need to call me J.P. No mister, please. This is baseball. We go by first names. I don't know what your wardrobe is like but it was nearly 80 degrees in Louisiana yesterday. Better get ready for warmer weather. I'll fax you additional details, as well as my direct line phone number."

Yellow Pad Entry: #8 1-30-2003 9:20 a.m.

Mr. J.P. Bellevue, Player Personnel Director for the Montreal Expos baseball team called at 9:20 a.m. Discussed issues concerning the job. Wants me to fly to New Orleans on Friday morning (2-7-03) to attend the wake and funeral of LaChance. Will return Sunday.

Hope I indicated strongly enough to Bellevue that I can only work for one employer at a time.

Need to get laptop computer and warm-weather funeral attire.

That damn phone is ringing again, thought Peg as she answered.

"Hi, Peg, Stu Mirkin here. I'm at Edwards' office. He just released the cause of death on his website: cardiac and respiratory failure caused by an overdose of the prescription drug oxycodone hydrochloride."

"Thanks for the info, Stu. Any clues in the stuff that Doc Edwards brought with him for testing?"

"Well, Peg, that's where it starts to get interesting. Everything tested negative except for one of the two little nip bottles of LaChance's Hi-Heat Hot Sauce that were in the glove compartment. The contents of one bottle were a little 'higher heat' than advertised. The 'hot' bottle was about 60 percent oxycodone. We think it was a fairly new version of the drug in liquid form. You can mix it with juice or something like pudding. The bottle had 50ml of liquid, of which 30ml was drug. The bottle still had its safety seal so I don't think LaChance put the stuff in there himself. Both bottles are still being examined for signs of tampering."

"That paints many interesting scenarios, Stu. According to what I read, not many people have much use for LaChance, but to murder him, that's another level. Too bad Sarek can't talk; he seems to be the only eyewitness to this whole sordid tale. Let me know if you hear anything about the bottle."

Yellow Pad Entry: #9 1-30-2003 9:50 a.m.
Doc Mirkin called: States that Dr. A. Coronet Edwards, Chief of Forensic Pathology, State Medical Examiner's Office, just released the cause of death for William LaChance. Overdose of the prescription drug oxycodone hydrochloride, a.k.a. Oxycontin. Other details, such as tampering of the LaChance's Hi-Heat Hot Sauce bottle, were not included in the news release.

A light snow again began to fall as dusk came quickly to North Troy. This reminded Peg of last Sunday afternoon, or was it a week, a month, perhaps a year ago? So much had transpired during the last four days.

Peg glanced over at Sarek as Bertha crunched across the two inches of new snow on the parking lot. Sarek, alert as always, scanned the road as the snow started to blow at an acute angle. Peg spoke aloud, "An excellent night for a warm fire, a good book, and a faithful companion to share the evening. Right, Sarek?"

Briefly, Sarek looked at Peg but then stared straight ahead at the falling snow.

"You're right, Sarek, Louisiana never looked like this."

January 31, 2003
"Good morning. U.S. Customs, North Troy, Vermont. Agent Randall speaking … Yes, Doc … Okay, I'll transfer you to her phone … Peg, phone call on line one. It's Doc Mirkin."

"Hi, Stu, Peg here. What's up?"

"Peg, I'm back in Boston. Ace just called me. Very interesting info on the hot sauce bottles. As I mentioned yesterday, one bottle was 60 percent oxycodone hydrochloride. Tests determined that is a relatively new variation of the drug called Oxyquick. It's manufactured by Wellingham-Joyce Pharmaceuticals of Durham, North Carolina. This version of the drug is in solution."

"That is interesting, Stu. Any ideas on how the drug was introduced into the bottle? Was it opened and resealed?"

"Ingenious, Peg—simple, but ingenious. The plastic bottle with the drug had a hole in the label area. Ace said either a #28 or #29 needle. About 30ml of LaChance's Hi-Heat must have been removed using a syringe, and the drug replaced the hot sauce by reversing the process.

Then the label was sealed by wrapping a piece of two-inch clear tape entirely around the bottle. The hole was so minute that it was only noticed when they X-rayed both bottles. The bottle cap was never removed."

"Stu, what does the 28 or 29 mean? In non-medical terms."

"Sorry, Peg, that's how we measure needle diameter. It's an archaic throwback to the early days of medicine. Identical needles are placed on a ruler. The number of needles needed to fill one inch gives the needle its size. A #29 needle takes twenty-nine needles to equal one inch. Twenty-nine is about the smallest we use. Common sizes usually range from #20 to #29. If someone wants to give you a flu shot with a #8 or 10, better run! I'll call you if I get more news. Think about the menu for next week in Boston. Talk to you soon."

"Bye, Stu. Sarek says good-bye also."

Yellow Pad Entry: #10 1-31-2003 8:43 a.m.

Doc Mirkin called. States that Doctor Edwards, Chief of Forensic Pathology, called to inform Mirkin that one bottle of LaChance's Hi-Heat Hot Sauce had a small diameter hole that was covered with two-inch clear tape to prevent leakage of contents.

Mirkin said that a #28 or #29 needle probably caused the hole in the plastic hot sauce bottle. Hole appears to be caused by a needle puncture rather than a hole made by a drill bit of the same size.

A #28 needle is 1/28 of an inch in diameter; which equals .0358 inch.

A #29 needle is 1/29 of an inch in diameter; which equals .0345 inch.

Chapter 18

South Station

Perhaps Peg would have considered the job interview this morning more of a success if she hadn't had the assignment with the Expos in hand. Both Lindahl and DeBillare were pleasant, and she was sure a job offer would quickly follow. But the boredom associated with a position with Apex was apparent during this initial interview.

The interior of South Station could be cruelly cold during February. Passengers walked in all directions, triggering the automatic door openers. Each open door invited a rectangular shaft of icy air to rush into the cavernous confines of the station, enveloping the awaiting multitude and chilling them to the bone.

Washington, D.C., had Union Station; New York had its Pennsylvania Station and the station of stations, Grand Central. Boston, never far from its typically Puritan practicalities, had South Station and its geographically situated cousin, North Station.

Two six-foot-high by twelve-foot-wide black schedules hung from the curved ceiling, one announcing commuter rail and the other for Amtrak long-distance service. A large crowd stood silently watching the commuter display. Ticky, ticky, ticky emanated from the overhead display every few minutes as train numbers, departure times, and track platforms were updated.

The sound of the changing letters and numbers was accompanied by a verbal announcement that seemed to be a voice from the heavens and at least that far away.

Ticky, ticky, ticky; Train Number 067 to Plymouth. Departure 2:45. Platform 12.

Part of the horde started to move to the left side doors. In unison, like ants.

"Attention, please. The 2:45 commuter rail to Plymouth, with stops in: Braintree, South Weymouth, Abington, Whitman, Hanson, and Halifax, is now boarding on track 12."

Ticky, ticky, ticky; Train Number 114 to Attleboro. Departure 2:48. Platform 3.

Another large group headed for the right side of the station. Shafts of cold air rushed across the station interior with each door opening.

"Attention, please. The 2:48 commuter rail to Attleboro continuing service to South Attleboro and Providence, Rhode Island, with stops at Back Bay, Ruggles, Hyde Park, Route 128, Canton Junction, Sharon, and Mansfield, is now boarding on track 3."

Ticky, ticky, ticky; the Amtrak board on the left, with its own particular display, announced that Dr. Stu Mirkin's train was twenty minutes late.

Arrivals

Time	Train Number	From	Status
2:35	170 ACELA REGIONAL	WASHINGTON, D.C.	ARRIVED
3:05	2154 ACELA EXPRESS	NEW YORK CITY	20 MIN. LATE
4:44	172 ACELA REGIONAL	NEW YORK CITY	ON TIME
5:30	174 ACELA REGIONAL	WASHINGTON, D.C.	

Departures

Time	Train Number	From	Status
3:03	2167 ACELA EXPRESS	WASHINGTON, D.C.	ON TIME
3:20	449 LAKE SHORE LTD.	CHICAGO	ON TIME
4:10	2171 ACELA REGIONAL	WASHINGTON, D.C.	

Railroad terminals have always provided a unique atmosphere to engage in people-watching. This afternoon was no different. The cast of characters was gathering. East of the commuter arrival/departure display, with its standing throng peering upward, as if in anticipation of divine intervention, were twenty-five to thirty circular dark-green metal tables, each with four matching green metal chairs. A book seller's kiosk bordered the area of tables. Two tables away was a couple in their early twenties. He was wearing Buddy Holly glasses and an orange shirt, and blonde streaks highlighted his hair. The girl had long blonde hair and was wearing a bright red hat and a sad expression. She and her work boots seem tired … very tired.

At the edge of the seating area sat a cool dude with an expensive three-piece suit. His cell phone conversation was so loud that those around him were simultaneously annoyed and curious. He might have been taken seriously were it not for the fact that wearing reflective dark glasses while sitting in the interior February shadows of South Station looked downright silly.

"Attention, please. The 3:17 commuter rail to Framingham with stops at Back Bay, Newtonville, West Newton, Auburndale, Wellesley, Natick, and West Natick, is now boarding on track 1."

At the book kiosk, a man in his fifties, with a white shirt and pea-green tie, thumbed through a book from the self-improvement section. His frayed tweed sports coat had leather elbow patches. A double string, perhaps from a tag inside, hung three inches below the unraveling hem on the right side of his jacket.

"Attention, please. Amtrak Acela Express, train number 2154, will be arriving momentarily on track number 8."

Peg met a rather tired, hungry Stu as he entered South Station after departing 2154. A seven-minute taxi ride brought the couple to a quaint Italian restaurant in Boston's historic North End. Ricardo's had been a fixture in Boston for nearly seventy-five years and was a pure gem, frequented mainly by locals. It was rare to see a tourist here, unless accompanied by one of the regular patrons. Stu Mirkin might not have been one of the regulars but he dined there often and was instantly recognized by the staff as he entered.

Stu ordered a red wine, 1995 Chianti Classico Riserva, and then suggested, "I'd like you to try my favorite meal here. May I order it for you?"

At first, Peg was a bit irritated by his forwardness. How could Mirkin possibly know her tastes when considering Italian cuisine? But then, based on his boldness on the ski slopes, she wasn't really surprised.

Augusto, the waiter arrived with antipasto salad, which was followed by lasagna with Italian gravy. Cappuccino and tiramisu. What a finale to a fantastic dinner. As it turned out, Stu's menu choices were impeccable! The Italian gravy was a sauce that was so rich and robust, it was like nothing Peg had ever tasted.

Although exhausted from the train, Stu Mirkin was not at a loss for words. Peg, in typical U.S. Customs Agency efficiency, decided to ask the questions this time. Mirkin proved as proficient talking about himself as he was getting others to answer his questions. Not bragging, just the facts. Peg had to admit that she was rather impressed with the doctor's accomplishments.

It was a most enjoyable evening, and Peg was satisfied with her strategic planning. She now knew as much about Dr. Stuart Mirkin as he knew of her. After dinner and a quick hug, Peg taxied to her hotel near Logan Airport for an early flight to New Orleans in the morning.

The cab turned right off Hanover Street; Stu Mirkin was still at the curb waving as the taxi entered the Sumner Tunnel and headed east toward the airport.

Chapter 19

Smell of the Spanish Moss and Cypress

The planned three-hour snooze on the boring flight from Logan-Boston to Louis Armstrong International in New Orleans, via Hartsfield-Atlanta, failed to materialize, due to two crying infants and an obnoxious neighbor who talked the entire flight. Peg thought to herself, *Everyone (at least those over thirty years old) knows of Louis Armstrong but who the heck are Logan and Hartsfield? Someone should write a book about those obscure names of airports, bridges, and tunnels. How many children must think the Holland exits in Amsterdam as they head to New York City from New Jersey?* Peg wondered as the 757 taxied to gate 45.

Trying to put some thoughts to paper, Peg considered who might be responsible for the demise of one William No Chance LaChance. A very meager offering of likely villains was developed.

Yellow Pad Entry: #11a 2-7-2003 10:44 a.m.
With the now known facts the strongest possible candidates are:
  William LaChance, An Irate Fan, and Walter Qaqish
  With the now known facts the weakest possible candidates are:
  Montreal Expos and the Hot Sauce Company
Somewhere in-between strongest and weakest is the possibility that
  LaChance's death could be caused by: A Random Act of Tampering
  or LaChance's Ex-Wife.

The opening of an automatic door was a reminder of yesterday while waiting for Stu at South Station. The contrast between South Station in Boston and the Louis Armstrong International Airport were extreme. Wow! The taste and the smell. The dankness of Spanish moss growing atop nearby old cypress stands and the 92 percent humidity ignited the chemoreceptors of Peg's nose and tongue. *Lady, you're no longer in Vermont, or Boston for that matter,* Peg thought to herself.

One word described the topography of lower Louisiana—flat, or to be more emphatic, perhaps three words—flat, flat, flat, or maybe flat-cubed. The only noticeable indications of ground elevation were mile after mile of levees which, with major attention and repair, prevented the Mississippi and its many tributaries, which splayed out across the delta, from flooding the lowlands.

Louisiana Route 39 from the airport to the town of Luisi was one thirty-mile diameter semicircle. Starting north-northeast, the rural highway constantly drifted to the right and ended at a compass heading of due south in the mighty metropolis of Luisi and the location of Peg's overnight accommodations in Louisiana. Peg confirmed her reservations at the motel desk and was given a phone message.

PHONE MESSAGE
For: Peg McCarthy, Montreal Expos,
Date: 2-5-03
From: Sheriff Franklin Ames
Time: 2:25 p.m.
Message: Check your e-mail

On the table in the motel vestibule, a stack of local weekly newspapers, with a sign announcing 'Complimentary Copies,' evidenced the grieving of the community.

Here, No Chance was more than a local hero. He was the community. Interesting how the media, both print and visual, could influence the human psyche to believe what they painted as the truth. Reviled, detested, loathed, abhorrent, despicable, and despised were all included by the sarcastic sports pens of the major media markets to describe the late William. But here, in the heat and humidity of the Mississippi Delta, William LaChance, the late Dollar Bill, was revered as a saint. Perhaps, rightfully so.

The St. Bernard & Plaquemines Weekly Banner
Week of February 2, 2003
Local Hero Returns Home for Burial
By Staff Reporter Jayme Charpentier
One of our own, Mr. William "No Chance" LaChance, will be laid to rest at Dellacroix Memorial Cemetery & Gardens on Saturday, February 8, 2003.
(See Obituary on page 7.)

Pitching ace dies at age 36.

A funeral service and internment will be conducted on Saturday at 11:00 a.m. at the Dellacroix Memorial Cemetery & Gardens in LaChance's hometown of Dellacroix. Mr. LaChance was discovered in his vehicle near the U.S./Canadian border at approximately 5:00 p.m. on January 26 by a U.S. Customs Service agent. The motor vehicle of Mr. LaChance had been involved in a minor accident at the scene. He was transported to the Orleans County (Vermont) Hospital but was declared dead soon after his arrival. An autopsy was conducted on January 28 but, as of our going to press, the results were inconclusive, according to Sheriff Franklin Ames of Orleans County. Toxicology results could take a few weeks and could shed more light on the matter.

Bill LaChance was much more than a local boy who was born across the river in Belle Chase. No Chance never forgot where he came from and was always there to assist with any deserving project in the delta area. His philanthropic foundation, Take a Chance, has been responsible for underwriting all, or part, of the following programs:

Dellacroix Health Clinic in Dellacroix—Sarek's Spot Animal Shelter in Reggio

Make a Wish Chapter for St. Bernard & Plaquemines Parishes

Mississippi Delta Boys and Girls Clubs in Belle Chase and Braithwaite

Delta Regional Library Project, Sponsor of the Mississippi Catfish Legion Baseball

Founding Member of the Delta Jazz Preservation Society

These were only a few of Mr. LaChance's favorite charities.

As a baseball player, Bill LaChance was known as "No Chance." His Hall of Fame statistics include:

Eight years with the Houston Astros in the National League

Five years with the New York Yankees in the American League

Three years with the New York Mets in the National League

316 career wins, 51 career shutouts, 4300+ strikeouts, 5-time Cy Young winner

Thirteen years as an All-Star Starting Pitcher in seven All-Star Games

Mr. LaChance had recently signed a three-year contract with the Montreal Expos. Baseball and Southern Louisiana will miss No Chance LaChance.

The St. Bernard & Plaquemines Weekly Banner, page 7
Week of February 2, 2003

OBITUARIES

William Emeril LaChance

William E. "No Chance" LaChance died on Sunday, January 26, 2003, at the age of thirty-six. Devoted father of Marie LaChance of Hanover, Mass. Son of the late Waylon E. LaChance and the late Hazel Troolard LaChance of Dellacroix, La. Brother of Waylon LaChance Jr., Noel (LaChance) Poydras and Renee L. LaChance. Nephew of Mr. and Mrs. Jolie LaChance. Family and friends are invited to attend a funeral service at the Chalmette Funeral Home, 1505 W. DeLeon Street, Chalmette, La., on Saturday, February 8, 2003, at 11:00 a.m. Visitation will take place on Thursday, February 6, and Friday, February 7, from 5:00 p.m. until 9:00 p.m., and on Saturday from 9:00 a.m. until 11:00 a.m., followed by a funeral mass in St. Eloi Catholic Church, Dellacroix. Internment will follow in Dellacroix Memorial Cemetery & Gardens on Boudreaux Bayou Road in Dellacroix. In lieu of flowers, please make donations to the William LaChance Take a Chance Foundation c/o Crescent City Federal Savings Institution, 120 Hartsuff Blvd. New Orleans, LA 70130.

From:	"Sheriff Franklin Ames" <fames@orleanscty.vt.us./gov>
To:	"Peg McCarthy" <mccarthypeg@rcn.com> | This is spam | Add to Address Book
Subject:	🔗FW: wallet contents list
Date:	Thu, 6 Feb 2003 18:20:19 –0400

Peg—Sorry I didn't get to see you before you left for Boston and New Orleans. Attached is that wallet contents list that we discussed earlier this week. See you soon. Frank

Orleans County Hospital—Newport, VT
Patient's Personal Belongings List
Patient Name: William E. LaChance
Emergency room admission date: 1-26-2003

Clothing: pair of pants—green, shirt—white, undershirt and underpants (boxers) —white, pair shoes (size 11) —black, pair of socks—black, light jacket—blue (with New York Mets logo)

Other Items: set of eyeglasses—prescription, wallet—Buxom (see contents below)

Wallet contents include: $47 cash

MasterCash Credit Card ****-****-****-8926

Vista Credit Card ****-****-****-2331

Arco QuikGas Card ***-***-***-748

Two wallet-size pictures of teenage female (one is marked To Dad—Love Marie)

Emergency Notification Card listing Buckley Roberts @ 617-282-5660 as person to contact Four restaurant receipts

Two lodging receipts

Louisiana driver's license w/ picture —# 234716844—Expiration Date 11-17-2005

Dental appointment card for 3-31-03—Julia Emig, DMD, 54 North Ave, Rockland, MA

Three #71 baseball cards—William "No Chance" LaChance

Six business cards from various parties, bound together by a large paper clip

After digesting the obituary and article in the February 2 issue of the *St. Bernard & Plaquemines Weekly Banner*, Peg revised her list of potential murderers:

Yellow Pad Entry: #11b – Addendum 2-7-2003 6:23 p.m.
With the now known facts the strongest possible candidates are:
William LaChance, An Irate Fan, and Walter Qaqish
With the now known facts the weakest possible candidates are:
Accidental Poisoning, Montreal Expos, and the Hot Sauce Company
Somewhere in-between strongest and weakest is the possibility that LaChance's death could be caused by: A Random Act of Tampering, LaChance's Ex-Wife, LaChance's Daughter Marie, and the 'Take Chance Foundation'.

As Peg typed the info from her yellow pad into her new laptop, the one with all the bells and whistles, she pondered the criminal possibilities that seemed to be expanding exponentially.

"Daughter? Why is it that I learn of LaChance's daughter in the obituary? Why is it that no one knew of LaChance's daughter? The Take a Chance Foundation? Perhaps someone who was denied a financial request? The list goes on."

Chapter 20

Brass Band Funeral

Music filled the streets and professional mourners wailed as the procession for one William Emeril "No Chance" LaChance entered the old cemetery at the end of Boudreaux Bayou Road. The expected set of local and not-so-indigenous dignitaries associated with the death and disposal of a member of the "rich and famous" club were at the front of the procession, as they always were.

The parish elders, U.S. congressman from the District, the governor of the great state of Louisiana, representatives from the New York Mets, Major League baseball, and Peg McCarthy, as the designated griever from the Montreal Expos, followed the two-horse hearse into the cemetery. Leading the procession was the parade marshal, the Honorable George "Blind Lemon" McSplivins, and the Delta Jazz Preservation Society Brass Band—all fourteen members. Other funeral marching groups included the Linden Street Outlaws, Misery Loves Company Brass Ensemble, and the Unified High School jazz band. A large eight-wheel-rack body trailer carried renowned jazz pianist Miles McDougal, his ebony grand piano that he referred to as Grace, and the twenty-four member choir from the Ebenezer Baptist Church of Dellacroix. The entire vehicle was festooned with flowers, front to back. The trailer was pulled by a bright yellow Mack ultra-torque tractor with the lettering "Cajun Food Specialties—Ponchatoula, LA 70454" stenciled boldly on each door. In the center of the logo was a two-foot chili pepper with a sinister smile, greeting the street-side multitude. As the entourage completed its final left into the cemetery, all band members, Miles McDougal and Grace, and the twenty-four soulful sisters of the Ebenezer Baptist Church began "Nearer My God to Thee."

The width of the flatbed from Cajun Food Specialties measured exactly ninety-six inches and the ornate entrance arch of the Dellacroix Memorial Cemetery & Gardens was a scant 4¼ inches more. With only two feet of trailer remaining to safely clear the arch, the driver started to turn left and up the cobblestone path, where the LaChance crypt was located. With a loud crack the trailer suddenly stopped. The largest of the twenty-four soulful sisters of the Ebenezer Baptist Church lurched into three of her semi-siblings in the back row, pitching the lead soprano into the flowers at the rear. The throng gasped. Miles McDougal mournfully stared at Grace, the front leg of which had buckled under. Grace sat at an oblique angle, her shiny black lid propped open, exposing her innards, which continued in sympathetic vibration caused by her fall. Three of the mourners assisted McDougal as Grace was uprighted and balanced on several cinder blocks, which were found behind the archway. Both Grace and the principal diva were shaken from the ordeal, but both seemed ready for their graveside performance.

The motel manager had told Peg, "You can measure the status one had in the community by the number of instruments played in his or her funeral procession." If this was true, No Chance had been big—very big.

More surprising to Peg was the large number of ordinary folk who took time from their Saturday morning to pay their condolences. Most had only watched LaChance pitch on TV; few had had the opportunity to personally view his exploits. Although portrayed as a pompous ass by members of the media, Bill LaChance remained a hero to his community, not because of his achievements in baseball but for his devotion to his roots.

The Honorable George "Blind Lemon" McSplivins, as part of his funeral parade marshal duties, assumed the role of master of ceremonies of this event. Between eulogies, each of the participating musical entourage performed its special tribute to its fallen champion.

Blind Lemon added his own words of respect and then announced, "Our final eulogy will be delivered by Ms. Patricia Tremblay, CEO of Cajun Food Specialties of Ponchatoula, Louisiana."

"Good morning, everyone. Although, I'm associated with the Cajun Food Specialties Company of Ponchatoula, of much more importance is that I chair the seven-member board of Bill LaChance's Take a Chance Foundation.

"Who was Bill LaChance? Father, All-Star pitcher, soon-to-be Hall of Fame honoree, business associate, philanthropist, and friend. As the chairperson of the Take a Chance Foundation, I cannot begin to tell you of the good that Bill and his foundation have done for so many, not only in the Mississippi Delta but throughout North and Central America. The committee would like to thank all those who have contributed and will continue to contribute to the Take a Chance Foundation. I'm sure we share sincere gratitude to Bill for his kindness and devotion to his roots.

"Bill ... No Chance ... LaChance ... you will be missed."

It was obvious to all that Patricia Tremblay was a major-league fan of LaChance and what he represented to his community.

On the Mississippi Delta, cemeteries are referred to as "Cities of the Dead" because the dearly departed are buried in family tombs built above the ground. These cemeteries were designed this way not because they looked good in the movies but because of the problems experienced as a result of flooding. At one time, graves in the Louisiana Delta were beneath the ground, but when flood waters rose, so did the coffins.

The casket of LaChance was slowly carried on its final journey into a large ornately decorated crypt by six former team mates who, in their role as pallbearers, wore the cap of their respective teams—Mike Goldstein and Jose Duarte, coaches from the Yankees, McHugh, Oliver, and Natola from the Mets, and Nicky "Hot Wheels" Maganser, now retired but who was LaChance's catcher when he was in Houston. McSplivins once again stepped to the podium. "James DiMarino and Adrianna Lomysh, friends of the LaChance family, will conclude these services by singing one of Bill's favorites, "To Where You Are."

Miles McDougal, attired in a lime-green tuxedo, climbed the seven steps onto the rear of the Cajun Food Specialties trailer and slowly approached Grace. Lomysh and DiMarino flanked the doors the LaChance repository. McDougal and Grace, with her amputated leg, played the intro as Lomysh and DiMarino began.

DiMarino and Lomysh sang the first stanza together. DiMarino completed "to where you are" alone. Adrianna Lomysh was inconsolable. Peg wondered about the reasons for her profound grief. It was obvious to all that No Chance LaChance meant a great deal to Adrianna Lomysh. McCarthy made a mental note to check into this later.

At the end of Boudreaux Bayou Road, just before it joins with County Road 37, is the McCarrick Elementary School. Nearly all of the hundreds of attendees at the funeral service walked behind the music to the school, as the musicians played "When the Saints Come Marching In."

A wall plaque at the entrance read: "This school is named in honor of War of 1812 naval hero Captain Robert McCarrick, who in the early morning of the 8 January 1815 engaged the superior fleet of British Vice-Admiral Cochrane. Attacking with his diminutive force of five gunboats, Captain McCarrick damaged one British frigate and caused two British troop transports to go aground. The regiments on these British transports were unable to join the ranks of the 8,000 others that were in battle with Americans, led by Major General Andrew Jackson. A week later the British force withdrew from the New Orleans area. The area to the rear of this school and continuing east to the end of Boudreaux Bayou Road is the actual location of the last battle of the War of 1812, the Battle of New Orleans."

The cafeteria of the McCarrick School was not the most ideal location for the gathering of the funeral participants. However, the ice tea, lemonade, and cookies provided by the Delta Jazz Preservation Society were welcome and necessary in the eighty-degree heat.

"Hi, I'm Peg Mc McCarthy. I'm with the Montreal Expos."

"What position do you play?" joked Patricia Tremblay. "Tu parlez francais?"

"Oui," Peg answered with her own smile.

"Mm-m-m. I wondered if everyone associated with the Expos spoke French. Do you live in Montreal?"

"No, actually I'm originally from Maryland, just outside of D.C. Could I ask you to a few questions about Bill LaChance and the Take a Chance Foundation?"

"Perhaps another time, Ms. McCarthy. I'm emotionally wiped out. When are you returning to Montreal?"

"I understand. I have a flight late tomorrow afternoon."

Hoping that the Expos might be forthcoming with a sizable donation to the LaChance foundation, Mrs. Tremblay offered, "I'll be in my office all day tomorrow. Why not stop on your way to the airport? The plant is just off the I-10, right near the I-55 interchange."

"That will work, Mrs. Tremblay. Say 2:30? Are you sure Sunday is okay?"

"See you at 2:30. Here's my card; the directions are on the back."

Chapter 21

Ponchatoula
PATRICIA Tremblay

Not far from the intersection of Interstates 55 and 10 was the tiny Louisiana town of Ponchatoula, home of Cajun Food Specialties Company. A long, single-story, nondescript building in the LeJeune Industrial Park was identified by two twelve-foot chili peppers—one red, one green—flanking the heading "Cajun Food Specialties—Ponchatoula, La."

A circular manicured garden included three flags: the Stars and Stripes, the flag of the great state of Louisiana, and the company logo flying at half-staff. In the center of the logo flag was the two-foot chili pepper with the sinister smile. A pleasant aroma of spices cooking permeated the air, something sweet yet spicy hot. Employee parking was along the left side of the building. Five angled parking spaces faced the garden. Two spots were marked "visitor," one had a handicapped symbol, one was marked "Foreman," and the last was lettered in capital letters: "PATRICIA."

Sunday afternoon found Patricia Tremblay dressed casually in slacks and a white T-shirt emblazoned with the Cajun Food insignia.

"Good afternoon, Ms. McCarthy," greeted the chili pepper baroness as Peg entered the reception area.

"Please, call me Peg." Peg looked at her watch, the time was 2:27 p.m. "You have a long day in the world of hot sauce."

"Yes, Peg, I've a lot of things to catch up on. This week has been very hectic, with the wake and then the funeral. I prefer to be informal as well, so please, call me Patricia. You said yesterday that you are from the D.C. area. Maryland?"

"Actually, Pat, I now live in upstate Vermont. I grew up in Maryland."

"I prefer to be called Patricia. I do business with a company in northern Vermont. Ames Wood Products. Ever hear of it? They build all our oak casks for aging sauce."

"Wow! What a small world! Ames Wood is only about nine miles from where I live. George Ames is the brother of our local sheriff."

"I've never met George Ames. We have dealings over the phone. But I can tell you this: he's one of the most honest people that I deal with. His prices are fair and he delivers exactly as promised. What questions bring you to Ponchatoula on a Sunday afternoon? I'm sure it's not to buy hot sauce."

"Well, Patricia, as you know, I was sent to represent the Expos at the funeral."

Patricia Tremblay, with an obviously pained expression, asked, "Do you have any idea what really happened to Bill? The media is full of conjecture. Overdose, steroids, suicide."

"That's my main reason for coming to see you on my way to catch a return flight to Boston. Do you know anyone who may have disliked Bill LaChance? Any recent issues down here on the Delta?"

"Peg, Bill LaChance was a close friend of mine. This company was founded by my late husband's family over 150 years ago. My husband, Jo-El, and Bill LaChance graduated from high school together. Bill LaChance was the best man at our wedding in 1985. When Jo-El was diagnosed with Hodgkin's disease five years ago, it was Bill LaChance who flew from California to be with him during his final days. After Jo-El's death, it was Bill LaChance who advised me as to how to run this company. I don't know how I could have gone through those most difficult days without him. I will miss him. The media has, over the past fifteen years, tried to portray Bill LaChance as a money-grubbing, heartless, cold individual. Nothing could be further from the truth. His association with this company was only to provide a means of generating funds for the Take a Chance Foundation. Bill LaChance received no monies from the sale of his Hi-Heat Hot Sauce."

Patricia Tremblay, the tough, determined CEO of Cajun Food, looked out into the parking lot to hide the tears running down her cheeks.

"I'm sorry, Mrs. Tremblay. I didn't stop by to stir up memories."

"Ms. McCarthy, what was your reason for stopping here on a Sunday afternoon?"

"I don't believe that Mr. LaChance's death was suicide, and I don't believe that he accidentally overdosed. I believe he may have been intentionally poisoned."

Regaining her composure, Patricia Tremblay became agitated and angry. "Who? Why?"

"I'm sure, Mrs. Tremblay, you've heard all the media reports concerning Mr. LaChance's toxicology report. It's public knowledge that his cardiac and respiratory failure was caused by the drug oxycodone hydrochloride, better known as Oxycontin. It has been determined that it was a new variation of the drug called Oxyquick. Who knows? Perhaps the intent may not have been to kill Mr. LaChance, just to make him ill. Do you have any ideas who may have poisoned Mr. LaChance?"

"Ms. McCarthy, yesterday's proceedings, I hope, demonstrated the true feelings that the people of the Delta had for Bill. He was considered by many to be our personal hero. Please don't do anything that may tarnish his image with the people who loved him."

"Patricia, you and I share the same goal. We want to find the real story behind Bill's death. My reason for stopping to speak with you today was to ask if the Take a Chance Foundation had any unusual or curious requests that may have been denied or rejected."

"We do get an occasional weird request for cash or support from a dubious charity. If you leave your fax number, I'll forward you a list. It won't be lengthy. Most requests we receive are very appropriate. Any other issues?"

"Yes. Bill LaChance had a daughter?"

Patricia Tremblay visibly stiffened. "Please don't go there. Marie is only thirteen years old. She and her dad were extremely close. That's one of the reasons Bill was hoping to go to the Red Sox—to be closer to Marie. During the off-season, Bill lived in Massachusetts, but you probably know that."

"Was there any bitterness between Mr. LaChance and his ex?"

"Dianne? None that I ever heard of. Bill always spoke very highly of her. When the marriage ended, there was no noise or notice. She's a trauma-room nurse back in the Boston area."

Peg continued adding notes to her ever-present yellow legal pad. Before noting all the details of the former Mrs. LaChance, she asked another question. "Were Adrianna Lomysh and Bill LaChance more than just friends? She seemed extremely distraught at the internment service yesterday."

"Bill was a big supporter of the arts here on the Delta. I believe he was instrumental in the development of both Lomysh's and DiMarino's singing careers. I don't think there's any more to it than that. Ms McCarthy, I think you'll be hard pressed finding any murder suspects here in Louisiana."

"Thank you very much, Mrs. Tremblay, for sharing your insight. Oh, one other question, if I may. Do you know a Walter Qaqish?"

"*Qaqish!* That cretin! Never met him. Don't want to! He called here yesterday wanting me to ship five cases of Bill's Hi-Heat Hot Sauce. He e-mailed a similar request. What nerve! He was a so-called friend of Bill's. I can't imagine why. He and Bill did baseball shows during the off-season. Bill had us ship Qaqish cases of hot sauce, the small sample bottles, to be given out at the shows. I'm sure Qaqish wants to hustle a buck, probably going to sell them for five or ten dollars a bottle. Claimed Bill had told him to call us before his death to order more of the product."

"Do you have Qaqish's shipping address?"

Patricia jotted the address of Walter Qaqish on a sticky pad and handed it to Peg.

Walter Qaqish, 443 Warren St., W. Warwick, R.I. 02889
email: cardman@popcorn.com

"Well, Patricia, thanks again. You have my number. If you could fax me that list of odd requests to LaChance's foundation, that would be appreciated. Thanks again."

Peg thought it best not to mention that the drug that killed LaChance was found in one of the small sample bottles of Bill LaChance's Hi-Heat Hot Sauce. Patricia Tremblay didn't need to know those facts. It was clear why Ace Edwards' office never mentioned the hot-sauce bottle in its release of the cause of death. That information could put a small-sized company like the Cajun Food Specialties out of business and its workers out on the street. Besides, the product-tampering didn't seem to have happened at the point of manufacture. It was illogical that if someone at the hot-sauce plant wanted to dope the small plastic bottles, he or she would not have needed to infuse the Oxyquick with a syringe and place clear tape over the injection hole.

While waiting the final twenty minutes before boarding Flight 8129 to Montreal via Philadelphia, Peg rewrote her list. The funeral of William LaChance and the later conversation with Patricia Tremblay had altered her inventory.

Yellow Pad Entry: #11c Addendum 2-9-2003 5:27 p.m.
With the now known facts the strongest possible candidates are:
Walter Qaqish
With the now known facts the weakest possible candidates are:
William LaChance, Accidental Poisoning, Montreal Expos, A Random Act of Tampering, LaChance's Daughter Marie (only thirteen yeas old) and the Hot Sauce Company

Somewhere in-between strongest and weakest is the possibility that LaChance's death could be caused by: An Irate Fan, LaChance's Ex-Wife, Patricia Tremblay, and the 'Take a Chance Foundation', and Adrianna Lomysh-the singer at service?

A short list of possible culprits was forming in Peg's mind, and Mr. Walter Qaqish, a.k.a. CARDMAN, seemed to be moving to the head of the class.

Chapter 22

7:24 a.m.
Tuesday, February 11

P eg's thoughts went to her own situation. *This coming Friday will my final day of work. It seems as if I started only a few years ago; and yet it seems like I've done this my whole life.*

The flight was uneventful and, mercifully, not crowded. To Peg, it seemed as if she had been away from Vermont for a month. First the job interview in Boston, then the trip to New Orleans for the LaChance funeral and on to Montreal Sunday night for a breakfast meeting with J.P. Bellevue at the Montreal Bonaventure Hilton at ten o'clock Monday morning. At brunch, Bellevue discussed the fact that the payroll supervisor of the Expos had noticed that LaChance had recently requested continuation of a directed deduction from his payroll check be made monthly to Allied Abington Insurance Company. He asked Peg to notify the ex-Mrs. LaChance that, when Bill LaChance was with the Mets, he had purchased a one-million-dollar life insurance policy from Allied Abington as a trust fund for his daughter, Marie. This insurance policy was the first indication that LaChance had any dependants. Both Peg and Bellevue were surprised that LaChance had a daughter. After updating Bellevue, a Monday afternoon limo ride, courtesy of the Expos, brought Peg McCarthy back to North Troy. *It's all a blur*, she thought.

Peg arrived at the Customs Station at 3:30 p.m. Bill reported that Sheriff Ames had called twice. Of all those in the office, Sarek seemed the happiest with Peg's return. Hard for Peg to believe that it'd been just two weeks since Sarek arrived. Seemed like he'd been there forever. The few people that Peg talked with in New Orleans couldn't give much information concerning Sarek. Patricia Tremblay knew of the dog but said that to her knowledge, Bill LaChance never had the dog with him when he visited Louisiana.

Yellow Pad Entry: #12 2-11-2003 7:24 a.m.
Patricia Tremblay mentioned that LaChance never had the dog with him on his last several visits to New Orleans.

Check kennels south of Boston to see if Sarek was boarded. Perhaps Sarek stayed with daughter and ex-wife.

The weather in northern Vermont in February was a repeat of January: cold followed by snow followed by cold followed by more snow. But at 7:45 a.m., the day brightened considerably when Sheriff Ames entered the Customs Station with a box of Grandma Joan's blueberry muffins—baked fresh about an hour before. Sweet.

"Hi, Peg. Welcome home! How did the job interview go?"

Sarek had his nose high in the air as the smell of the freshly baked muffins wafted across the office.

"Well, Frank, I have a message on my answering machine to call Apex. I'm sure they will make me a reasonable offer. But I'm just as sure that I will be intolerably bored with whatever Apex has me doing. Meanwhile, I have this deal with the Expos which I find intriguing."

"Well, Peg, as I mentioned in our phone conversation last night, the Vermont State Police are impounding LaChance's Range Rover. Dr. Edwards has declared this a suspicious-death investigation, and, because LaChance was found in the vehicle, they will be transporting the SUV to Montpelier by car carrier. They said the carrier will be here by ten o'clock on Friday. I received several calls from that guy Qaqish. He's still wanting 'his' baseball cards. He's also looking for the cases of hot sauce."

"What could be so special about those baseball cards, Frank? They're all the same number; some signed, some not. Qaqish is probably just trying to hustle a buck."

One of the cards was in a clear plastic page in the LaChance scrapbook. Looking at the reverse side gave no clue as to why Qaqish might want these cards.

No. 71
LaChance, William "No Chance"   Born 11/19/67   Belle Chase, LA

Height: 6'3"   Weight: 233   Bats: Right   Throws: Right

YEAR	TEAM	W	L	GS	IP	H	BB	K	SO	ER	ERA
1987	Houst. NL	8	3	15	130	126	31	94	1	54	3.74
1988		16	7	28	236.1	221	93	173	3	81	3.09
1989		22	9	36	258	214	86	288	3	77	2.67
1990		26	3	36	273.2	193	68	338	6	63	1.88
1991		18	9	34	252	277	86	226	1	81	2.89
1992		21	8	35	261	232	77	274	5	65	2.24

Year	Team										
1993		**25**	7	*36*	**280.2**	205	83	**309**	4	71	**2.28**
1994		19	12	34	269.1	246	101	216	1	84	2.81
1995	NY AL	**22**	8	**36**	253	227	82	273	6	82	2.92
1996		17	8	30	231.1	198	80	258	2	83	3.23
1997		21	10	37	284.1	229	107	243	3	91	2.88
1998		15	15	*35*	247	252	98	239	1	104	3.71
1999		12	8	27	211.2	223	75	197	0	68	2.89
2000	NY NL	**23**	4	33	253	189	62	**317**	4	67	**2.38**
2001		*18*	9	31	246	208	59	254	2	83	3.04
2002		20	5	33	233	178	67	301	3	90	3.48
Totals		293	125	516	3920	3428	1256	4000	45	1244	2.86

Pro*Star Sports Cards, Plano, TX

Walter Qaqish was becoming more than a grungy chum of Bill LaChance. His constant pressure to retrieve articles from the SUV and his efforts to have Cajun Food Specialties send him more of the small sample bottles of LaChance's Hot Sauce were, to say the least, fishy. Perhaps Qaqish's interest in obtaining more bottles of hot sauce, the same bottles associated with the death of No Chance LaChance, was just an unfortunate coincidence.

Picking up the phone, Peg enlisted the assistance of directory assistance. "What city and state?"

The phone listing of SPORTSCARD HEAVEN, 443 Warren Street, West Warwick, R.I. revealed a robotic message: "The weekday hours of SPORTSCARD HEAVEN are 11:00 a.m. to 7:00 p.m. Friday's until 9:00 p.m. and Saturdays, 9:00 a.m. to 6:00 p.m. Please note: we are closed on Sundays and selected Saturdays for baseball card shows."

Peg also knew, as the bureaucratic wheels started to turn in the formal investigation of LaChance's death, that the homicide detectives of the Vermont State Police would also be traveling south to West Warwick, Rhode Island. Peg McCarthy suspected it might be more productive to chat with Qaqish prior to the visit from the police. Qaqish would probably be speaking through his attorney very soon. Peg also realized that, if Qaqish was responsible for the death of LaChance, it would be wise not to visit him alone. A phone call to Boston quickly enlisted the immediate assistance of close friend Dr. Stu Mirkin. Mirkin told Peg his only restriction would be that he had to be back in Boston to catch a flight out of Logan at 8:20 p.m. He had to jet to the West

Coast for a one-day speaking engagement. Peg and the dear doctor planned to visit Walter Qaqish on Thursday, mid-afternoon.

The *Boston American Record*, the undeclared daily tabloid of the Beantown print media, had begun a five-part series on the dirty little secret of professional sports (baseball in particular) on Sunday, the ninth. The skeleton in the closet was the use and misuse of performance-enhancing supplements. Ephedrine, steroids, and now the possible misuse of Oxycontin by a now very deceased future Hall of Fame pitcher were discussed in part one of the series. Later installments promised to name names. To be sure, one of the headlines would include the name of No Chance LaChance.

As Peg laid a large map of southeastern Massachusetts and Rhode Island out on the counter, she remembered that both Bill and Chip had asked for a list of people who should be invited to the yet-to-be-planned retirement celebration. Typically, Peg recorded her thoughts onto her trusty yellow pad.

Retirement Note: 2-10-2003 9:13 a.m.
The location will have to be a motel or country inn in nearby North Troy. Invitees should include C.A. Ed Hawley and wife Brenda, C.A. Clare Murphy and friend Chet Columbo, C.A. Bill Atwood and wife Amy, C.A. Homer (Chip) Randall and his brother James (the researcher from U. of Maine in Orono), who is staying with Chip while studying the owl population, C.A. Scott. Mom and Dad, Kate and Rich, Mary and Patrick, maybe Jim (I did invite him verbally last time we talked). Maybe Stu?

Journal Entry
Monday, February 10, 2003
I had no idea what a philanthropist LaChance really was. Oh, well, hopefully his foundation will continue with the positive work that he began.

So, about my retirement party. I really need to move forward with these plans! The guest list is almost done. Two questionable invites: Jim and Stu. Jim and I started our careers together so it seems only appropriate that he should be here when I conclude mine. Jim—yes.

Dr. Stu Mirkin, I wonder. Skiing was fun. Dinner in Boston was nice, very nice. He's so easy to chat with. It seems I've known him forever, and we've actually just met.

Hm-m-m. Make a decision—yes or no? It's just a party invite. He probably won't come to it anyway. Always so busy! Okay—yes.

There—the guest list is done! Now just the place, food, date, etc. Well, I'll think about that later.

Chapter 23

02-13-03, 02889
3:15 p.m.

West Warwick, Rhode Island, like so many New England towns, looked as if it had had a purpose in an era long ago. One hundred years past, in Massachusetts, the City of Lowell had been known for its textiles and Brockton for its shoes. It was difficult to visualize what claim to fame West Warwick may have had. Peg McCarthy and Dr. Stu Mirkin arrived at 443 Warren St. at 3:15 p.m.

The string of stores that were the downtown of West Warwick, Rhode Island, appeared to have been denied TLC since the late 1950s or early '60s. Every town that called itself a town had a Woolworths or a W.T. Grant. The store that was Walter Qaqish's SPORTSCARD HEAVEN looked as if, in an earlier life, it might have been a J.J. Newberry's. The store adjacent to Qaqish's had Old English-style lettering on the glass, proclaiming "Dark Dungeon." In the window was an array of medieval helmets, battle axes, halberds, knives, and swords. Unlike the Dark Dungeon, the window display of SPORTSCARD HEAVEN was barren. Peg could see four cases stamped "Cajun Food Specialties—Ponchatoula, LA 70454" through the unwashed window.

A bell over the door announced the arrival and departure of patrons. Upon entering, Peg was surprised to see that Dark Dungeon and SPORTSCARD HEAVEN were actually joined, and that one could walk from one store to the other through a portal that was emblazoned with "Prepare to Meet Thy Maker." A large portrait of a king cobra with an ominous smile flanked each side of the walkway into the Dark Dungeon section of the store.

The store seemed empty. However, Peg could hear several voices speaking on the other side of the cobras. Stu Mirkin was revisiting his youth as he peered into the glass cases of baseball cards.

"Wow! Look at this, Peg! 1967 Pirates. I remember these guys. They were my favorite team back then. Only $28. That seems fair."

"Stu, we're here for information, not to buy baseball cards. Hello! Hello! Is anyone here?"

"Peg, they're all here: Willie Stargell, Roberto Clemente, Bob Veale, Vern Law. There's even a Don Schwall. I remember when he first pitched for the Red Sox. I forgot all about Bill Mazeroski."

Peg was bemused that a forty-eight-year-old former pediatric surgeon and world-renowned forensic scientist could, in an instant, revert back to his years as a Little Leaguer.

"Over here," a voice beckoned from beyond the king cobras with the menacing smiles. Peg entered the other side of the store, which could be described as the other side of the universe, dark and dreary. A display of T-shirts and posters adorned with skulls, flames, dragons, and other associated monsters filled the far wall. Black lighting produced a forbidding glow to the rear of the store. A deep-maroon curtain was pushed to the right, and a thin youth of less than sixteen years with nearly that many pieces of facial jewelry approached Peg and Stu. Beyond him, past the burgundy drape, Peg could see three others standing around a four-foot oval table. The sweet smell of burning incense flooded into the room when the curtain was pushed aside.

"Hi there. Welcome to the Dark Dungeon. I'm Jason. Do you play Magik?"

"Excuse me?" answered Peg. "I'm looking for Mr. Qaqish."

The attire of Jason and the three Magik players could be definitely be defined as Gothic.

"Oh, Uncle Wally. He's at lunch; he'll be back at 3:30."

Stu asked, "What's that incense scent you're burning? Checkerberry?"

"No, juniper, I think," replied the youth. "We need it. Uncle Wally's got a water problem in the basement. I'm trying to cover the musty smell. Besides, it adds to the atmosphere of the Magik game."

The personable, facially adorned adolescent proceeded to describe the trading-card game known as Magik. He also enlightened Peg and Stu regarding the artists of the various fantasy art wall posters. "Fantasy art developed in the late 1960s, some of it in comics of that era. It all started with Boris Vallejo. That's one of his posters there. The one with the beautiful maiden riding a tiger. I have signed posters drawn by Brian Doyle Mackey, Andrea Haney, Christopher Pearce, and Pat Odom. Can I show you anything?"

"I'd like to see that set of 1967 Pittsburgh Pirates cards in the showcase. Should I wait for Mr. Qaqish?" asked Mirkin.

"No, I'll get them out for you. I take care of Uncle's side when he's not here, and he watches my store from 11:00 until 2:30, when I get out of school."

Looking at her watch—3:25—Peg asked, "What year of high school are you? You seem young to have your own business."

"I'm a junior at Champion Charter School. It's an alternative school for misfits like me and the other Goths behind the curtain." Jason laughed uncomfortably. "This is more like a hobby than a business. Uncle says it keeps me busy and off the streets. We do card shows together."

"Oh, you did card shows with your uncle and Bill LaChance?"

"I only did a couple with Mr. LaChance. Too bad about him. I liked him. He was a nice guy. I usually only do non-sports card shows with my uncle."

"What cards are classified as non-sports cards?" asked Peg.

"All kinds of stuff," offered Jason. "Non-sport cards have been around longer than those with sports personalities. Years ago, there were bird sets, flowers, and butterflies. Then, later on, airplanes like the Wings and Jets series made by Topps. All kinds of stuff on non-sports cards. Uncle has a mint Elvis set from the early 1970s in the case."

Peg was examining a medieval weapon—a spiked steel sphere (tennis-ball size) attached to a wooden handle by a fifteen-inch chain. *How can they sell things like this?* she wondered to herself.

"Oh, that's not real," exclaimed Jason. "It's only a replica. We have a double-ball version also."

"That's comforting." Peg could only imagine the ruckus such an item would cause at a boarding gate at Logan Airport.

The bell on the door of SPORTSCARD HEAVEN announced that Walter Qaqish was back from lunch.

"Uncle, can you show this customer the 1967 Pittsburgh Pirates set in case number two?"

Through the store-connecting threshold, Peg McCarthy noticed that Walter Qaqish did not look nearly as disheveled as he had two weeks ago.

Stu Mirkin thumbed through the set of eighteen cards. "Jim Pagliaroni, Pete Mikkelsen, Roy Face, Woody Fryman's rookie card. Twenty-eight dollars. Why so cheap?"

"Condition. Condition means everything. The Clemente card alone would be worth $65 if it were mint. Investment collectors only want cards that are perfect. Those cards are far from perfect. But if you're a 1960s Pirates fan, those are for you."

"Do you have any No Chance LaChance memorabilia?" Dr. Mirkin was doing a bit of investigating on his own. Peg continued looking at the strange assortment of medieval implements of Jason's Dark Dungeon emporium.

"LaChance stuff is very pricey, especially since his death. Seventy-five bucks for a signed card and thirty-five for a signed bottle of LaChance's Hi-Heat Hot Sauce. If you're interested, hundred bucks for the pair."

Peg entered the baseball side of the store. Qaqish hardly noticed. Jason returned to the Magik game behind the wine-red curtain. "Would you take twenty dollars for the Pirates set?" Mirkin placed two tens on the counter.

"Deal," mumbled Qaqish. He removed his infamous crumbled handkerchief from his right pants pocket, followed by a wad of bills to which he quickly filed Mirkin's two ten-spots.

"Good afternoon, Mr. Qaqish. Do you remember me?" Peg entered the card store from the dimly lighted side.

"Maybe. You look familiar." He put a mint Roberto Clemente card in a plastic protector onto the counter. Stu Mirkin was starting to drool. "This is what mint looks like. Look at that. Did you notice, they called him Bob Clemente back then?"

"I'm Peg McCarthy from the U.S. Customs Station up in Vermont. You stopped there a couple of weeks ago."

Without even blinking, Qaqish retorted, "You're a long way from Vermont. What brings you to West Warwick? Are you delivering my stuff that was in Bill's car?"

"Well, Mr. Qaqish, as far as I know the vehicle is still impounded by the Vermont State Police. Mr. Qaqish, you seemed to know Bill LaChance pretty well. Did you ever suspect he was taking drugs?"

"Bill LaChance? Drugs? No way! LaChance didn't have many bad habits, no drugs, no booze, no chew, no nothing. He thought too much of himself and the money he could earn to ever be involved with anything like that. The only bad habits I know of were eating those damn sunflower seeds and his ability to tick off members of the media. He was an expert at doing both."

"Do you think LaChance could tick off someone to the point of poisoning him?"

The card dealer scratched the left side of his head. "A member of the press or TV? No, Bill was the press' bread and butter. Always a controversial story, whether he spoke to them or not. Down deep, they loved, well, respected No Chance LaChance. Why all the questions? You sound like some kind of cop. Why is the Customs Service involved?"

Peg picked up the Clemente card and wondered what was so special about it. The sixty-eight-dollar sticker on the corner of the plastic protector seemed outrageous for the paper card inside. "No, I'm not a cop. I'm retired from the Customs Service. I'm working for the Montreal Expos. The Expos are very concerned about Mr. LaChance's death."

Qaqish, always ready to react to a possible business opportunity, reacted to Peg's Expos connection. "Wow! The Expos! Maybe you and I can do some dealing. I'm always looking for interesting baseball memorabilia. You don't have any LaChance items, do you? He probably wasn't with them long enough. Too bad. Really too bad. You and I could have made some serious bread. Do you really think somebody poisoned Bill?"

"You were one of the last to see Bill LaChance alive. What do you think?"

Qaqish scratched his head once more. It was then that Peg knew what was so different about the cardman. A toupee! Qaqish was wearing a rug and not a very good one at that.

"I don't know, Ms. McCarthy, I just don't know. Mr. LaChance and I made a lot of money in our years of knowing each other. Well, I made a lot for me, and Bill made a lot for his foundation. Lately, everything he was involved with was for that damn charitable foundation. I don't know who would want Bill dead, but I do know it's going to hurt my business. Going to cost me a lot of money. That's life."

Peg nodded in agreement, then asked, "Do you know anything about Mr. LaChance's dog?"

Qaqish's oval face turned prune-like under his ugly hairpiece. "I don't care much for dogs. Especially that dog! Bill thought the world of that mutt. I wouldn't trust that fleabag, Sarek, any further than I could throw him."

"I see, Mr. Qaqish. Did Mr. LaChance ever mention where the dog stayed when he was away?"

"I didn't trust him. Bill mentioned that the dog stayed with someone while he was on the road. He often said he had to pick up the damn dog at Jule's or maybe Jude's place. I'm not sure what that means. Maybe a friend or perhaps a kennel. I don't care much for that dog."

Stu drove the return trip to Boston, a trip that was, for the most part, very quiet. About the time that route I-295 intersected with I-95, Stu asked, "What are you thinking about, Peg?"

"Just trying to figure how, and if, Qaqish fits into this picture. I was so sure we were hot on the trail of the murder motive of Bill LaChance. I'm not so sure now. Qaqish didn't act like he might have been involved. Just a poor slob trying to make a buck, like the rest of us. One other thing is bothering me."

"What's that, Peg?"

"Checkerberry. Why checkerberry? The incense in Jason's side of the store. Why would you think of checkerberry."

Stu Mirkin had to smile, although Peg couldn't see his grin. It was nearly 5:15 and dark. "Oh, checkerberry. An old friend of mine, an autopsy colleague, Jim Gilmore, better known as Bones Gilmore. Every time he got a tough one, you know, well decomposed, he burned checkerberry incense to cover the stench. The smell of that incense reminded me of Bones. He retired last year, to a life of golf. What a great friend and a great teacher!"

Chapter 24

02-13-03
Route I-95 Northbound,
5:55 p.m.

"I hate cell phones. Said I'd never get one. Look at me now, fumbling around in the dark, trying to retrieve messages from who knows who."

Peg McCarthy was pressing buttons on her phone like a steno typist from Carla Crawford's Secretarial School, a place Peg had taken summer courses while in high school at the insistence of her mother. Rather than argue all summer, she agreed to the daily train ride to downtown Washington. Besides she loved, still did, the urban environment.

"Please enter your password. You have three new messages and one saved message. To listen to your messages press 1."

"First new message …"

"Hello, Peg, J.P. Bellevue. Just wondering how things are going. Talk to you soon. Au revoir."

"To save this message press 7; to delete, press 9. Message saved."

"Next new Message …"

"Hi, Peg, Frank here. Muriel, in my office says Buckley Roberts, LaChance's agent, has called here twice today (2-13-03) and once yesterday. Something about the dog. I didn't know if you wanted your cell phone number spread around. Here is his number if you want to call direct: 617-282-5660."

"To save this message, press 7; to delete, press 9. Message saved. Next new message …"

"Good afternoon. It's 3:30 on Thursday, February 13. This is Dave Lindahl with Apex International. I'm calling to see if you have made a decision concerning our offer of a position with Apex. Please call me with your intentions within the next couple of days. Thank you. 617-435-7711."

"To save this message, press 7; to delete, press 9. Message saved. First saved message …"

"Hi, Peggy. Mom here. It's Monday the 10th, 1:35 in the afternoon. We were wondering if there are any details on your retirement party. Love you. Bye-bye."

"To save this message, press 7; to delete, press 9. Message saved. You have no more messages."

The vehicle was stone silent for about six miles, until Stu asked, "Anything important?"

"I guess that's it for Sarek. LaChance's agent, Buckley Roberts, has been calling Frank and asking about the dog for the last couple of days. It was only a matter of time. That will teach me to get close to another animal."

The remainder of the ride back to the airport consisted of occasional chitchat. After a dinner at Dickie O'Doherty's Eatery & Irish Pub in Southie, the shortcut to Logan through the new Ted Williams Tunnel brought the couple to Terminal C at 7:55. Stu exited the driver's door and Peg, the right side. Mirkin removed his overnight bag from the rear seat, checked his shirt pocket to be sure that his set of 1967 Pittsburgh Pirates was accounted for, and met Peg at the curb. He kissed Peg softly, and they hugged. All Mirkin could say was, "I'm so sorry about your dog."

Peg, fighting back tears, replied, "Thanks. I'll miss that dog."

"I should be back from L.A. before noon Saturday. Want to do lunch?"

"I'm not sure. I'll have to see what happens tomorrow. I have a lot of people to talk to. I'll check with Buckley Roberts in the morning. I have your number. I'll call you to let you know about Sarek. Have a good trip."

The Regency Estates in Braintree, about fifteen miles south of Boston, was the ideal accommodation for the business traveler. Large rooms, mini-refrigerator, restaurant, Internet access, easy on/off to the major arteries. The three-night rate was cheaper than a downtown hotel, and, most important to Peg tonight, it was quiet.

Before turning in for the evening, Peg, as usual, jotted down her tentative agenda for Friday.

Yellow Pad Entry: #13 2-13-2003 9:49 p.m.
Is Qaqish less of a suspect than noted earlier? Or more? Q. claims his business partner (LaChance) is deceased and this will cost him dearly.

Maybe Q. is sitting on a ton of LaChance memorabilia. Is he hoping the value will increase? Is this reason enough to poison LaChance?

Perhaps LaChance was dropping Qaqish in favor of a new arrangement. Q. is only a small-time operator. LaChance seemed to look out for his foundation over other considerations.

Did Q. skim profits from the foundation. This would certainly prompt LaChance to dump him.

Q. had the opportunities; did he have a motive?

Things to do:

 # 1—Return call to Buckley Roberts, 617 282-5660.

 # 2—Return phone calls to Apex, Bellevue, and Mom.

 # 3—Check on local kennel (Jule's or Jude's) to see if Sarek may have been boarded there during LaChance's trip away from home. Call Ashodod Animal Hospital in Easton, Mass.; maybe they know where Sarek was boarded.

 # 4—Set up an appointment with Dianne (ex-LaChance) and possibly Marie (LaChance's daughter) to discuss the insurance policy and also ask if dog should be coming to them.

 # 5— LaChance had an appointment card from his dentist in his wallet. Stop at LaChance's dentist (Julia Emig, DMD, 4 North Av, Rockland, Mass.) to ask about LaChance's recent tooth extractions that were noted in the autopsy report. (Call first.)

With all intentions of watching the eleven o'clock news, Peg dozed off, while the television remained on Channel 4 until the early morning hours. Peg McCarthy was exhausted. Totally exhausted.

Chapter 25

4:38 PST

A ringing woke Peg at 7:38 a.m. The sound seemed to be in four-ring cycles. R-ring—R- ring, then a short pause of about ten to twenty seconds before starting again. On or about the fourth cycle, Peg realized that the sound was coming from her fanny pack. It was her cell phone.

"Hello, Agent McCarthy here." Peg remembered that this was her last official day with the Customs Service.

"Good Morning, Peg. Did I wake you? It's Stu."

"That's okay, Stu. I needed to get started. What's up?"

"I guess you haven't been watching the news."

Peg was still trying to remove the cobwebs of sleep. "I had every intention of watching it last night but I fell asleep."

"That attorney who's been calling you, Buckley Roberts, LaChance's agent. Somebody murdered him in his car last night. Shot twice."

"What's next, Stu? Any details?" Peg McCarthy was awake. Wide awake.

"Here's the weird part. He was shot across the street from Dickie O'Doherty's in Southie, where we had dinner last night. My friends at the South Boston Police Precinct tell me Roberts also had dinner with a client at O'Doherty's. He must have arrived just after we left."

"That's weird, really weird."

"I'd say that! I already talked with Barbara Lyons this morning. She's the assistant DA for Suffolk County. They asked me in on the autopsy tomorrow afternoon. I'm catching the red-eye back late tonight. What do you say we do dinner tomorrow night at O'Doherty's and see what we can find out?"

"Sounds rather morbid, even macabre, but could be interesting. See you tomorrow. Call me when you're ready to go to dinner."

Peg's after-breakfast schedule started with a call to the Ashodod Animal Hospital. No boarders, thank you. The receptionist asked how Sarek was doing. She added how much she adored him. That helped counterbalance the feelings of Uncle Wally Qaqish.

The second call Peg made was to Mom. Left message: "Hi, Mom! Thanks for the call. I finished the guest list for the retirement party. Still need to find the place, finalize the best date, and figure out the food. Sorry the plans are taking so long, but with this new job and all, I'm swamped. I'll keep you posted. Love you. Bye."

The next call was to Dr. Julia Emig, DMD. Interesting that, at 9:04 a.m., this dentist answered her own phone. Dr. Emig stated that her 10:00 a.m. patient had rescheduled, and she would discuss, within the limits of patient confidentiality, William LaChance.

The fourth and final call was made to the home of Dianne Banks (formerly Mrs. William LaChance) and Marie Chance, daughter of William LaChance. After three rings, Peg left a message informing the parties of her affiliation with the Montreal Expos and the need to discuss several financial issues. The time was 9:35 a.m., and Peg started her fifteen-minute ride to 54 North Avenue in Rockland.

Traveling from north to south on Union Street, there was a set of traffic signals at the Holy Family Church. This set of lights controlled the intersection with North Avenue. North Avenue met Union Street but did not cross it. When turning right onto North Avenue, the dental practice of Julia Emig was located in the third house on the left. The dental office occupied the bottom floor of a white-sided Cape from the mid-1800s, while the upper appeared to be a residence.

Entering the office, Peg was greeted by Dr. Emig's receptionist. "Hi there, you must be Ms. McCarthy from the Expos. The doctor is finishing up with a patient. She'll be with you in a few minutes."

The decor of the waiting area supported the fact that Dr. Emig catered to younger patients. The far wall, from about two feet above the chair rail, was covered with autographed photographs of sports celebrities. Men and women were equally represented on this Wall of Athleticism. Some of the photos were signed "To Doctor Emig," but the vast majority were penned to the "Patients of Doc Emig." Peg noted that the picture of No Chance LaChance was prominent in its location within the collection: "To My Friend Julia Emig and Her Young Patients—Be Brave—No Chance LaChance." Most of those photographed were taken in their playing uniforms at various sport venues. LaChance's picture was unusual. Extremely unusual. It looked as if it had been taken in an ancient Greek or Roman ruin. LaChance and his dog, Sarek.

Mid-thirties, attractive, 5 foot 8. Peg was surprised when Julia Emig, DMD, entered from the rear of the office. She'd expected someone older. "Quite a collection of sports photographs. Hi there. I'm Peg McCarthy from the Montreal Expos."

"Yes, but I'm afraid it won't be growing much larger. I just learned that Buckley Roberts was killed last night. He's the second patient that I've lost in the past three weeks. First Bill LaChance, now Mr. Roberts. Those two provided 90 percent of the photos you see. Glad to meet you, Ms. McCarthy. How can I help you?"

Peg and Emig entered a small office. Emig sat in her chair; McCarthy in an overstuffed leather.

"Well, Dr. Emig, I'm here as a private investigator for the Expos. I'm trying to piece together the last week or so of Bill LaChance's life to see if any conclusions can be determined concerning the circumstances of his death. He had one of your appointment cards in his wallet, and the autopsy noted that Mr. LaChance had two recent tooth extractions. That brings me to your office this morning."

Julia Emig paused for a long moment before responding. "Let me preface our conversation by telling you that what we may discuss today is just between you and me and should not be construed as public knowledge. My association with Bill LaChance was far greater than a dentist/client relationship. Bill was a true close friend."

Peg also paused. She knew that this conversation with Dr. Julia Emig was going in a direction that was completely unexpected. "Did you and Mr. LaChance date?"

"Something about dating implies that our relationship was romantic. It wasn't. Bill and I had many similar interests: sports, the arts, and jazz. For the past two years, we attended many functions together. When Bill had to travel away on business, I watched his dog, Sarek. We were close friends, and I miss him."

"You mentioned Sarek. The dog has been with me since the accident. Do you know what Mr. LaChance might have wanted done with the dog? Are you interested in keeping him?"

"Sarek? No, I don't think that's a good idea. He would remind me of Bill. I just got two kittens, and Sarek is not a feline lover. I'm not sure who would want Sarek. Sorry."

"I understand, Dr. Emig. How long prior to Mr. LaChance's accident did you perform the tooth extractions?"

"Oh, I didn't do those procedures. I have an oral surgeon who does extractions. We schedule the patients here, and the surgeon travels from dentist to dentist. He might do five to seven extractions on the day that he comes here. Bill LaChance had those two wisdom teeth removed about two months apart. One about two weeks before Thanksgiving and the second, mid-January. That's also a sad story. The oral surgeon I use has taken an undetermined sabbatical from his practice. He had a rough couple of months. Became ultra-nervous. Had a tough time controlling his hands from trembling. Lost a son to leukemia. I'm looking desperately for someone to replace him. Haven't heard from him in over a month."

Peg thanked the dentist and headed for the door.

"Oh, Ms. McCarthy, maybe you should take this with you. This was delivered the Tuesday after Bill's death."

Dr. Emig handed Peg an 11x14 manila envelope with a hand-written address:

Erik Santagati
c/o Dr. Julia Emig—World's Best Dentist
54 North Avenue
Rockland, MA 02370

The return address was:
Buckley Roberts
Maye & Associates
473 Peterborough Street
Suite 7204
Boston, MA 01812

Puzzled, Peg asked, "Why give this to me?"

"That's Bill LaChance's handwriting. That was sent to our traveling oral surgeon. I was hoping he would return. Bill said he was going to get an autographed picture for Erik. I bet that is what is in the envelope. Both parties on that envelope and the person that signed the photo inside are deceased, and Dr. Santagati has postponed his practice. I think I'd rather have that envelope gone. It's all rather creepy."

Peg couldn't help noticing that the manila envelope had been propped up by two small, nip-size bottles marked "No Chance" LaChance Hi-Heat Hot Sauce; Prepared by Cajun Food Specialties, Ponchatoula, LA 70454; 1.7fl. oz. (50ml).

"These little bottles are cute." Peg picked up one bottle, then the other and looked at them with the recessed ceiling light shining directly on the label. Stu Mirkin had told Peg that the bottle containing the Oxycontin had a decidedly dull finish on the label.

Both these bottles seemed shiny, and Peg presumed that they had not been tampered with.

"Those are bottles of Bill's hot sauce. He used the stuff on everything. He would ruin good food by smothering it with his hot sauce. He gave those little bottles to everyone. The only one that liked that hot sauce more than Bill was his dog. Sarek had one of those small bottles of sauce on his food every night. It's a wonder it didn't kill the poor dog. Take those if you like. I have others."

Peg could only think of Qaqish's thirty-five-dollar price tag on the little bottles that probably had a phony No Chance signature.

"Is that your oral surgeon—Erik Santagati?"

"No, that's his son, the one who died of leukemia. The surgeon is Sebastian. Sebastian Santagati."

Before leaving the dentist's parking lot Peg updated her Yellow Pad.

Yellow Pad Entry: #14 2-14-2003 10:46 a.m.

Julia Emig, DMD, states she was a close personal friend of Bill LaChance. States the recently deceased Buckley Roberts was also a patient.

LaChance's recent extractions, as noted in the autopsy, were done at Emig's office by a visiting oral surgeon, Sebastian Santagati.

Emig has no recollection of Walter Qaqish.

Julia Emig might be the Jule (Jude) that Qaqish mentioned as taking care of LaChance's dog, Sarek.

As Peg retraced her route back to the highway, her cell phone rang. The former Mrs. LaChance was at home and would be for the next hour or so. Rockland to Hanover was only a ten-minute ride. Peg found herself quickly at 399 Cedar Street. It was just down the street from Hanover High School. At 11:00 a.m., Marie Chance, Bill LaChance's daughter, was in school.

The former Mrs. LaChance was not surprised by the news of the insurance policy for her daughter, Marie. She was stunned to hear on the morning news of the death last evening, of Buckley Roberts. Dianne Banks openly discussed her two-year marriage with William LaChance. Both she and Bill had been in their early twenties, and both had needed to mature. Neither had been ready for a commitment. It had been Bill's idea that Marie should drop the "La" from her last name just so every kid in school wouldn't be asking, "Are you related to No

Chance LaChance?" There had never been any hostility between the formerly married LaChances; Bill had always been emotionally close to his daughter and supportive financially.

Peg was reluctant to ask, "What about Sarek? He's been staying with me for the past several weeks. Should I bring him here?"

"I'm sorry, Ms. McCarthy, Marie and I are both allergic to dogs. Marie couldn't ride in Bill's car, even without the dog. If you supply me with a list of expenses I'd be happy to reimburse you."

"Don't worry about the expenses. I'd love to keep the dog myself He's a real sweetheart, but I need somebody's authorization."

"I guess that would be Marie. I don't think she will have any issues, as long as Sarek is going to a good home. I'll discuss the matter with her after school. Leave me your number and I'll call you in the next day or so. If you desire something in writing to adopt Sarek, we can provide that also."

When Peg returned to the Regency Estates she filed her latest notation.

Yellow Pad Entry: #15 2-14-2003 12:53 p.m.
Dianne Banks seemed both warm and forthcoming concerning her two-year marriage to W.L.
I wonder if there is reason to suspect a motive with the ex-Mrs. LaChance: Greed? Revenge? Slow or no child support?
She stated that she and daughter (Marie) could not take dog due to allergies. Will talk with daughter about letting me adopt Sarek.
Mrs. Banks has heard of, but never met, Walter Qaqish.

Journal Entry
Friday, February 14, 2003

Well, this whole Buckley Roberts affair is down right unsettling!

I wonder why he kept calling about Sarek?

I guess I'll never know.

It looks like I may get to adopt Sarek! LaChance's daughter is allergic to dogs, so hopefully she won't object. I'll keep my fingers crossed. I sure miss Sarek. I guess it will be a while before I return home to see him. I'm sure he and Ed are doing fine while conducting the biscuit dance around the desk. I just wish I knew what Buckley Roberts wanted with the dog. I'll contact Maye and Associates, Roberts' law firm, on Monday. Perhaps someone there can shed light on why Roberts was trying to reach me concerning the dog.

Chapter 26

Return to 888 Broadway

Feeling that her patience was being tested, Peg had been waiting at Dickie O'Doherty's Eatery & Irish Pub in Southie nearly half an hour. Still no Stu Mirkin. Twice she had gone to the hostess and revised her reservation. Saturday night was always busy at O'Doherty's. The later, the busier. As Peg was heading for her car to get her phone, a Boston police cruiser did a loud U-turn and stopped abruptly at O'Doherty's green entrance awning.

"Thanks for the lift, Cookie." Doctor Stu Mirkin had arrived. "Sorry I'm late. We just finished. Belated Happy Valentine's Day."

A kiss on the cheek, a big hug, and a bigger bunch of roses erased Peg's annoyance. She had forgotten Valentine's Day. She usually called her Mom and Dad on Valentine's.

"Peg, this is Officer George Cook. Everyone calls him Cookie. Cookie, this is who we stopped to get the flowers for."

George Cook reached through the open window to shake Peg's hand, saying with his rich Boston accent, "Miss McCarthy, you must be special. You're all he talked about on the ride over. I've known the doc for nearly twenty years, and this is the most excited I've seen him. I must warn you about the dear doctor. He has a problem. He's a workaholic. He needs to get a life."

The radio of the cruiser crackled; Cookie responded, waved, and merged into traffic as he sped north on Broadway with lights flashing and siren wailing.

"That's the parking lot across the street, where Roberts got shot. Some of these hoods got a lot of gall. Right there in the parking lot of Boston PD, Precinct 7. Bang! Bang! They got surveillance cams but they probably won't see much on the tapes. Pretty dark over there on the side where Buckley was parked."

Peg peered into the inky darkness of the right side of the parking lot beyond the brightly lighted thoroughfare. "What do you think? Robbery? Anything unusual with the autopsy?"

"Robbery is the best guess so far. Roberts' wallet is missing. I'm not sure about the autopsy. Two wounds, one penetrating, the other perforating. The wound size has me wondering."

"There you go again, Stu, with your technical terms. What's the difference between penetrating and perforating?"

"Sorry, Peg. Penetrating shots make only an entrance wound. We found that slug in Roberts' chest wall. Went through his shoulder area. Looks like .25 caliber. Perforation has an exit wound as well as an entrance wound. The perforating shot was through the head, an inch behind his left ear. That's the one that killed him. The crime-lab people called as I was leaving the morgue. They found a second bullet on Roberts' front seat. Looks like a .25 to them as well."

"Well, Doctor, what's bothering you?"

"I'm not sure. Instincts I guess. I can't recall that much trauma caused by a undersized slug. Just looks like a large caliber wound, although they found two spent cartridges at the scene. Both matched and both .25 cal."

As Peg admired her roses, Dr. Mirkin entered the zone. Forensic science was his life, and the challenge of an unusual case was what he lived for. "Peg, if you were Buckley Roberts' assailant, what would you do after the event?"

"I'm not sure. I do know what I would *not* do. Head toward the front door of the police station. I'd go north."

"Exactly. Let us assume that the shooter went up the street. Maybe he parked his getaway there. Maybe he ran down the stairs to the Red Line subway at Broadway Station. What else would you do, Peg?"

"Guess I'd get rid of the evidence. The gun and the wallet. Any water around here?"

"Fort Point Channel is a few hundred yards beyond the subway. Brackish water. Very murky, especially with all the Big Dig work around it. Ideal spot to dump something. I'll call Tim Snow in the morning. He's head of homicide and a friend of mine. He's probably having the Boston Fire & Rescue Dive Team look in the channel. We should come back here in the morning and look around that parking lot."

In between the appetizers and the entrees, Stu Mirkin's cell phone buzzed. The din of the Saturday evening crowd made him dash to the front door.

"Interesting. That was Snowman calling. Tim Snow, the homicide detective I was telling you about. The transit police just called him. They found a .25 caliber "Saturday Night Special" stuffed behind a seat cushion on an Ashmont train. Same subway train that would have gone through Broadway Station about 9:30 last night. He says the dive team is scheduled to search the channel on Monday morning. They love to dive in the winter. Br-r-r-r! Not for me."

Stu was making interesting designs with his spoon in his clam chowder, trying to cool it.

"Stu, what do you think we might find in the parking lot?"

"I don't know. Something seems odd in this case. Very odd. It looks like a simple robbery gone bad, but the wound damage has me baffled. Looks like someone really wanted Buckley Roberts dead."

Sunday morning brought a different perspective to the parking lot across from Dickie O'Doherty's Eatery & Irish Pub. A few cars were parked adjacent to Precinct 7, but the remainder of the lot was vacant. Several dilapidated police cruisers pushed to the rear fence that separated the lot from the railroad tracks beyond. Masking tape on the asphalt still marked the wheel location of Roberts' Lincoln Mark VI.

"Left ... left ... a little more ... good. You're parked about where Roberts' was last Friday."

Stu walked around the vehicle twice, counterclockwise, then reversed until he was standing next to the driver's door. Peg remained in the rented Kia with the heater fan on high. Mirkin seemed oblivious to the outside temperature of twenty-two degrees Fahrenheit.

The side door of the police station opened. Sergeant Lawrence Bulger, a desk sergeant for the Boston PD, exited and headed for the beige Kia. A scowling Larry (a.k.a. Tiny) Bulger, no relation to South Boston's infamous Whitey Bulger, wasn't thrilled with tourists in his parking lot. "This is police property. Why are you here and what are you doing?"

"Good Sunday morning, Sergeant. I'm Stu Mirkin. I did the autopsy on the shooting victim of Friday night. I'm looking over the scene before I make my final report this afternoon." Doc Mirkin handed the sergeant his card.

"Oh. Sorry, Doc." Tiny doffed his sergeant's hat to Peg inside the Kia. Peg moved the heater control to a lower position.

"Well, your rapid deployment to the parking lot this morning tells me your surveillance camera is working. Did you see anything last Friday?"

"Yeah, Doc. I guess we got the shooter on tape. Typical, had a hood on. Never turned towards that camera." Bulger pointed to a pole in O'Doherty's parking lot across the street. "Was only on tape for about thirty-five seconds. Just enough time to pinch a guy's wallet and shoot him. Twice. Headed that way. Just walked away." Tiny was looking toward the Broadway 'T' Station a block away. "Well, Doc, have fun. I got a cup of coffee waiting for me. See you later, miss."

"Peg, you're Roberts, and I'm the shooter. Put the other window down. Snowman said both windows were open. If I shoot you in the shoulder what are you going to do?"

Peg demonstrated as she spoke, "I'd lay down, trying to get away from the gun."

"Exactly! That's why I think the first shot was the one to the head. Close range. Not an actual contact wound but no more than four or five inches away. Initial autopsy report cited 'some soot' around the wound in Roberts' skull. That still doesn't explain the wound diameter. I'm going to call the Snowman. He only lives over on G Street."

Annoyed, Peg barked, "Stu, it's Sunday morning. Not everyone has your enthusiasm. Give that Snowman a break."

"He won't care … Hello, Timmy? Stu Mirkin. I'm at the parking lot across from O'Doherty's. Can you come over? I got some questions for you. Yeah, I know it's Sunday. I'll spring for brunch. Okay. See you in ten minutes." Stu Mirkin smiled.

"All you have to do is mention food to the Snowman. Gets him every time. The guy consumes 4000 to 5000 calories per day."

Peg could only shake her head. "Bet he weights over 300. Doesn't he know that's not healthy?"

"You won't believe it, Peg. Wait until he gets here. You won't believe it."

A brown K Car, circa 1982, careened into the parking lot. Its bent tailpipe emitted sparks as it scraped the sidewalk. The driver's door, primed red-oxide, opened before the car came to a complete stop. Enter the Snowman.

Tim Snow faced the light pole across the street in O'Doherty's parking lot, stood at attention, and saluted the security camera. "Okay, Mirkin, what do you want? When do we eat?"

"Okay Snowman, okay. I want you to meet a friend of mine Peg McCarthy. Peg just retired from the Customs Service."

Peg surmised that Tim Snow was probably in his mid-thirties but looked about five years younger. Five foot ten, 160 pounds, perhaps less. He seemed to be in perpetual motion.

"Tim, did you look at the weapon the MBTA found on the Ashmont train?"

"Yeah, I got curious last night, went over to see it. It's a suicide special called a Zack 'Pit Bull,' caliber .25, a real piece of crap.

Genuine white plastic hand grips, seven-round magazine. Made in Spain. Had five rounds in the magazine, none in the chamber. This gun had one bizarre aspect to it. Every other round of ammo was backwards. Never saw that before."

"Backwards? What do you mean, backwards?"

"Every other bullet had the projectile turned around so the pointy end was facing inside the cartridge. Bizarre. I wouldn't dare shoot something like that. Must cause a wound that you could drive a truck through. Have you ever seen or heard of anything like that?"

Stu and Peg both shrugged.

"Why would someone do that?" asked Peg. "Doesn't seem like typical mugger diversion, reversing slugs to cause more damage."

Stu was still looking toward the far end of the parking lot. "That might explain the large wound. Roberts' head wound was large, but the bullet didn't curve. The projectile path seemed straight. In and out. Seems a reversed bullet would go in anywhere but in a straight line as it swapped ends traveling, even in a small caliber like a .25. The entrance and exits wounds were approximately the same size."

Snowman was eying the front door of O'Doherty's.

"Tim. Sit in the car. You said both the driver's and passenger's side windows were open when they found the car. Let's say I'm the shooter and I ask for your wallet. Then I shoot you right behind the left ear. Let's say I'm using a larger bore than a .25 cal. It's a perforated wound. What happens to the projectile?"

"I'd say the bullet goes right out the passenger-side window."

"Exactly. Peg, you're the shooter. Point at Tim's ear. Where's the bullet going?"

"Over into the railroad yard."

"Exactly. If the shooter is six foot six, then the bullet goes into the ground somewhere between here and the fence. If I'm the shooter at five foot ten, then the slug goes nearer to those wrecked cruisers."

Stu, the Snowman, and Peg walked the three hundred or so feet to the back of the lot. The three police cruisers were parked nose to tail. The first two had damage, and the third looked like it was ready for service. "Snowman, what's wrong with this one?"

"Oh, that's Rusty Dennis' car. He took out the oil pan on a raised manhole cover over on Tremont Street last week. We'll probably lift a motor from one of these other cruisers. We used to get two, maximum three years, out of a vehicle, but with budget constraints we push them to four or five years. They are really beat when we're done."

Stu looked at the left side of each vehicle, the side facing the street. He stopped midway on each vehicle, and examined the side in the glare of the February sun. "When did Rusty's car get a bullet in the side?"

Tim Snow looked surprised. Both he and Doc Mirkin knelt down on one knee as if genuflecting to the god of police cruisers. Right there, between the O and the N was a hole large enough to insert a ring finger in, up to the second knuckle.

"Damn if that doesn't look new," said the Snowman. Looking through the windshield, he added, "I don't see a matching hole on the inside. If that's a bullet hole, then the slug must be inside the door. I'll call Rusty Dennis later to see if he knows about that hole. I'll make a call and have Dennis' cruiser towed to the lab. I'll call inside the precinct and have someone come out and secure the vehicle. I'm sorry Stu, that's it for me. I'm too cold and too hungry to hike any further. Let's eat."

With the brunch orders having been taken, Peg noted on a yellow Post-it pad:

Yellow Pad Entry: #16 2-16-2003
Send Valentine's basket to Mom and Dad—Maybe a coffee assortment from Blue Hills Coffee Roasters. Check for online catalog. Better late than never!

Mirkin and the Snowman were in the midst of a heated baseball discussion when Peg's cell phone rang. She exited in order to hear.

"I tell you Timmy, it's the same old story. All hitting. They're two pitchers short, and what's this closing by committee crap? They got *no* bullpen. It's the middle of February, and I'm already saying wait 'til next year. *Closing by committee?*"

By the time Peg returned to the table, Tim Snow had inhaled about half of his food.

"That was Dianne Banks. I told her if she needed anything to call me and the Expos would provide any assistance during this traumatic time for Marie Chance. Never expected to hear from her. They were scheduled to fly to Scottsdale, Arizona, for a week's vacation but had a garage fire early this morning. She says the daughter is having a tough time. Nightmares. She was wondering if the Expos could help to reschedule their flight. Ready to take a ride, Stu?"

Chapter 27

Return to 399 Cedar

The Southeast Expressway splits in Braintree, near the Regency Estates. The left hand lanes become Route 3 South, headed to Cape Cod. As Peg drove, Stu called his old mentor, "Bones" Gilmore.

"Hi, Bones. Stu Mirkin here. How's your golf game? Eighty-three? That's pretty good. Is that for nine holes or eighteen? Yeah. Yeah. I got a question for you. Have you ever seen the projectile reversed in a cartridge? Yes, removed and replaced pointed end toward the inside. Yeah, seems like it would cause some real crazy bullet track. This one went straight, like an arrow. Yes. Really! Interesting. Well, I'll let you return to your golf game. Thanks, Bones. Talk to you soon. Bye."

Mirkin was quiet. Thinking. "Gilmore says he never saw a bullet reversed, but he says he read about it in a murder mystery. Fiction. Says he thinks the author is either Higgins, Dunham, or Cernach. He'll call back when he looks it up. Bones has more murder mysteries than the Boston Public Library."

The detached garage, actually pieces thereof, of Thomas and Dianne Banks was scattered in a giant oval of about fifty by thirty yards. The roof had collapsed onto a Jeep Cherokee, which was visible inside. Both overhead garage doors, still intact, were lying in a heap, halfway up the driveway. Hanover Fire Department Pumper No. 1 was leaving as Peg and Stu pulled up to the Banks home.

A youthful police officer addressed them as they exited the rental car, "Sorry, no visitors."

Stu reached into his pocket and handed the rookie his card. A card which stated boldly: STUART MIRKIN, M.D. STATE CRIME LABORATORY

"This is Agent McCarthy, U.S. Customs Service. Mr. and Mrs. Banks called us."

"Okay, Doc. The Bankses are out back with the State Fire Marshal's investigator."

There were pieces of the garage and its contents everywhere. "Be careful where you step, Peg."

"Thanks, Stu. Please, no more of the Agent McCarthy bit. I'm retired. Remember?"

"Yeah. Yeah. Sometimes it's just easier than explaining. I hate wasting time explaining."

Mr. Banks, Mrs. Banks, and Marie Chance peered from inside the bay window at the rear of the house.

A voice bellowed from the back of the debris field that had been the Banks' two-car garage. "Hey! Old Blood and Guts Mirkin! We got no stiffs here. What's going on?"

"Deputy Chief Fire Marshal Peter V. Austin, I haven't seen you in about two years. It was that woman they found cooked in the trunk of that Mercedes, wasn't it?"

"That's the one, Stu. You got a good memory. What brings you to Hanover?"

"Oh. This is my friend, Peg McCarthy. Mrs. Banks called her. What happened here?"

"Well, Stu, this is a prime example of what is known in the business as a low-order explosion. Diffused rather than concentrated. Propane gas. The tank is behind the garage. Mr. Banks had the garage heated. Kept his antique car warm for the winter. Lucky for him, the old car is in the upholstery shop. He had the heat turned off, seeing the old car isn't here. Looks like the feed line broke where it comes in from the rear. Filled the garage up and, when Mrs. Banks hit the remote to warm up the Jeep, wooooosh. Deflagration. I'm taking some debris samples back to the lab for testing. I haven't seen anything suspicious yet. Good thing the garage wasn't attached to the house."

Meanwhile, Peg entered the home and talked with the Banks family. Dianne explained that Marie was a real mess. "She really believes this was not an accident. She thinks someone is following her. Says she has seen an unfamiliar pickup truck in the neighborhood. I think the stress of the past three weeks is getting to all of us. That's one of the reasons we were going to Arizona for the week."

Peg listened, then looked at her watch and offered, "I talked with J.P. Bellevue, of the Montreal Expos. He thinks you should continue with your vacation. It's 1:00 p.m. now. You'll never make your 2:15 flight from Logan. Bellevue says the Expos will have a private jet meet you at Plymouth Airport and get you into Scottsdale at about the time you were expected. I'll contact a public insurance adjuster to handle your claim, and we'll get someone in here to monitor security until the cleanup is complete. The mess will be gone by the time you get back. We can rent a large storage container and put it on site until your garage is rebuilt. What do you think?"

"Thank you so much, Peg. And, please, thank the Expos. I think you're right, Peg. We need to get away, especially Marie."

"Can I use your phone book? I'll see about getting you a limo to Plymouth Airport."

During the entire conversation, Marie stood at the den window looking out at the rubble that was, until earlier that morning, the Banks' two-car garage.

Journal Entry
Saturday, February 16, 2003

Damn, this case is really getting strange. Two murders, one garage explosion, and one orphaned dog. A dog of unusual interest to many parties. I wonder if there is any connection.

I definitely feel the CARDMAN is not involved with this whole matter. Seems he just wants his autographed hot-sauce bottles. I'm not going to forget Qaqish, just put him on the back burner.

Patricia in New Orleans and Julia the dentist? Both seem to be true friends of LaChance. Just a gut feeling, I don't think either could be implicated in this mess.

Peg pulled out her yellow pad and revised her possible villain list. LaChance was crossed off the list. Suicide or accidental overdose is a doubtful possibility.

Peg had to laugh at herself when she realized that LaChance couldn't have killed Roberts or blown up the Banks' garage. Would LaChance's ex cause a garage explosion to deflect suspicion? Was Marie at risk from her mother?

Yellow Pad Entry: #17 2-16-2003 7:00 p.m.
With the now known facts the strongest possible candidates are:
The events of the past couple of days seem to eliminate Qaqish from the strong side of candidates. An irate fan? Someone with an issue with LaChance's Foundation.
With the now known facts the weakest possible candidates are:

William LaChance (deceased), Accidental Poisoning, Montreal Expos, A Random Act of Tampering, LaChance's Daughter Marie (only thirteen yeas old) and the Hot Sauce Company or an employee of the Hot Sauce Company? Possibily, but why?

Somewhere in-between strongest and weakest is the possibility that LaChance's death could be caused by: Walter Qaqish (seems to have more to loose than gain with LaChance's passing), Ex-Wife (probably wouldn't blow up own garage), Patricia Tremblay, and the 'Take a Chance Foundation', and Adrianna Lomysh.

New addition: Dr. Julia Emig.

Chapter 28

Ballistics Report
.25 versus .455

" **P** lease enter your password. You have two new messages and five saved messages. To listen to your messages, press 1. First new message ..."

"Hi, Peg. Bill Atwood. It's 7:30 in the morning on February 18th. Update on several items. Number one! The moving van was here and picked up your stuff for transit to a storage facility in St. Johnsbury. The four boxes you wanted to remain here are locked in the closet at the station. I figured I better keep them in a heated area. Don't know if you had anything that might freeze.

"Item number two! Someone called this morning at 7:00 looking for the whereabouts of Bill LaChance's dog. Wanted to know why the dog is being detained by the U.S. Customs Service. I did mention that the dog was in your custody and in good health. I also told the guy that he must contact you. He refused to give a name or number. Our government tracking system says it was a Massachusetts area code. Could it have been Qaqish?

"Item number three! Everyone around here is asking about your retirement party. Any idea where and when?"

"Next new message ..."

"Good morning, Peg. Stu here. Can you meet me at the Boston PD crime lab, 723 Columbus Avenue, at 1:00 p.m.? Snowman has a ballistics report for us. See you there, unless you can't meet us. Let me know if you are tied up."

"End of new messages."

Mother Nature couldn't decide. Rain or snow? While deciding, she was doing both, and the traffic responded accordingly. The normal twenty- to twenty-five-minute commute slowed to forty-five. Peg pulled into a parking spot at Boston Police Headquarters at precisely 1:03. Stu and the Snowman were just inside the revolving door, and their conversation of yesterday had hardly progressed. "... and what's this 'closing by committee' crap? They got *no* bullpen."

The walk down a long, poorly lit corridor led to a door stenciled: BALLISTICS LAB. Led by homicide detective Tim Snow, the threesome entered. Expecting to see a large laboratory, Peg was surprised by the sparse accommodations: three work stations, two with binocular triple-turret microscopes, and a large green barrel with the words "Bullet Trap" handwritten on the side with a Magic Marker. A placard on the door at the rear announced Dark Room—Do Not Enter When Light Is Flashing.

"Stu and Peg, this is our ballistics person, Anita Ivarson. Ms. Ivarson, Peg McCarthy—retired U.S. Customs Service—and Dr. Stu Mirkin—forensic scientist, self-proclaimed baseball authority, and friend. Tell us what you found."

Ivarson was not your typical firearms expert. Twenty-nine years old, tall. One word described her: *striking*. John Ivarson, Anita's father, had been a participant in the 1968 Winter Olympics in Grenoble, France, and again in the 1972 games in Sapporo, Japan. His sport, biathlon. Anita Ivarson shared her dad's passion for both sports, skiing and competition shooting.

Anita looked over the top of her half-rimmed eyeglasses. The frames matched her lime-green Levis and lime-green Salvatore Ferragamo athletic shoes. "The firearm found behind the seat on the Ashmont subway train is a Zack 'Pit Bull,' caliber .25, semi-automatic, seven-round magazine. Manufactured by Ego Armas of Elgiri, Spain, circa 1978. Imported into the U.S. by Zack Armament Ltd., Perrine, Florida. Both companies, if they are still in business, must be operating under different names. I can't find either listed as current. This thing is a cheap Saturday Night Special, probably sold new for less than fifty dollars. Both recovered bullets were fired from this handgun. The marks on the slugs match the land and groove pattern from the gun. One interesting thing was that neither of those recovered projectiles was like the reversed ones found in the magazine. Both had left-hand twist lines. If the projectile had been reversed, the twist marks would be opposite."

Ivarson handed a Ziploc bag containing the Pit Bull to the Snowman; it looked like a toy. She continued, "The gun was clean, no prints, no blood, no nothing."

Peg examined the piece through its plastic protector. "No prints from the person who located it? Who found the gun?"

The Snowman picked up the folder marked Evidence ID # 03-19737 Zack Pit Bull—2-13-03—.25 cal. Serial Number 29108Z.

"Report says weapon was spotted by crew cleaning Ashmont train number 1349. This unit left Alewife yard at 8:55 p.m., heading south and arrived at Ashmont yard 10:02 p.m. Weapon was noticed in the second of a four-car concise. Picked up with a pencil by MBTA employee, John Christie, put into trash bag and given to shift supervisor Mary Wilson. Wilson called MBTA police at 11:00 p.m., and they picked up the weapon at 11:22 p.m. We ran a NCIS firearms check with the Feds. Nothing back yet. May take a couple of days. Anita, did you see Dr. Mirkin's preliminary autopsy report?"

"Yes, read it this morning. I agree. The head wound of the victim seems to be caused by a bullet much larger than .25 caliber."

At the rear of the lab, propped against the wall, was the left front door from the police cruiser that Stu, the Snowman, and Peg viewed at the rear of the lot across from O'Doherty's. The door with the hole between the O and the N big enough to insert a ring finger up to the second knuckle.

"The garage guys brought that cruiser over yesterday. I had them remove the door after I received your e-mail about a possible slug being inside. Here's what I found." Anita handed a small evidence bag to Tim Snow.

"Wow, looks like a .45. What do you think, Stu?"

"Interesting. What do you make of it, Anita?"

Anita placed an overhead transparency on the projector. "The hole in the door is fresh. No rust around the entrance hole. The bullet exited the inner door metal and lodged in the padding of the armrest. There's no recent record of shots being fired at a police vehicle. It's larger than a .45, a .455 Webley to be precise. British ammo."

Peg and Stu were unfamiliar with .455 caliber. Peg asked, "Are you saying that this was probably fired by a British pistol?"

Ms. Ivarson adjusted a second transparency. "No, I don't think it was British. British gun barrels, in fact most European firearms, have left-hand rifling. This bullet has right-hand marks indicating the pistol was U.S. manufacture. My guess is a Colt semi-automatic, Model 1911 manufactured between 1915 and 1919. The original finish was blued, and, when you find it, the gun should be marked CALIBRE 455 on the left side of the receiver. This gun is a collectors' item. World War I. Nearly ninety years old and, in today's market, very expensive. The slug was checked for DNA with inconclusive results. Fired that close, then passing through the door skin and inner liner, you're probably not going to see much brain matter on the bullet."

The Snowman smiled. "I told you Anita is the best."

The phone on the wall vibrated twice with an annoying buzz.

"Detective Snow, phone."

"Snow here. Hi, Gonzo. Yeah, Yeah. That's interesting. How much? Okay. Put it in a bag. I'll be over to pick it up. Yeah, I know where you are. On Northampton, behind the Cathedral, right? Okay, see you later."

Snow hung up the phone, and looked at the group. "Strange. That was Gonzo Legendre. He says his dive team just finished. No weapons, but they found Buckley Roberts' wallet. $150 inside along with his credit cards. It's safe to conclude that robbery was not the motive. Any thoughts?"

It was Peg who answered first. "Assuming the motive was to kill Buckley Roberts, not rob him, why plant the Pit Bull on the Ashmont train?"

Stu responded, "I bet the killer planted the gun on the first train that came through Broadway Station. Wouldn't have mattered if it was a southbound train to Braintree or Ashmont or a northbound to Alewife. The shooter was probably hoping some punk from Dorchester would see the gun on his way home and just pocket it. Some time later, the gun would be used in another crime and, if found, the poor sap holding it would get tagged with the Roberts hit. He never figured we'd get the weapon so quickly. The slug found on the seat of Roberts' Lincoln was dropped there by the killer; made it look like two slugs and two matching cartridges. Very clean. Ms. Ivarson, nice meeting you. Thank you for your rapid response to this situation. Tim, thanks for allowing us to see the ballistics information."

The snow had now turned to sleet as Peg and Stu came down the steps of Boston Police Headquarters.

"Stu, I have a three o'clock appointment with Monique Maye. She heads the law firm where Buckley Roberts was a partner. Her office is closed until after the funeral proceedings on Wednesday, but she is willing to discuss things. She mentioned something about Sarek and the fact that someone in LaChance's family has been trying to locate the dog.

As usual, Peg updated her yellow pad entries prior to one-mile hop to Monique Maye's office on Peterborough Street.

Yellow Pad Entry: #18 2-18-2003 2:18 p.m.

Boston Fire Department Dive team recovered a wallet in the Fort Point Channel. Contents suggest that it is the wallet of Buckley Roberts. Found approximately ¼ mile from the location where Roberts was shot. $150 cash and credit cards were found in the wallet.

The projectiles and cartridges found in Roberts' car are the same caliber as the pistol found in the subway train.

Anita Ivarson, Boston PD firearms and ballistics expert located large caliber (.455) projectile in the padding of the armrest (left front door) of an out-of-service police cruiser that was parked at the rear of the location where Roberts was killed.

Chapter 29

Maye & Associates
473 Peterborough Street
Suite 7204
Boston, MA 01812

The printed note on the door of suite 7204 simply stated:
DUE TO THE DEATH OF OUR FRIEND AND COLLEAGUE,
BUCKLEY ROBERTS, THE OFFICE OF MAYE & ASSOCIATES
IS CLOSED.

WE WILL REOPEN AT 9:00 A.M. ON THURSDAY
FEBRUARY 20, 2003.

A pink Post-it was affixed to the glass: Ms. McCarthy—Please
knock when you arrive. M.M.

Monique Maye. Isn't it strange how one pictures someone when
one hears her name, the location of her office, her occupation? Peg
fashioned an image of an older, matronly, plus-sized woman with salt-
and-pepper hair wrapped tightly in a bun, wearing a dark business-style
suit that would look like proper attire for an attorney, male or female.
When a tall, attractive black woman, perhaps in her late twenties,
opened the door, Peg automatically asked, "Is Monique Maye in? I'm
Peg McCarthy."

"I'm Monique. Please come in. Nice to meet you."

Dressed in black sweatpants, athletic sneakers, and a long-sleeved
T-shirt embossed with the head of a growling bear and lettered
"Dorchester High—Men's Basketball," Monique Maye's look was not
that of your stereotypical lawyer.

"I'm heading for basketball practice at four o'clock. Please sit
down."

"Oh, you play basketball?"

Monique Maye laced her sneakers as she spoke. "Oh. yeah, I still
play. Started when I was about four. But today I'm coaching."

"Girls' basketball at Dorchester High?"

"No, actually I'm the men's coach. Junior varsity."

Peg felt that her questions thus far were presumptuous and her investigating skills surely must have seemed amateurish at best. She handed the manila envelope to Monique. "Julia Emig, a dentist in Rockland and a friend of Bill LaChance, asked me to return that to you. She says that is LaChance's handwriting, and that both the addressee and the addressor are deceased."

Ms. Maye used her scissors to slice open the envelope. Inside was an eight-by-ten black-and-white photograph of Bill LaChance wearing his infamous number 13. The photo was signed in bright orange ink:

To Erik,

Hang in There and Keep Pitching.

Your friend,

"No Chance" LaChance

In addition to the LaChance photograph, there was a signed baseball card (No. 71) of LaChance and several other signed baseball cards from players that Maye & Associates represented.

"Bill and Buckley must have put that packet together. We keep signed cards on file from players that we represent. You say Mr. Santagati is deceased? What happened?"

"I've been told leukemia. Ms. Maye, do you have any clue who may have wanted Mr. LaChance and Mr. Roberts dead?"

"Someone with a motive? No one comes to mind. It's a known fact that there are weirdos out there who get their kicks by stalking celebrities. We have no knowledge that Mr. LaChance had any issues like that. As for Buckley, this firm represents athletes both professional and pre-professional. We work with our clients in contract negotiations, endorsements and the legal aspects of their professions. We advise our clients in the area of investments and other legal issues. We don't handle criminal or civil litigation cases, although we do refer our clients, if they have those problems, to specialized counselors for these matters. Can you make a connection with both homicides?"

"No, Ms. Maye, as yet, no connection. But it seems more than ironic that these two gentleman, who were closely associated, met their deaths within three weeks of each other. Unusual? More than unusual. Weird. Real weird."

Thru a window to the right of Monique Maye's desk, Peg could see Fenway Park and its new "monster seats" perched atop the legendary left-field wall. Although Peg was not an avid baseball fan, Fenway and the area of Boston that enveloped it brought back memories of being a student teacher of French at Snowden High School for International

Studies, a public school down on Newbury Street. Seemed like only a few years ago, not twenty-seven.

"Ms. Maye, do you know the ex-Mrs. LaChance?"

"No, that's one aspect of Bill LaChance's affairs where our firm did not provide services. Bill was very private about all dealings with his ex-wife and daughter. Do you suspect that his ex-wife might be involved?"

"No, Ms. Maye, but I do worry about the daughter. She's very stressed by the death of her father and now her father's business manager. They also had a garage explosion and fire on Sunday, and Marie is a mess, according to the mother."

"Hopefully, his daughter will feel better when Bill's dog is returned. That's the reason Buckley was having a dinner meeting last Thursday, the night he was gunned down."

Adrenaline suddenly made Peg's senses shift into overdrive. "Mr. Roberts had dinner with Marie LaChance and Mrs. Banks the night he was murdered?"

"Not Mrs. Banks but someone who was representing her and the daughter. Mr. Roberts and I both find that dinner meetings with clients are often informal and relaxing. Buck liked O'Doherty's. I use Thornton's Fenway Grille, right across the street." Ms. Maye went to the adjoining office and returned with a leather book. "It's right here in Buckley's appointment book. He had two meetings at O'Doherty's that evening. The first with a Mr. H. Sumner Smyth at 7:00 of S.S.S. and a second at 8:00 with Mr. and Mrs. Peter Fine and their son Pete Junior. Pete Jr. is a six-foot-seven tenth grader from Worcester Academy. The parents wanted to discuss their son's scholarship options. The kid is getting letters and calls from every college basketball program around. We work with many high school athletes to help parents decide on all the possibilities. I'm sure Buck said that his other meeting at O'Doherty's that night was to meet someone concerning Bill's dog. I have no idea what S.S.S. stands for. Buck mentioned that someone representing LaChance's daughter wanted to discuss the whereabouts of LaChance's dog. He said this party pointed out that the dog was being detained by the Border Patrol in Canada. Ms. McCarthy, I faxed the last fifteen pages of Mr. Roberts' appointment book to the Boston PD last Friday."

"Ms. Maye, you faxed this information to Detective Snow of the Boston Police?"

"No, it wasn't Snow. I wrote the name on a note and slipped it in the back of Buck's appointment book. Here it is. Detective Ruiz, Boston PD."

Monique Maye and Peg glanced at their watches simultaneously. It was time for men's junior varsity basketball practice at Dorchester High, and time for Peg to tie up some loose ends at 339 Cedar Street in Hanover.

"Ms. Maye, sorry to have met you under these circumstances. My condolences to you and to Mr. Roberts' associates. Call me if anything new develops, and I'll contact you if anything interesting turns up. Good luck with the Dorchester Bears."

At 3:45 p.m., southbound traffic on the Southeast Expressway was always heavy. With today's messy precipitation, it was worse.

"Dr. Mirkin, please. Peg McCarthy. I'll hold. Hello, Stu. I'm heading to Hanover to check on the status of the cleanup at the Banks' house. Yeah. How about dinner at O'Doherty's when I get back? My treat. You know the wait staff at O'Doherty's. Ask them if they recall who Buckley Roberts might have had dinner with last Thursday. Just curious. See you there around 7:00 p.m. Bye."

Thinking aloud, Peg slowly proceeded down Cedar Street. "Without the reference of the Hanover High School, I might have missed the Banks' driveway. Everything is different in the dark."

A long strip of yellow CAUTION tape was pulled taut from the corner of the house to a thirty-five-foot blue spruce on the right side of the long driveway. Everything was gone. The Jeep Grand Cherokee had been towed. The two garage doors and all the assorted flotsam and jetsam that had been the garage of Tom and Dianne Banks had been put into two roll-off rubbish containers. All that remained was the concrete floor that marked the dimensions of the garage and the large propane tank that had been undamaged by the explosion that it caused. At the rear of the cement slab was a large white box that looked like a trailer truck body without the wheels. This was lettered South Shore Storage Rentals.

Everyone hates rental cars. Finding a simple thing like the knob to turn on the overhead light turns into a project. Fortunately, there was a light on the mirror of the pull-down visor which allowed Peg's next yellow pad entry.

Yellow Pad Entry: #19 2-18-2003 5:37 p.m.

Monique Maye—Maye & Associates states that Buckley Roberts met with two clients at O'Doherty's the day of his murder.

Client 1: H. Sumner Smyth—a representative of Dianne Banks and Marie Chance to discuss Bill LaChance's dog. (SSS)

Client 2: Mr./Mrs. Peter Fine and son Pete Fine, Jr., concerning athletic scholarships.

At 399 Cedar Street, all debris from the garage explosion has been put into two large removal bins. Both are covered with blue tarps and appear ready to be taken to a landfill.

Maye also states the contents of Buckley Roberts' appointment book (last fifteen pages) had been faxed to Boston PD Detective Ruiz on 2-14-03.

A loud metallic snap-snap-snap jolted Peg out of her scribbling. Outside the vehicle she could barely make out the form of an individual with a flashlight. Snap-snap-snap again as he tapped on the driver's door glass. "Excuse me, miss. Can I help you?"

Cracking the window, she said, "I'm Peg McCarthy from the Montreal Expos. I'm checking to see how this project is going."

"Oh, hi there, Ms. McCarthy. Chief Calderwood said you might come by. Do you have some type of ID?"

Peg handed the youthful uniformed officer her Expos card.

"Thanks. I'm Joe Franey. I live next door. I'm a summer police officer for the Town of Marshfield. Because I live close and am off from school for spring break, the chief gave me this detail of watching the place until the Bankses return."

"Very good, Officer Franey. Is that your partner with you?" Peg was staring at an enormous canine that must have tipped the scales at least 130 pounds.

"Oh, Ms. McCarthy, this is Rufus, he's a bull mastiff. He's harmless."

"I certainly hope so. Can you tell me what's been happening here?"

As soon as Peg exited her car and started her conversation with Officer Franey, Rufus, the harmless 130-pound wonder dog, sat on Peg's foot.

Officer Franey removed a note pad from the upper left pocket of his black leather jacket.

"Yesterday, 2-17-2003, at 9:12 a.m., an insurance adjuster from Beacon Insurance, Ms. Anne Garabedian, arrived with M/M Banks' insurance agent, Paul Nisula, of Hanover. Ms. Garabedian took photographs and discussed the damages with Mr. Nisula.

"At 9:40 the Hanover fire chief Sidney Goss was here with three Hanover firefighters.

"At 10:05 a representative from the State Fire Marshal's Office arrived. Deputy Chief Fire Marshal Peter V. Austin and Chief Goss examined the site and a permit was issued for clean-up.

"Those are the highlights of what happened yesterday. Now for today—"

"Excuse me, Officer Franey, you certainly keep a detailed journal. Can you put that info in writing when you e-mail me your total hours? Have you kept track of your time on site? Will we be paying you directly or through the Hanover PD?"

"I think you'll have to pay me direct; I'm not on the Hanover PD detail list yet. I have ten hours for yesterday and ten more for today. Do you want me to continue tomorrow, Ms. McCarthy?"

"Tomorrow? Yes, stay for the day tomorrow. Please note the time that the debris containers leave. Why don't you look the place over for the remainder of the week until the Bankses return? Put in for five hours per day until they get back."

"Thank you, Ms. McCarthy, that's more than fair. I've been parking my Toyota at the end of the driveway near the street for the past couple of nights, just to deter the curious."

"Well, Officer Franey, thanks again for being so conscientious. Now if you could remove Rufus from my foot. My toes are starting to lose circulation. Anything else?"

"Oh, sorry! Rufus, come here."

Looking at his notepad with the purple cover, Joe Franey flipped the page. "Yes, there were two other visitors today. At 12:10, the Hanover fire chief was here. At 4:15, a gentleman was here looking for the Bankses' dog. He thought Rufus might belong to the Bankses. Kind of odd; he showed me his business card but put it back in his pocket. He was shaky; his hand trembled. I didn't catch his name, but I did see that he parted his name off to the side, rather than in the middle."

"What do you mean, his name was parted to the side?"

"Well my name is Joseph F. Franey, middle name Frank. If I parted my name on the side, I would be J. Frank Franey. He was driving a small Ford pickup truck, mustard yellow. He was parked across the street, so I didn't see the tag number. The truck did have identification, however—Scrimshaw Security Service—and a phone number, 857-285-5426."

"Can you give me a description of this guy?"

"He was average, five foot eight, maybe five foot nine, 150 to165 pounds, Caucasian, no more than forty-five years old. Hard to tell his hair color and style, as he was wearing a hat. He had a suit and tie with a long topcoat with a cloth belt. You know the kind that a Gestapo agent would wear in a World War II movie."

Chapter 30

7:11 @ the 7-Eleven

Will wonders never cease? Dr. Stu Mirkin was waiting at O'Doherty's and greeted Peg with a big hug. "Hi, Stu. Find out who Roberts had dinner with the other night?"

"Denise was his waitress. She said he had dinner with a couple and a very tall juvenile. That's all she remembered."

"That was his eight o'clock appointment. I'd like to know who his earlier guest was. Stu, do you know the bartender in the lounge side?"

"Yeah, that's Eddie. Let me check to see if he was on duty last Thursday. Hey, Eddie, were you here last Thursday, the 13th?"

"Let me check the calendar, Doc. Yup, I was here, 5:30 'til closing. What's up?"

"Did you see Buckley Roberts? You know, the sports attorney, at the bar?"

"Oh, yeah, Doc. He was at the bar, waiting for a client. About an hour, I'd say. Drinking his usual—Coke and coffee. Decent guy. Lousy tipper."

"Eddie, did you notice anyone with him?"

"Nobody in particular. There were other people at the bar, but I don't know if they were with Roberts. It's a bar. Everybody chats with everybody. Hard to tell, especially when it's busy. He's been coming here for a few years. Always wants his coffee for free. Lousy tipper."

"Why did he want his coffee for free?"

"See Dickie's sign." Eddie pointed to a placard over the mirror: MAKE THE LAST ONE FOR THE ROAD. COFFEE—ON US.

"Buck Roberts only drank Coke and coffee, nothing alcoholic. Not that I ever saw."

"Thanks, Eddie. Oh, Eddie, here's a quarter for your tip jar."

"Yeah. Thanks, Doc. Very funny."

Stu Mirkin couldn't contain his grin when he returned to the table.

"What's so funny, Stu?"

"Peg, I think I found your killer. Eddie the bartender. He had the opportunity. Most of all he had the motive. Buckley Roberts was a lousy tipper."

"Yeah. Thanks, Doc. Very funny."

"Hm-m-m. That's exactly what Eddie said when I left him a quarter. Eddie didn't notice anyone special with Roberts. Traffic tough coming up the expressway? How's the clean-up going?"

"The mess is gone—the car, the debris, everything. They got a young kid watching the place, a neighbor, a police wannabe. Summer Intern Officer Joe Franey. Super-efficient kid. Guarding the place with his wonder dog, Rufus, like it was his own. One strange thing though."

"What's that, Peg?"

"He said someone was there earlier today looking for Sarek. Someone from the Scrimshaw Security Service."

"Never heard of that company."

"Here's the weird part. I stopped for gas at that 7-Eleven. The one near Morrissey Boulevard. When I came out from paying, there was a vehicle sitting in the Dippin' Donut Shop, next door, with the same lettering. Scrimshaw Security Service. I waited about five minutes to see the driver, but never saw him. I drove once around the block, and when I went back, the car was gone. It wasn't the same vehicle that Joe Franey saw in Hanover. His Scrimshaw Security vehicle was a pickup. That's why I'm a tad late. Don't you think that's weird, Stu?"

"Coincidence, I'm thinking. The Snowman is supposed to call me soon. I'll ask him to run a check on Scrimshaw."

The lobster roll with french fries and cole slaw was the specialty of the house at Dickie O'Doherty's Pub. None better. Nothing in the confines of North Troy, Vermont, could match the cholesterolic assault provided by the morsels from Dickie's kitchen. Once again, Stu sought the quiet of Broadway when his cell phone vibrated on his left hip. Caller ID indicated it was Tim Snow. He returned with a curious gaze.

"When I mentioned Scrimshaw Security Service, Snow said, 'Don't move, I'll be right over.' I told him we already ate, and we were not springing for dinner."

The front door opened less than five minutes after Doc returned to the table. Tim Snow looked uneasy. He was carrying a laptop computer case.

"What's this about Scrimshaw Security, Peg?"

"Coincidences, I guess. I visited Monique Maye this afternoon. She said that Buckley Roberts had two appointments here at O'Doherty's the night that he was shot. Roberts' calendar said the 1st appointment was with an H. Sumner Smyth, who was associated with S.S.S., but he didn't include what S.S.S. stood for. Later this afternoon, I went to Hanover to check on the home of LaChance's daughter to see if the mess from the explosion had been cleaned. The security person we hired told me that a gentleman with a pickup truck, lettered Scrimshaw Security Service, was at the site earlier today asking about LaChance's dog. On my way here tonight, I spotted another vehicle, a green four-door, lettered Scrimshaw Security Service. Weird?"

Tim Snow stood, turned, and said, "Follow me. Hey, Eddie, can I use Dickie's office for about five minutes?"

"Sure, Snowman. Here's the key."

Dickie O'Doherty's back room reminded Peg of Julia Emig's dental office. Sports memorabilia on all the walls. Many of the photos were of Dickie O'Doherty himself in his glory days of football at Stonehill College. Dickie O'Doherty was not, nor was he ever, a large man. But it was said that while playing linebacker at Stonehill, Dickie played large, very large. Perhaps that's why the lounge side of the Eatery & Irish Pub had very few incidences of unruly customers.

Tim Snow unzipped his laptop case, placing the computer on the side table. "You need to look at this. I put this on DVD. This is part of the Boston PD's tape of the parking lot taken last Thursday, the night Roberts was whacked. It's about fifteen minutes total. Five minutes before and ten after someone, the killer, approached Roberts' Mark VI. Let me speed this up. Okay, this must be Roberts walking to his vehicle. Remote unlock. Lights flash, and he enters the car, starts it, reverse, stop, now forward. Look at this. Here comes someone from the rear of the lot to the passenger door. This must be where Roberts lowers the window on the right side. Now the person comes around the front of the car to the driver's window, talking with Roberts. Driver's window must be down now. Vehicle still running—see the vapor from the tail pipe? Headlights are on. Right there, see that flash? That must be the first shot. The vehicle must be in park, engine running, headlights on, just like we found it ten minutes later. Bang! Second shot. Watch the shooter. Take a good look. Exit stage right. The time on the tape says 9:22. Did you notice anything odd?"

The Snowman paused the DVD. Stu looked at Peg and she at him. They didn't see anything revealing. Stu shrugged. "Okay, Tim. What did we miss?"

"It seems obvious to me that Roberts and the shooter knew each other. Seems that if it was a simple robbery, the shooter would have tried to get in the vehicle on the passenger side after Roberts had stopped and opened the window. But no, he comes around the front of the Lincoln. If Buckley Roberts thought this person was going to mug or kill him, he had the opportunity to run the shooter over, flatten the assailant right there in the parking lot."

Tim restarted the DVD player, and the tape track continued with the time indicator flashing in the top right corner: 9:22, 9:23, 9:24. Tim fast forwarded to 9:30, 9:31.

"Okay, watch very carefully. Look at the entire picture. It's 9:31:20. The vehicle has been sitting there with its lights on, running for about nine minutes since the event. Here comes our cruiser into the parking lot. He has to slow to maneuver around the Lincoln. He drives to the empty part of the lot at the rear, does a 180, and comes back to Roberts' car. The officer gets out, flashlight in hand and discovers the now-deceased Buckley Roberts. Did you notice anything else?"

"Sure, Snowman, there was something else. Reverse the tape back about thirty seconds. Right there, as the cruiser heads to the back of the lot. Here's another vehicle leaving the lot. You can only see part of it; the rest is out of frame. Now he's gone. That what you mean, Tim?"

"Right, Peg, but watch. See the vehicles on the street going by? You can only see the southbound side and then only the upper portion of each. We counted sixty-seven from the time the shooter walked away until now. Many of the units we were able to identify. One Broadway 'T' bus, a Yellow Freight tandem going to Gillette, Rothchild's Sewerage truck, four taxis of various liveries, a flat-bed car carrier lettered N.E.L. hauling a damaged U.S. Postal Service van. Let me rewind a little. Now watch. Here's the cruiser turning and the other car leaving the lot on the right side of the screen. Now watch the street. Dark Ford pickup, McHale's Cab, nothing, nothing, car with small lettering on the door, next, compact car, full-size car."

Stu scratched his left ear. "Is there more than this, Snowy? You got down here pretty quick, and you haven't mentioned food once. Very unusual."

"Yes, Stu. Yes, Peg. I think that car with the small lettering is the one that left the parking lot as the cruiser arrived. Let me bump the CD until I get that sedan in the frame. Here it is."

The three huddled around the laptop. Tim advanced the frame until the four-door, which appeared to be a Saturn, was in the middle of the screen. "Awful blurry. Lettering is not that clear. Advance another frame, Tim. One more."

On the last frame just before the four-door Saturn disappeared on the left side, the lettering on the driver's door came into better focus. "There it is. You can just make it out. Damn. I don't believe it."

There it was fuzzy, very fuzzy, but legible: Scrimshaw Security Service.

"Stu, I looked at this tape a dozen times. I never made the connection 'til you mentioned Scrimshaw. Doesn't that vehicle leaving the lot look similar to the one marked Scrimshaw Security Service? Looks like lettering on the left front door but the angle and the headlights wash it out. I swear that's the same car."

Peg continued staring at the blurry image on Snow's laptop. "There's the possibility that this whole deal with Scrimshaw Security Service is legit. Somebody hired them to locate LaChance's dog. Maybe relatives in Louisiana. This guy Smyth calls Buckley Roberts. Maybe that's even his car leaving the parking lot. Still doesn't mean he shot Roberts. Maybe he stayed at the bar and left after Roberts, and that would explain the time lapse. Scrimshaw certainly isn't trying to hide. When I went to Hanover, I only missed them by an hour. They seem to have several vehicles."

Tim Snow slipped the laptop back into its case and pocketed the CD. "I'm hungry. Let's eat! Only one problem with that scenario, Peg. I called into headquarters on my way here. No listing on Scrimshaw Security Service. Nada! Zippo! It doesn't exist. No webpage. No phone listing. No nothing. I think the whole thing is bogus, and it has me worried, Peg. I worry about you."

"Why worry about me? I'm only an observer to this whole affair."

"Sorry, Peg, you're more than a simple observer. This guy Smyth, who claims he is with Scrimshaw, is looking for you. That worries me."

"Looking for me? Why me?"

"Because you have the dog. He could be out to get you or Sarek or both."

As they followed Tim out of O'Doherty's office, Stu asked, "Tim, why do you think this is one person when we see several different vehicles?"

"I bet he has magnetic signs that can be moved from car to car. Cars could be stolen, borrowed, rentals, anything."

"How about the phone number that Officer Franey got off the pickup truck?"

"Okay, Peg, I'll run a trace on the phone. I bet that's a phony, too. Don't call that number. If it's active, we may be tipping him off."

A few minutes later, in the cold outside under O'Doherty's green awning, Peg told Stu the lingering questions that bothered her. "What do you think, Stu? Do you think Tim is overreacting?"

"Peg, I think Tim Snow is a tough detective. I think you should heed his warning. I also think you need to be careful. Why don't we switch cars this evening in case someone is looking for your rented Kia? When did you say you were returning to Vermont?"

"I was going to drive back on Thursday. Bellevue wants me to fly to Montreal, and the Expos will provide a limo ride back to North Troy. I need to pick up my car, my stuff, and my dog. I really need to find an apartment or something I can call home. I'm just not sure where. Vermont? Around here? Maybe near D.C."

"Peg, I was hoping it would be in Boston."

They hugged. Peg could feel his strength. She also could sense his deeply felt concern. That worried Peg. Perhaps this situation was becoming more dangerous than she imagined.

Peg thought to herself, *Perhaps it would be wise to return to Vermont tomorrow. I need to get my bits and pieces out of there, and I do miss Sarek.*

Yellow Pad Entry: #20 2-18-2003 10:45 p.m.

At 399 Cedar Street—Security being provided by next door neighbor who is a part-time police officer. He is keeping a detailed log of happenings at the site.

See Attached Report of Special Police Officer Joseph F. Franey.

Scrimshaw Security Service (S.S.S.?) 857-205-5426—Possible link to B.R. murder?

Also been asking about Sarek at Hanover explosion site.

(See above mentioned report.)

Decided to return to Vermont via Montreal. Booked ticket via Internet. Canadian Air – Flight No. 3301; departure time 6:45 a.m. 2-19-03—confirmation # 1983452.

"To leave a message, simply press 1, or you may wait for the tone."

"Hi, Stu. Thanks for the use of your car. I've decided to get back to North Troy tomorrow morning, 6:45, Canadian Air Flight No. 3301 via Montreal. I'll leave your car at your office and take the water shuttle over to Logan Airport. You said you had a second set of keys. I've really got a lot of loose ends that I need to take care of. Flying into Montreal for a morning meeting with Bellevue at 10:00. Can you have the rental company pick my car up at your office tomorrow? Call me if you get any more info on Scrimshaw. Hugs. Bye."

Journal Entry
Tuesday, February 18, 2003

Boy, I thought this day would never end! Those anonymous phone calls about Sarek are very concerning. These calls, combined with today's meetings. First, with Stu and Snowman about the ballistics of the Roberts murder; then with lawyer Monique Maye; the visit to the Banks' home and the impromptu update by Police Intern Franey; and concluding with dinner at O'Doherty's with Stu and Boston PD Detective Snow. What a day! I'm exhausted just thinking about it. I do wonder if Tim Snow is overreacting to the situation? Am I in danger?

I do look forward to returning home tomorrow. Can't wait to see Sarek. I do miss that dog and the quietness of the northern woods. I also worry that someone seems to be looking for him. All this interest in a dog seems odd. I don't get it.

Tomorrow, I'll pick a date for my party. I'm too tired tonight. What a day!

Chapter 31

Wednesday 2-19-03
Flight 3301

Oh, the advantages of airline travel with just a carry-on bag! The first thing Peg noticed as she left the security perimeter of Canadian Air was a gentleman holding a sign at chest level. It read "Peg McCarthy—Expos." She nearly walked past. "Oh, that's me! I'm Peg McCarthy."

"Good morning, Ms. McCarthy, I'm Oscar. Your limo is right outside. Do you have any baggage to claim?"

"No. No baggage, thanks."

"Mr. Bellevue will meet you at Café De Paris on Sherbrooke Street. I hope you didn't have breakfast on your flight."

Peg could see Oscar's toothy grin in the rear view mirror. "Right, Oscar, you wouldn't believe how little they serve on flights these days. I can remember when you could get a full meal on a flight. Those days are gone."

At 9:40 a.m., the quick ride to downtown Montreal ended. "Here we are, Ms. McCarthy. Café De Paris. Please let me know when you are ready to go to Vermont."

J.P. Bellevue waved from his table at the left rear of the Gold Room. "Peg, so good to see you." Bellevue offered his hand, then changed his mind, and hugged Peg. "I've been worried about you. Let's order. You have several phone calls to answer. A Tim Snow from the Boston Police Department has been trying to reach you since about 7:30 a.m. He says you must have had your cell phone off while flying. He's called three times and wants you to return his call ASAP."

"J.P., I'm going to make this call outside so I don't disturb anyone."

"Boston PD. How may I direct your call?"

"Yes, Tim Snow, homicide, please. Hello, my name is Peg McCarthy, and I'm returning a call to Detective Snow. Yes, I'll hold."

"Good morning, Peg. Are you in a quiet spot so we can talk?"

"Yes. Tim, I'm outside the Café de Paris in Montreal. What's cooking? Must be important."

"Peg, I called the Regency early this morning, and they said you had checked out. Stu mentioned yesterday that you might return to Vermont via Montreal. Peg, I'm afraid I have bad news. Stu Mirkin's been involved in a serious accident. Just after he left us last night at Dickie O'Doherty's. He was heading east, on Dorchester Avenue and was forced off the road at Summer Street. Vehicle passed him, then turned right on Summer, forcing him onto the sidewalk. He hit a concrete streetlight pole, and it came down on the car. It took a half hour to extricate Stu from the car. He's in the intensive care unit at Mass General Hospital. I just talked with the trauma surgeon, Dr. Wallace Heleen. He says the next twenty-four hours are the most critical. Peg, are you there?"

"I'm here, Tim. Should I return? Did the other vehicle stop?"

"No, Peg. Hit and run. Someone followed the vehicle. It was a pickup truck that headed south on Summer and turned left onto Falcon Pier. Went down Drydock Avenue. That's a dead end. There's a Navy frigate, the USS *Lusby*, in dry dock for repairs with a ten-member security crew aboard. One of the sailors on watch said the vehicle went right past his position at a high rate of speed and continued to the end of the road. He thinks it went into the water at the end of the pier. I got Gonzo Legendre and his rescue team going into the water as we speak. Why don't you wait a day or so before you head back. I hope this is an unfortunate accident, but I think we should examine all these events to see if there is any connection."

"You know, Tim, Stu was uneasy about my driving to Braintree last night. We switched cars at O'Doherty's. That was my rental he was driving!"

"That worries me, Peg. Perhaps someone's stalking you, and Stu just happened to be driving your rental."

"It worries me as well. Okay, Tim, let me know if you hear anything about Stu's condition. You'll get hospital updates quicker than I would."

Peg's knees went weak, and she suddenly felt ill. Bellevue came out to tell her breakfast had arrived. Peg's facial expression explained her distress.

"Bad news?"

"I'm afraid so. My friend, Dr. Stu Mirkin, was involved in a car wreck. He's in intensive care at Massachusetts General. I hope this is not connected to the other violent events that I've been investigating."

Peg no sooner sat down when her phone rang.

"Peg, Snowman again. Good news. Bad news. Doctor Heleen just called me; Stu's condition is much improved. They changed his status to stable. He has a concussion, compound fracture of the right femur, broken ribs, collapsed lung, and a broken right thumb."

"Tim, if that's the good news, I hate to ask about the bad news."

"Okay, Peg, the bad news. They just got that pickup truck winched out of the drink at the end of Falcon Pier. Ford, mustard yellow, magnetic sign on one door. Hazard a guess what the name on the truck was?"

"Don't tell me! Scrimshaw Security Service?"

"You guessed it, Peg. Empty, no driver. I bet it's clean as a whistle inside. Peg, do you still have a sidearm?"

"All Customs agents were issued a new Glock 9mm about ten years ago. I still have my own revolver that I used prior to the issue of a standard firearm. Back when I started, everybody had his or her own weapon. Mine was a Smith & Wesson 357 Magnum revolver. Still have it. It's in my stuff, back in Vermont."

"Sorry to say, Peg, but I think you better dig it out. I think we got a sociopath on our hands. One who's a killer. This time I think he was out to get you, Peg. Stu just happened to be driving your car."

"Why me? I have no connection with either LaChance or Buckley Roberts."

"There must be a connection. Perhaps the killer feels you're getting too close to him."

"Tim, you say 'him.' There's always the possibility that LaChance was drugged by a woman."

"I agree death by poison is often perpetrated by a woman. Oh, Peg, we ran a check on that phone number that was on Scrimshaw's placard. Came up listed to Scrimshaw Security Service, with a billing address in Ledyard, Connecticut. We ran a call with number blocking to that phone. Answering service in Boston. Scrimshaw pays their monthly bill by money order. Those money orders are very difficult to trace unless we see a copy to find the location of purchase."

All different methods of violence were used: LaChance by drug, Roberts by gun, Banks' garage by explosion, and Doc Mirkin's accident. The only commonality is the motor vehicle aspect, and that's probably coincidental. It's almost as if the killer is playing games. Quite unnerving!

"J.P., please excuse my interruptions to your breakfast. That was Detective Snow. Stu Mirkin seems better. I feel better. In fact, I'm hungry. This whole story, starting with Bill LaChance's death, is beginning to take on the flavor of a murder mystery. Three weeks ago, I thought we would find a jilted lover, an irate fan, or someone with financial gain who was responsible for LaChance's demise. I seem to be in the middle of something far more disturbing and complicated and tangled and *big*."

"Peg, perhaps you should get out of the line of fire. Let the police handle this. I'm concerned about your safety."

"You're right, J.P. That's the main reason I came back a day early. That, and I do miss Sarek. If anything good came out of my investigating this case, it's the fact that LaChance's daughter Marie is letting me have Sarek. He's such a great dog."

"Peg, it's 11:15. I'll call Oscar and tell him to head this way in about twenty minutes. You must be exhausted. How long have you been away from Vermont?"

"Thanks J.P. Seems like I've been away for about two months, but it's been less than two weeks."

"Peg, have a good trip back, and please stay safe. It might be best to stay away from Boston until this whole affair is resolved."

About the time that Oscar and the azure-blue limo with the Province of Quebec vanity license tag that read "Expos 3" reached South Bolton, it started to snow. The final twelve miles to the Vermont/Canadian border seemed to take hours. The crunching sound of the tires on fresh snow as the limo pulled into the parking lot of the Customs Station was a comforting reminder of what was, until two weeks ago, home. There were no other tire tracks in the snow, indicating that this, in fact, was another quiet day in the boonies.

As soon as Peg entered the office, the smell of Ed Hawley's old coffee hit like a brick. Oh, to be home!

"Welcome back, Peg. Sarek. Hey, Sarek! Wake up! Look who's here."

"Thanks, Bill, it's so good to be back. Seems like I've been away for months. I see the weather hasn't changed. Where's my dog?"

Sarek couldn't race across the office faster. His actions were the best homecoming gift. Sarek's cries of joy were almost mournful. "Peg, I missed you. I missed you. I missed you. I didn't think you were ever coming back. I thought I was an orphan again. Where have you been?"

"Oh, Sarek, I missed you too. I guess you really are my dog."

"Peg, there may be some parties that might argue that point. About your being Sarek's owner."

"What do you mean, Bill? Are you saying all those phone calls have been trying to locate Sarek?"

"Those calls and the fact that some guy has been here twice today looking for you and the dog. I think it was the same person who called me earlier this week. Voices sounded alike. There was something about the guy that didn't seem right. Tried to control the conversation. You know. Like the dope dealer we nabbed last year, the one who tried to boss us around. It's a technique, you know. Trying to show that he is the one with the power. I gave him an I.B.B.Y. and told him that you retired from the Customs Service and that you and your little dog, Sarek, were no longer in the area. Sorry and good-bye. He muttered something about taking me and the U.S. Customs Service to court for kidnapping his client's pet."

"That's not what I wanted to hear. Did you notice what he was driving?"

"He had a lime-green Saturn, later model, four-door sedan, Rhode Island tag # MG 2910. Had those magnetic signs on the doors."

"Let me guess—Scrimshaw Security Service."

"No. Something like that, though. Stone Investigative Services. He showed me his business card. I wrote the information down, and he put the card back in his pocket. Like it was the only card he had. Here it is right here."

H. Sumner Stone. Stone Investigative Services. 370 Main Street, Suite 24. Milton, MA 02345. 617-283-8000.

"What do you make of it, Peg?"

"There's an excellent possibility that this guy Stone, Smyth, or whatever his name is, killed both LaChance and Buckley and could be responsible for an explosion at the home of LaChance's ex-wife and daughter. Not to mention the fact that he ran a friend of mine off the road and put him in Mass General. He seems to be after me now."

"Why you, Peg?"

"I'm not sure, Bill. I was advised to get my sidearm. Do you have the key to the storage closet? Any idea how long my federal firearms license-to-carry lasts?"

"The end of the year in which you retire. Then you can request an extension if you have reasons associated with your employment, like this deal with the LaChance murder. Peg, please be careful. This nut could be right down the street. I'm calling Frank. He needs to know about this bird running around God's Northeast Kingdom.

Journal Entry
Thursday, February 19, 2003

Oh, *my God!* What is going on here? It seems that someone really is after me all because of a dog! And because of me, Stu is run off the road and is now in the hospital! I can't believe it—he could have been *killed!* Thank God, he's doing better.

Maybe J.P. is right. Maybe I should leave this whole matter to the authorities. I concluded, incorrectly for that matter, that I'd be safe back here in Vermont. Now I find that someone is searching for me and Sarek here as well. And now someone attacks Stu! What if that concrete pole landed on Stu, head on? He'd be dead right now. This is starting to get personal—and scary. I'll tell you one thing. This stalker isn't getting me or Sarek. And quite frankly, I think Stu is just too damn stubborn to die; especially this way. I need to take care of business here so I can get back to Boston and check on him. Of course, that's assuming he remains stable. Timmy said he'd call if anything changes. Psycho or no psycho, I need to be there for Stu as soon as I can.

Not to change the subject, but finally a date for the retirement party has been decided! July 4th weekend. Seems appropriate.

It has been good to see Sarek and everyone at the Customs Station.

Chapter 32

Estimated 7-8 Months Pregnant

Before Sheriff Ames arrived, the fax machine started its familiar warm-up ritual.

"Here it comes." Bill Atwood, newly appointed director of the Customs Station, watched the paper feed slowly, line by line, and read the incoming information on Rhode Island tag # MG 2910.

"That's no surprise. Stolen plate. Someone in Cranston, Rhode Island. Peg, you think Qaqish might be involved. Cranston isn't that far from West Warwick."

"I don't think so, Bill. Everybody in Rhode Island seems to live next door to each other. I talked to Qaqish a week or so ago. When he was here, it looked like he might gain financially from LaChance's death. But he had more to lose than gain with LaChance's passing. Besides Qaqish and H. Sumner Smyth-Stone are not the same person, according to those who have seen both. There doesn't seem to be anything that indicates they're working together. You didn't see Qaqish when he was here on the 28th of January. Ed was here when he arrived early that Tuesday morning. What did the Stone Investigative Services person look like?"

"Just an average-looking guy. Very neatly dressed. White shirt. Power tie. No coat, even though the temperature was twenty degrees. Five foot eight, 150-160 pounds, Caucasian, forty to forty-five years old, slight build. He looked like a Republican candidate running for office. You know how they look when they come through here during primary season?"

"That's definitely not Walter Qaqish. Good, here comes Frank."

"Afternoon, all. Welcome back, Peg. Did you miss us? Just about the time you think you've seen it all, something happens to displace that myth."

"What happened, Frank?"

"Oh, some woman took a car from Mike Caulfield's Truck Stop over near the interstate. Came out of the ladies room, went out to the pumps and hopped into a Chrysler that was fueling up. Told the kid at the pump her husband was inside, and she was going to move the vehicle so the next person in line could get gas. Just left the lot and got on the interstate going north. We got an APB out. I talked with Ernie over at the Interstate Customs Station. They've got the Mounties waiting for her. Should be easy to spot. New Brunswick tags with a very pregnant lady driving. You heard me right. Pregnant! According to the four witnesses that saw her, she's seven to eight months along. Don't that beat all? The state police up on I-91 were only a couple of minutes behind her."

Peg removed several boxes from the storage closet. In typical Peg McCarthy efficiency, all had the contents written on the top. The list on the third carton indicated a S&W .357 with ammo and holster were inside.

The revolver, wrapped in cloth and placed in a large Ziploc bag, was in its original orange box. The box flap was marked Smith & Wesson, Model 581, Blue Finish, cal. 357 Mag. Peg had forgotten how the short barrel of this handgun, a stunted four inches, made it appear almost toy-like. Yet the .357 bore made this a most potent, albeit not a long-range, defensive weapon. The gun box hadn't been opened in five or six years.

"Hey, Bill, if you were me, where would you put the key for the trigger lock on my old Smith & Wesson?"

"Knowing you, Peg, it's over there in the key cabinet with a tag on it. Do you really think you'll need that pistol?"

"I'm hoping no, but with what has happened over the past three weeks, everyone connected with this case is very jumpy. I have the holster and ammunition here also. I haven't fired this weapon in ten to twelve years. Maybe I should practice a little."

Frank looked at the deeply blued sidearm, raised the plastic bag to his nose, and inhaled. "You must have cleaned it before putting into storage. Boy, does that gun oil have its own particular aroma. Wow! Peg, thanks for all the e-mail updates. You've had a couple of stressful weeks."

As usual, Bill was right. The key for the trigger lock was in the cabinet and was neatly marked "S&W .357." Peg had worn a sidearm every working day for the past twenty-two years, yet now, after only three weeks away from duty, this heavy metallic object felt strangely foreign on her belt.

"Peg, two questions: How long are you back for, and where and when is your retirement party?"

"Good questions, Bill. I was going to stay around here for a few days, until the dust settles in Boston. But you remember that doctor who came up from Boston for LaChance's autopsy? Stu Mirkin? He and I have become friends. Doc Mirkin is in Mass General. Someone was trying to run me off the road, but we had switched cars. I feel the need to get back to Boston as soon as possible."

"He seems like someone real special."

"He is. Real special. I feel responsible for his getting hurt. As for my retirement party, I'm thinking the July 4th long weekend. Independence Day—appropriate day for a retirement party. Don't you think?"

"Well, Peg, you better stay over and get some sleep. Clare Murphy's on vacation this week and next. She said if you came back to use her place as long as you needed. Sarek is also welcome. Staying at the compound is a safe spot. I would imagine Stone, or Smyth, or whatever his name is has hit the road."

"I put an APB out on that lime-green Saturn about an hour ago. You said Stone Investigative Services, didn't you, Bill?"

"That's it, Frank. Stone Investigative Services, 370 Main Street, Suite 24, Milton, MA 02345. 617-283-8000."

"Let's call that number in to see what we get!"

Frank picked up his phone. "Hello, I'm trying to contact a Mr. H. Sumner Stone. Okay. What did you say the name of your firm was? Okay. Yes, I got that. Are you located in Milton, Massachusetts? No? Where? Thank you so much."

It was amazing how proficient Frank had become in the past three weeks with his new communicator phone. "283-8000 is the phone number for McLean's Carpet Cleaning Company, and they are located in Arlington, not Milton, Massachusetts. She said Milton is about fifteen miles south of Arlington. Never heard of H. Sumner Stone."

Frank tapped out numbers as if sending Morse code from a century past.

"Yes, directory assistance. Could I get the non-emergency number of the Milton Police Department in Milton, Massachusetts? Thanks. Yes, that would be helpful if you could connect me."

"Milton dispatcher. How may I direct your call?"

"Hi there, this is Sheriff Franklin Ames of Orleans County in Vermont. I'm working on a motor vehicle case here. I have a vehicle that has a Milton, Massachusetts, address on the side, but the phone number directed me to Arlington, Massachusetts. Can you verify the location?"

"I'll try. What is the information that you have?"

"Stone Investigative Services, 370 Main Street, Suite 24, Milton, MA 02345. 617-283-8000."

"Hold on a second. I'm going to call one of our squad cars to check."

Frank cupped his hand over the phone. "Squad car! Haven't heard that expression in twenty years. This lady must be older than me."

"Sheriff Ames. One of my officers is only minutes from that location. Hold on. Okay, he's in front of 370 Main Street and reports that it's a Mail Boxes for U location. That suite 24 must be their box number. He's going in to check with the clerk. Hold on. Sheriff Ames, officer reports box number 24 is rented to a Mr. H. Sumner Stone. His rent is paid up until April first. Just a mail drop, I'm sure."

"Thank you so much. You've been most helpful. Oh, I'm sorry, I didn't note your name."

"Beatrice Briggs; that's B-R-I-G-G-S."

"Thank you, Ms. Briggs. Could you ask your officer to check on one additional item with the clerk at Mail Boxes for U? Ask if they have a box rented to Scrimshaw Security Services."

"Hold on, Sheriff. I'll ask. Sheriff Ames, they do not have any box holder with that name. Anything else that I can help you with?"

"No, Ms. Briggs, that's it. Once again. Thank you."

H. Sumner Stone, a.k.a. H. Sumner Smyth, had the attributes of a chameleon: phony companies with bogus locations; phone numbers to answering services; multiple vehicles with magnetic identification signs. Customs Agent Bill Atwood and Summer-Intern Police Officer Joseph Franey, the only known witnesses, both described Mr. Smyth/Stone as a rather innocuous individual with average features. The darkened videotape of the Buckley Roberts shooting yielded a fuzzy hooded form at the driver's window of Roberts' Lincoln. Scrimshaw Security Service seemed to be everywhere, yet it didn't exist anywhere. The ballistics reports were just as confusing. A .25 caliber. Every other slug had been extracted from its cartridge and reversely reinstalled (for maximum damage?) and the bullet of .455 caliber, as suggested by Boston PD ballistics expert Anita Ivarson, fired from a rare Colt semiautomatic with British markings, and located in the door of an out-of-service police cruiser. So many facts with only slim threads of connection.

The ringing of Peg's cell phone caught her by surprise. "Hello, Peg McCarthy speaking."

"Hello Ms. McCarthy. This is Julia Emig, the dentist from Rockland. You said when you were at my office to call you if anything else came up. A woman called me about an hour ago and asked about

Bill's dog, Sarek. She said she represented Stone Security Service, and she indicated that she knew I had taken care of Sarek during some of Bill's road trips. She stated she was trying to locate the dog for Bill's daughter. I know for a fact that Marie is allergic to dogs—severely allergic. That's why Sarek stayed with me rather than with Bill's ex-wife and daughter. I told her I hadn't seen the dog in months."

"That is interesting, Dr. Emig."

"Well, Ms. McCarthy, that's only one of the strange happenings around here. I have the feeling that someone had been in my office two nights ago. Nothing missing, my script pads are accounted for. Drug inventory checks out. All door locks seem normal. Just a sense that things had been moved. This morning I finally noticed something missing in my waiting area—Bill LaChance's autographed picture. The picture with him and the dog. I thought that a patient might have taken it, but those frames are attached by screws, four each, to the wall. Someone would have noticed if it was taken during office hours."

"That is weird. Anyone else have keys to your office?"

"My receptionist, the dental hygienist, the cleaning service, my brother who lives in the apartment above my office. There's a spare set around here somewhere. That's all I can think of. I've checked with everyone except my brother, Carl. He borrowed my car yesterday to go to a job interview in Hartford. He should return this evening."

"Dr. Emig, could you keep me informed of any other happenings? Did you call your local police to report your suspicions of a possible entry to your office?"

"No, Ms. McCarthy, I didn't call the police. First let me talk to my brother when he returns. I'll be in touch. Bye."

Bill Atwood could sense the tension. "Peg, look at this. Look what we taught Sarek while you were gone. Sarek, look who's coming. Out the window." Sarek took two mighty bounds and leaped onto one of the three stools near the counter by the large bay window. "Pretty good trick for such a large dog."

Sarek peered out into the snow. Dusk was coming quickly, once again, to God's Northeast Kingdom.

Safely ensconced at the compound of the U.S. Customs Service, Peg tried to update her yellow legal pad entries. Sarek was sleeping at her feet. To be more precise, Sarek was sleeping *on* her feet. He wanted to be sure that if Peg was going anywhere, he would be alerted and would not be left behind again.

Ring … ring … ring …

"Hi, Mom. It's Peg."

"Hi, honey. How's everything with your case? We're worried about you. There's a lot on TV about that LaChance murder. This is the last thing you need to do just after you retire."

"Mom, I'm fine. I have a lot of people looking out for me. Just wanted to let you know, my retirement party is going to be on the 4th of July. Can you call Kate and Mary and let them know?"

"Sure, honey, no problem."

"Thanks, Mom. Gotta run. Love you."

"Love you, too. Be careful."

"I will. Bye."

"Bye."

Yellow Pad Entry: #21 2-19-2003 7:17 p.m.

9:30—Received call from Tim Snow (Boston PD) informing me of Stu Mirkin's accident and his condition at Massachusetts General Hospital.

Bill Atwood reports that a male (just an average-looking guy). Neatly dressed. White shirt. Power tie. Five foot eight, 150-160 pounds, Caucasian, forty to forty-five years old, slight build, had been looking for me and the dog at the North Troy Customs Station (twice). Bill says he seemed jumpy.

Bill noted the vehicle information of individual seeking Sarek.

Late model lime-green Saturn, four-door sedan, Rhode Island tag # MG 2910, with magnetic signs on the doors: Stone Investigative Services, 370 Main Street, Milton, MA 02345. 617-238-8000.

Sheriff Ames traced the phone to a cleaning company in Arlington, Mass. The address of Stone Investigative Service indicates a mail box drop at a Mail Boxes for U in Milton, Mass.

3:45 p.m.—Received call from Dr. Julia Emig. Stone Investigative Services has called her, checking on Sarek. Doc Emig also thinks someone had entered her office several nights ago. Emig just noticed LaChance's autographed picture (the one with the dog) is missing from her patient waiting area. She will check with her brother when he returns from Hartford.

Late call to Tim Snow finds Stu Mirkin improving by the hour. Tim looked in on him around 5:00 p.m. States that Stu is banged up, groggy, and hurting but awake.

I'm driving back to Boston in the morning.

Chapter 33

Rural Route 101 To 100
To Interstate 89 South

Four cardboard boxes and an elderly Chevrolet Monte Carlo didn't seem like much of a legacy for twenty-two years in the service of the United States Customs Service. As usual, Sarek sat at attention, riding shotgun, as Peg began her trek to Boston. Peg hadn't been driving more than four or five minutes when she was startled by another vehicle filling her rear view mirror. Sheriff Ames and his Crown Victoria gave Peg and Sarek an escort the twelve miles to the Orleans County border.

As the duo approached the county line, Frank put on all of his emergency lights. They were on their own. Perhaps not. Crossing into Caledonia County, another vehicle was suddenly behind her. A Caledonia County Sheriff's Department officer passed, giving Peg the thumbs up signal as both vehicles accelerated well beyond the posted speed. Fifteen minutes at 80 miles per hour brought them to the on ramp of Interstate 91 South, where another sheriff's vehicle joined the parade. Both drivers saluted as Peg approached the highway and the fastest route to Boston.

Sarek was scanning the morning horizon for trouble when Peg's cell phone rang.

"Ms. McCarthy, this is Officer Dave Corayer of the Vermont State Police. I'm your next escort. I'm in the southbound rest area at the Mile 122 marker, about four miles south of exit 10. Are you getting close?"

"Good morning, Officer Corayer. I'm only two miles from you. Older Monte Carlo, maroon two-door. Who arranged this special attention?"

"Ms. McCarthy, my dispatcher says he's had four calls concerning your safe trip to Boston. One from the U.S. Customs Service; one from the Orleans Sheriff's Office; one from the Boston PD–homicide division; and the other from the State of Vermont Chief of Forensic Pathology, State Medical Examiner's Office. Are you in the witness protection program?"

Peg could hear Officer Corayer's partner laughing in the background. This police presence only confirmed how seriously everyone was taking this situation. Peg wondered, *How did I ever get immersed into the center of this case?* The gravity of everyone's feelings was emphasized when a blue-and-gray Massachusetts State Police car fell in behind as the old Monte Carlo entered Methuen, Massachusetts, on Interstate 93. The police company continued to the Massachusetts General Hospital, where Peg was directed to a parking area that had two uniformed Boston police officers at the gate.

"You must be Peg McCarthy. Tim Snow just called down about five minutes ago. He'll meet you in Room 824C, Ellison Building. This is Detective Carol Vecchi. She'll take you up to the room. We'll watch your dog."

The elevator stopped at the eighth floor with a split second of zero gravity. Room 824C was at the end of the hall. As Peg approached the room, the door opened and, Nurse Karen Peterkin exited.

"I sure hope you're Peg McCarthy. He's not cooperating. He refuses to start his lunch until you can join him. He ordered for you; I hope you like institutional chow. Doctors are always the worst patients!" Nurse Peterkin winked as she left the doorway.

Peg was more than stunned. The list of Mirkin's injuries was beyond extensive: head shaved; leg in traction with stainless steel threaded rods, called Schanz pins, passing through the femur and attached to an external fixator to maintain healing alignment. Additionally, there were tubes connected to many orifices. Still another larger blue tube entered the chest wall at an odd angle. This blue tube was used to maintain the ballooning of the collapsed lung. Dr. Stu Mirkin was alive but not going dancing anytime soon.

"Oh, Stu, I'm so sorry."

"It's okay, Peg. What do you think of this new look I'm going for? Kind of retro, don't you think? Oh boy, it really hurts when I smile or laugh or breathe. Other than all the tubes, all the equipment, and how I look, I'd say I'm doing fine. Guess I'm lucky to be alive."

Peg was looking for a spot to hug Stu without inflicting more pain. This was a difficult task.

Tim Snow came into Room 824C, whistling. "Stu, you do look better now that Peg is here, but you still look like donkey droppings. Just got off the phone. We may have a break in this case. Friend of mine, Woy Lee—she's a Boston PD photographer—says she's working a suicide over in the South End at the McKinley School. In the parking lot. Peg, wolf down your lunch, and we'll go over and take a look see. Woy says nobody's going to touch a thing until I get there. Only ten minutes from here. What do you think?" Tim Snow, as always, was in perpetual motion. "I need a break in this case. I'm spending too much time on it. I've neglected my gym work. I've only two months to get ready."

"Ready for what, Tim?"

"Boston Marathon. April 21st. Didn't Stu tell you? Both of us are running this year, 26.2 miles. Hopkinton to Boston. Stu, I'm thinking you got more work to do to get ready than me."

"Right, Snowman. Peg, didn't I ever tell you? Tim does that masochistic sporting venue, Iron Man Triathlon. I told you he was more than a little strange."

The Snowman excused himself when his phone rang. He was only in the hallway a couple of minutes and returned with a worried look. "That was my friend Brian Newsom; he's also in homicide. Said he happened to be reading yesterday's *Providence Journal* and saw a brief article about some associate of Bill LaChance's being electrocuted the night before last. It killed the guy's nephew as well. Looks like an accident. Something about a faulty sump pump in the basement. Peg, didn't you and Stu talk with a Walter Qaqish back a few weeks ago?"

It is said that the sense of smell is one of the most powerful stimuli to imprint one's memory. Peg and Stu instantly recalled the aroma of checkerberry—or was it juniper.

Stu spoke first. "Qaqish dead? Tim, you better call Rhode Island authorities and have them have check the wiring at Qaqish's store real close. Perhaps it's more than an electrical malfunction that killed Qaqish and his nephew."

The ten minutes to the McKinley School took only six, with one of those suction-cup revolving blue lights placed on the roof and plugged into the cigarette lighter. Snow's battered K-car bounced down Clarendon Street. Sparks and noise spewed from the bent tailpipe with every dip in the road. Sarek slept, like a baby, in the rear.

"Why the old Aries, Tim? You know, with one red door and one beige door. Looks—well, you know what I mean."

"Respect Peg. Simple respect." Tim sensed that Peg was baffled by the respect statement. "People, when they see and hear a police car say, 'Hm, I wonder if I should pull over. I wonder if it's after me. Hm, I wonder. I wonder.' With my car it's 'Look at that thing. I better pull over. He'll run me over if I'm not out of the way. I sure hope his brakes work.' Respect, Peg. Simple respect."

Snowman continued, "Last year, the Commonwealth had a surplus property auction. I was looking for a newer vehicle so they told me to go bid on something with a lot of life in it. This car belonged to the MWRA—Massachusetts Water Resources Authority. Only had 65k on it. Cost the city $265.38. I always bid with change on the end. I wonder why? Well, anyway, the only thing I had to do was remove the MWRA insignias from the doors. I was going to paint over them but my cousin Marlene's husband has a junkyard in Chelsea, and he traded me even, his doors for mine. Even helped me switch them. Only problem is now I got four keys for this car; one for the ignition, one for the red driver's door, one for the beige passenger door, and one for the trunk. It's a pain sometimes. Did I answer your question, Peg?"

"Oh, yeah, Tim, thanks. Thanks a lot."

The entrance to the McKinley School parking lot was a narrow driveway that started by coming up onto the cobblestone sidewalk. Carrying a tad too much momentum, the multicolored ex-MWRA inspection car slammed into the pavement as it made its final approach to the suicide scene. The left rear hubcap suddenly passed them and proceeded ahead into the nearly vacant lot. Woy Lee, armed with a 35mm Nikon F, and two uniformed officers watched with amusement and alarm as the wayward disc struck the far wall.

"He's here," announced Mrs. Lee.

"What we got, Woy?"

"Tim, this lot is used by school personnel during the day. Residents with a South End residents' sticker use it at night. They have to be out of here by 7:00 a.m. The principal will be right back; he's the one who discovered the body. Here he comes now. Tim Snow, this is the principal of McKinley High, Mr. Joseph Brown."

"Timmy Snow. Wow! I haven't seen you since you were in my U.S. History class."

"Hi, Mr. Brown. Been a long time. Tell me what you found."

"Timmy, I got to work around 6:40 this morning. This car was sitting here empty with the engine running. I figured it was a local resident letting his car warm up. Good way to lose your car, I figure. I had a meeting at West Roxbury High this afternoon, and when I came out to go to my car, I heard this car still running. I looked inside and saw the deceased lying on the front seat. That's when I noticed the hose running from the exhaust pipe to the rear window. I called 911."

Snow turned to the older of the two uniformed officers. "Did you guys run the registration number and VIN?"

"Not reported stolen, Tim. Titled to a Julia Emig, 54 North Avenue, Rockland."

Upon hearing the name Emig, Peg's thought was that this must be the brother who'd gone to Hartford for the job interview. The car was backed into a parking slot along the rear of the depressed parking level. A two-inch flexible hose ran from the tail pipe to the right rear vent window of the Caravan. The powered rear vent window was only open an inch. An open duffle bag sat on the second row of seats. Without getting into the vehicle, Peg could observe at least six motor vehicle plates in the bag. On the floor was a short stack of magnetic signs. The one on top was lettered Scrimshaw Security Service, with a phone number: 857-285-5426. The sign underneath was partially covered by the first, but it was obvious that it was Stone Investigative Services. On the right front seat cushion was Julia's missing autographed photo of No Chance LaChance and Sarek. Two of the four screws were still in the frame.

Two criminologists arrived from headquarters and started to catalog the crime scene. The medical examiner's office was notified.

"We got a suicide note; he's still got the pen in his hand."

One investigator lifted the note with a long set of tweezers and gently placed it in a plastic evidence envelope. Its contents were visible. The note had two words: I'm sorry.

Personal effects identified the corpse as, Robert Carl Wells, 73 E. Water Street, Whitman, Massachusetts. All the pieces fit. If any evidence was needed to close a case, then this case was done, stick a fork in it, cooked, finished, a wrap. All that was needed was the discovery of a motive, the .455 semiautomatic, and a way to tie the loose ends together. This afternoon's discovery was anticlimactic compared to the events of the past three weeks.

As always, Peg added to her growing stack of yellow pad entries.

Yellow Pad Entry: #22 2-20-2003 5:30 p.m.
Send thank you notes to sheriff's departments, Orleans and Caledonia counties, for the escort.
Ditto to the Vermont, New Hampshire, and Massachusetts State Police.
Ditto to Ace Edwards.
Apparent suicide victim found at McKinley School parking lot, Warren Street (South End), Boston. Tentatively identified as Robert

Carl Wells, 73 E. Water Street, Whitman, Mass. Victim left two-word suicide note: I'm sorry.

    Vehicle: 2002 Dodge Caravan, Mass. Registration # 481-YAG
    Titled to: Julia Emig, 54 North Ave., Rockland, MA 02370
    Vehicle contained the following items that might be associated with the LaChance/Roberts murders:
    Set of two matching plates 12383 Vermont.
    Set of two matching plates DAS 523 New Hampshire.
    One plate 1 DB 450 Rhode Island.
    Two Massachusetts plates, GREAT 1 and 747 THU.
    Two pairs of magnetic signs:
    set one: Stone Investigative Services
    set two: Saugus Dental Laboratory
    One single magnetic sign: Scrimshaw Security Service
    Framed autographed photo of Bill LaChance and Sarek as reported missing by Dr. Julia Emig, 54 North Ave.,Rockland, Mass.
    Carl Wells is, probably, the brother of Dr. Emig. Confirmation of positive identity should be completed following an autopsy.

    Yellow Pad Entry: #22 – Continued
    Potential Suspects
    With the now known facts the strongest possible candidates are:
    The events of today seem to point to one possibility, Carl Wells and the possibility of Dr. Julia Emig. Perhaps a co-conspirator with brother?
    With the now known facts the weakest possible candidates are:
William LaChance (deceased), Walter Qaqish (deceased), Accidental Poisoning, Montreal Expos, A Random Act of Tampering, LaChance's Daughter Marie (only thirteen yeas old) and the Hot Sauce Company or an employee of the Hot Sauce Company?

    There seems to be no possibility that Patricia Tremblay, the 'Take a Chance Foundation', or Adrianna Lomysh could have any involvement with this series of violent events

Chapter 34

The Morgue
at 612 Albany

The Suffolk County Medical Examiner's Office and Morgue were located at the Old Boston City Hospital at the corner of Massachusetts Avenue and Albany Street. This section of the city had been rehabilitated and cleaned up over the past decade. The morgue at 612 Albany Street, however, looked as it did in the 1930s. By law, all public buildings had to have handicap access. An unsightly elevator had been added to the right front of the building, which didn't complement the other décor. The morgue and autopsy area were located in the basement of this antiquated structure.

Julia Emig and an elderly gentleman were coming down the front steps as Peg approached.

"Good morning, Ms. McCarthy. I never believed it would come to this."

"I am sorry, Dr. Emig. Did you suspect that your brother disliked Bill LaChance?"

"My brother only met Bill a couple of times. I just can't believe that he could be responsible for all these tragic happenings. And the suicide, it's not in Carl's nature. He's had a rough couple of years, job issues, marriage on the rocks, all fueled by a gambling problem. Carl probably went to one of the Indian casinos in Connecticut; he didn't have a job interview at all. I just can't believe Carl would do this."

"Julia, did your brother ever mention LaChance's dog?"

"Carl is—sorry, was—a cat fancier. I don't recall that he ever saw the dog. Why do you ask?"

"No particular reason. Just wondering."

Julia Emig excused herself and headed to make funeral arrangements. Peg made her way down to the basement of the building.

"Peg! Peg McCarthy—in here. You just missed Julia Emig and her father."

"Good morning, Tim, I saw her on the way out. Tough situation."

"You got that right. I'm putting the notes together for my report on this case. Doc Emig identified the body but couldn't confirm the handwriting on the suicide note. Only two words, you know. I faxed it to a handwriting analyst. Dr. Emig says she'll fax me a copy of a card that her brother wrote last month for comparison. Plus, we've got his signature on his driver's license. Oh, that wannabe cop, Joe Franey from Hanover, was already here to see if he could ID the body. He said it was hard to tell. There's a big difference between seeing someone in dusk with a trench coat and hat, and the bright naked lights of the morgue. He said it might be the same person, but he couldn't give a positive identification. Hey, Peg, where's Sarek?"

"He's in the car. I'm going to have to find a place for the two of us really quick. I snuck him into the Regency last night."

"Sarek can crash at my place if you don't find anything. Let's go over to Mass General and check on our patient."

Room 824C was vacant when Tim and Peg arrived just after 10:00 a.m. Stu Mirkin had been wheeled downstairs for an X-ray and MRI of the broken leg. Commotion in the corridor was noted as Stu Mirkin was pushed from the elevator. Dr. Mirkin was recovering.

"Good morning, Stu. You look much improved over yesterday."

"I'm doing well. Going to get my butt out of here in a couple of days. Now I know why I got out of pediatric medicine. It just came to me. I hate hospitals. Looks like you guys are doing okay, solving the LaChance/Buckley murders and all. The papers say it's all wrapped up."

"I hope so." Tim Snow had a doubtful tone to his voice.

"Peg, what do you think? You share Tim's misgivings?"

"I hope it's over, but I just don't know."

"Tim, was the autopsy routine?"

Tim Snow, pulling a small spiral-bound pad from his pocket, began explaining from his hen-scratch notes. "Yeah, Doc, pretty much. But he really wanted to be dead. The preliminary toxicology report detected Tubarine . It's a neuromuscular blocking agent used as a surgical anesthesia. Intramuscular injection given in the thigh. The syringe was in the car. Julia Emig identified it as the brand of hypodermic she uses in her practice. I wonder where the Turarine came from? That's not a dental product. He also had an elevated carbon monoxide level. The combo killed him."

"While you gentleman discuss things, I've got to get out and look for a place that will accept my four-legged friend. I can't leave him in the car overnight."

An animated Stu interjected, "Peg, I can solve your problem. Stay at my place in Kingsbury, right on Rocky Nook that overlooks Plymouth Harbor. You'll love it. When I get out of here, in a couple of days, I'll need company to help me around for a little bit. Tim, ask out at the nurses' station where my belongings might be. My keys should be in my pants pocket. How about it, Peg?"

"Well, if you don't mind. I do have some loose ends around here. Apex wants to talk to me about their job offer again. You don't mind a dog in your house?"

"Sarek will be fine. Just don't let him smoke cigars and play cards with his friends."

A couple of days grew to be a couple of weeks, but on the cool crisp morning of March 6, 2003, Dr. Stuart Mirkin limped away from the entrance of Massachusetts General Hospital. Physical therapy, started in the hospital, would continue three days a week at an outpatient program in Plymouth.

The view of Plymouth Bay from the Rocky Nook front porch was beyond spectacular. It was just as the Pilgrims might have observed the bay nearly four hundred years ago. Across the water to the left were the green hills of Duxbury, with the Standish Monument peering above the trees. Straight out, at the edge of the harbor, Saquish Beach with its Gurnet Point Lighthouse and Clark's Island. To the far right was downtown Plymouth in its secluded inner harbor. Even with the cold winds of early March buffeting from the northeast, Peg sat on the porch for hours. Sarek loved the cool taste of the salt air.

Journal Entry
Friday, March 7, 2003

The past couple of weeks have been downright relaxing and almost peaceful! It is absolutely beautiful here at Stu's cottage by the sea. I just can't get over the spectacular view! Early morning walks on the beach with Sarek have been blissful! Sorry to say, things will be getting busy soon. Some meetings for the Expos. More traveling ahead. Shouldn't be too bad, comparatively speaking.

Decided to call Jim last week to remind him of the upcoming retirement party. I was feeling a tad nostalgic and figured what the heck.

Surprise, surprise. Jim had gotten married. He and his bride had just returned from Hawaii. I wonder why he didn't tell me when I talked with him at the end of January. He sounded a bit evasive, but I figured it was because we hadn't talked in such a long while. I reminded him about my retirement party and insisted he bring his new bride. He was noncommittal, saying he'd let me know.

Jim also mentioned he had been following the LaChance case in the papers. He found this whole story rather weird and asked me to be extra careful.

I still can't believe it! Jim got married! Why am I so obsessed by this? I'm not jealous, or at least, I shouldn't be. I was the one who didn't want to pursue a more serious relationship. Time has passed so quickly. I don't know. I feel I've lost something. I do wish him and his wife the best. I sincerely hope they will be happy. I wonder what she looks like. I know they met at work. I wonder what she's like. Is she like me? I wonder. It's good to have Stu home from Mass General, but he's a terrible patient! He can be annoying as hell when he won't take it easy as the doctors have insisted. On the other hand, he can be quite endearing when he tries to make coffee in the morning in spite of his pain. He's so sweet! We have become close friends. Yes, friends.

Got to go. The visiting nurse is here to change the dressing on Stu's leg.

Chapter 35

4-1-2003
April Fool

Peg, you had a phone call from a Peter Kokolski. Says he's a friend of Monique Maye. He wants you to give him a call back. His number should be the most recent call on your list."

"Thanks, Stu. What a perfect day. I think spring is finally here. Did you get outside for a while?"

"Oh, yes, Sarek and I did a short tour of the neighborhood. Next-door John joined us; we went almost a mile. Going a little farther each day. This nice weather helps change my entire outlook."

Peter Kokolski and Matt Beals were the co-founders of Commonwealth Associates. This low-profile company was in the business of personal protection of high-profile customers. In Peg's return phone conversation with Mr. ("Please call me Koko") Kokolski, she received a brief overview of the company's mission and how the Democratic National Committee had contracted their services to provide discreet security for the candidates, delegates, and their families at the convention in Boston in August of 2004. Matt Beals' expertise was the physical protection of clients, whereas Peter Kokolski was an expert in electronic security, the protection of computer-based data. The reason for Koko's phone call was an invitation to interview for a position with his firm.

Another meeting, in March, with Apex International was no more exciting than the first. In the days following this second interview with Lindahl and DeBillare, Peg concluded that employment with Apex was not in the best interest of all concerned parties. There were a few things that the Expos wanted completed, mostly legal and financial items with Marie Chance. But when nearly concluding the second of her four-month contract with the Montreal Expos, it was obvious to Peg that come mid-June, she would be looking for a new employer. She accepted the invitation to interview with Commonwealth.

A call to Tim Snow confirmed the legitimacy of Commonwealth Associates. Matt Beals and Tim had been in the criminal justice program together at Teelin University.

"Matt calls me every now and then, trying to get me to do a part-time detail. Maybe I should call him about the upcoming convention. Probably make a few extra bucks. Hey, Peg, want to do lunch or something when you come to Boston? When is your appointment with Beals?"

"Four in the afternoon on Thursday. I'm going to take the train in from Kingsbury Crossing. How about dinner at Dickie O'Doherty's? Say six o'clock?"

"Six, it is, Peg. Give my regards to Bobo Beals. Call me if there are changes. Tell your rambunctious patient that I'm coming down to see him on Friday. I got the day off. I'll take you both out to lunch down on the waterfront. Have some lobster before the prices go up for the summer."

As Stu recovered from his injuries, Peg found herself away from the cottage by the sea more and more—thankfully, not at the frantic pace of the first few weeks following the LaChance murder. Occasional details from the Montreal Expos and J.P. Bellevue were addressed. Two flights to Montreal to pick up and return insurance documents. Several meetings with Dianne Banks and Marie Chance, Bill LaChance's now fourteen-year-old daughter, were also completed. The Expos had Peg meet with a possible draft choice, Edson Saint Vil, a Haitian immigrant who was a pitcher for the local Brockton High School team. Although Edson had limited English language skills, his 91-mile-per-hour fastball interested many major league scouts. Peg's French and Edson's Haitian Creole were not exact matches, but they did manage to discuss his future.

Perhaps Peg had lingering doubts that the LaChance/Roberts ordeal was over. It was just a little too clean, too easy. Although there was no reason to believe that anyone but Carl Wells, the brother of Julia Emig, was responsible for the series of violent events, the fact that the .455 Colt had not been located and that no motive had been discovered prompted Peg to carry her .357 Smith & Wesson whenever she left the house. Because of the security hassle, the only times Peg didn't carry her sidearm were on her flights to Montreal.

Stu's physical condition improved each and every day. As yet, he was not able to drive, due to the lack of strength in his leg. When Peg was away, the next door neighbor, John McCaig, took Stu to therapy. By his own admission, John McCaig was an "artist, author, poet, and general all-around great guy." In reality, John was an octogenarian who, on warmer days, still rode his old Indian motorcycle to the post office. In earlier times, John McCaig was a business attorney who'd specialized in corporate law. Now, he was acting mayor of Rocky Nook, a nonpaying honorary position. Watering plants or feeding the cat while folks are away, cleaning the beach of trash, or looking after Stu Mirkin with a daily game of chess and/or a cup of Darjeeling, John McCaig was the ideal neighbor, and, although he didn't live next to everyone, he was known by all as Next-door John.

This third day of April was described by meteorologist Rod Bilman, on the local radio station WATD, as "Chamber of Commerce weather." Noon temperatures approaching fifty-five degrees, absolutely zero wind, and the brightest blue sky made leaving the Rocky Nook shore a real chore. Sarek and Stu were awaiting the arrival of Next-door John for today's epic chess battle. John usually arrived with Sarek's favorite biscuit. It was difficult to determine for whom the dog was rooting. These afternoon sessions contained many sidebar arguments about the Red Sox, local and national politics, the Red Sox, and the comparison of indigenous eateries—but mostly the Red Sox.

The 2:25 p.m. commuter rail departed Kingsbury on time for its forty-one-mile trip to South Station. The four block walk to Commonwealth Associates at 617 Atlantic Avenue brought Peg to her appointment about fifteen minutes early. Matt Beals explained the need to train personnel for the upcoming Democratic Convention. Female security staff was an area in great need, and Peg was asked to consider the position of senior trainer. Monique Maye had mentioned Peg's Customs Service experience to Beals, and this had prompted Commonwealth to contact her. She left the Atlantic Ave office at 4:48 and called Tim Snow to let him know that she would be at O'Doherty's a tad earlier than planned.

"How did the interview go?" asked Tim as he arrived at O'Doherty's about 5:30.

"It went pretty well. Matt Beals was asking for you. Sorry to say the job didn't seem any more interesting than Apex's."

As Tim thumbed through his notepad, he offered, "I understand that, Peg. I guess that's part of the reason why I haven't talked with Beals myself. I think if I get a part-time job it will be something away from police work and/or security. Maybe teaching a criminal justice course at Bunker Hill Community College or maybe Northeastern. Are we still on for lobster lunch tomorrow?"

"Stu and I are looking forward to it. Tomorrow is his big day. They've okayed him to start driving again."

Chapter 36

4-3-03
Train No. 051

Tim dropped Peg off at South Station for the return train. This first week of Daylight Saving Time was a welcome confirmation that spring had arrived. Peg thought of her friends in northern Vermont who would still have two or three weeks of lingering winter. The 7:25 p.m. southbound left platform 12 with few riders. During off-peak times, only two or three cars of the six-unit train were available for passengers. The remaining double-deckers were dark, with a blocking bar that prevented riders from entering. Sitting on the upper level, Peg could observe four other riders. There was a large, burley, mud-encrusted construction worker with a rusty lunch pail and a hard hat. He started napping as soon as his butt hit the seat. Second, a college student with a fifty-pound backpack, wearing an open jacket that was lettered "Wentworth Institute" was reviewing his calculus text. His visible T-shirt announced "Five out of four people have problems with fractions." How true. How true. Two women, seated together, were carrying bags of bargains from Filene's basement. They were displaying the clothing deals-of-the-day to Peg and to each other, following what was obviously a very productive trip to the city. Finally, as the train started to move, a fifth passenger climbed the stairs to the second level. This noticeably pregnant lady in her late thirties or early forties waddled down the aisle and sat four or five rows behind. Peg had noticed her earlier while waiting at South Station. The woman's overuse of makeup and the dark maroon beret that covered the left side of her bleached blonde hair were noticed by all who cared to observe. Peg wondered if she had taken the time to consider how hair chemicals might affect her newborn.

The train made its scheduled stops at Braintree, then South Weymouth, where the Wentworth guy left this band of nocturnal travelers. Onward through the darkness: Abington, Whitman, Hanson, and Halifax. The two happy shoppers gathered their bags of goodies and headed for their cars in the nearly empty Halifax lot. As the train started on its final seven miles to Kingsbury Crossing, it was just Peg, the sleeping leviathan, and the expectant mother on the top level. In less than ten minutes, the 051 pulled into Kingsbury.

As Peg move toward the forward staircase, she noticed the pregnant woman was leaving via the opposite end of the car. The hard hat never budged when the train lurched and the final announcement "last stop" came through the speakers. As Peg passed the snoring Goliath, she tapped on his lunch box. "Last stop. Kingsbury Crossing."

The giant stirred and grunted like he was looking for Jack and his magic beans. "Oh! Thank you."

There were only five or six vehicles in the lot. Stu's car was located at the far end where those riders of later trains are forced to find a spot before the long walk to the platform. It wasn't until Peg was about ten paces from Stu's Grand Am that she noticed the bad news. Flat tire, left front. Looking around the lot, she observed several sets of tail lights leaving the parking lot onto Brook Road.

Peg removed her cell phone and tossed her fanny pack on the rear seat. "Hi, Stu. I'm in the parking lot at Kingsbury Commuter Rail Station. I've got a flat tire—driver's side front. 'Fix-a-Flat'? What's it look like? Okay, I'll try that. I'll be looking for John. Thanks, I'll see you in a little while."

As Stu had promised, in the left corner of the trunk was an aerosol can marked Fix-a-Flat. *He's so efficient*, thought Peg. As she headed for the deflated Goodyear, another car slowly approached. Approaching at an acute angle, its headlights illuminated the deflated tire.

"Thank you for stopping," Peg said as she knelt at the deflated tire.

The driver stepped from the vehicle and into the shafts of light from the halogens. All Peg could determine were the shape and form of this Good Samaritan. It was the blonde pregnant lady from the train. Peg was instantly uncomfortable. Peg offered a second "Thank you." She stood between the headlights and seemed to lean against the hood and grille of her car. "When's the baby due?"

She never moved and only uttered one word: "Soon."

Removing the cap, Peg tightened the end of the hose from the aerosol to the brass tip of the valve stem. Hissing, the canned air started to inflate the tire. The rim lifted from the pavement, and she could feel the container cooling as it slowly accomplished its task.

The next few moments were a fuzzy blur. Peg wasn't sure if she felt the pain in her right shoulder or if she dropped the can first. As she stood, Peg could feel tugging at her right rear, as though someone was grabbing her jacket and shaking her forward and back. It was as if someone had poured hot coffee on her. She could feel warm liquid running down her back and front at the same time. Warm liquid ran down the inside of her bra, all the way to the beltline. Instinctively, Peg reached for the pain with her left hand; it was then that she detected the cause of her extreme distress. The outline of about two inches of cold steel could be felt through her jacket. The warm liquid was Peg's bleeding profusely, front and back. She had been stabbed. Her assailant was trying to pull out the knife that had impaled Peg through her right shoulder. The pulling suddenly stopped, and as Peg turned, the pregnant woman returned to her vehicle and opened the left rear door. Peg imagined Stu's voice saying, "Now that's an example of a perforated wound."

Peg could not raise her right arm. Opening the rear door with her left hand, Peg grabbed the open fanny pack. The texture of the grips of the Smith & Wesson was exhilarating. She could defend herself. Peg slowly backed out of the illumination, trying to present a less visible target. The attacker's blonde pageboy hair was backlit. She had a second weapon—a black machete. Standing like a samurai, the wide matte-black blade crossed her belly.

Peg continued to retreat from the light. Her would-be killer was thinking—thinking before hacking her to pieces here at the rear of the commuter rail parking lot.

Peg thought, *I'm only three minutes from home. Where is Next-door John?*

The demonic woman slowly advanced.

Someone was screaming. "Don't take another step! Don't take another step!" Peg wondered out loud, "Who the heck is yelling? Oh, it's me."

Ten feet, eight feet, six, then five. The machete blade was raised to the stars, then lowered and pointed.

Just then another loud voice echoed through the parking lot. Peg's .357 spoke for the first time in nearly eleven years. Its detonation reverberated from each of the three wooded sides of the lot, like thunder from an approaching squall. The woman stopped as the first shot struck the 18-inch machete with a shower of sparks. The machete leaped into the air and spun onto the asphalt. The intense silence following the discharge of Peg's .357 was replaced by distant springtime peepers, croaking in the nearby swamp. The pain was unbearable. Substantial blood loss was starting to cloud Peg's consciousness.

Her assailant took one more step. Misters Smith and Wesson spoke on their own. Peg didn't remember squeezing the trigger. Spark and flame exploded from the four-inch barrel. The woman stopped. Beyond the echoing gunshot, Peg heard an audible groan—like a loud exhale. Peg had just shot this woman and her baby. Peg was instantly nauseous. The pregnant attacker calmly turned and re-entered her vehicle, the left rear door still open. The drive wheels spinning, the blue sedan backed across the desolate lot—straight back, forty or fifty feet. Peg tried to place as much distance between her and the Grand Am, in case the assailant rammed Stu's car. Squealing wheels heralded the fact that the car had gone from reverse to drive. Holding her weapon with both hands, Peg tried to raise the sights to eye level. Her right arm wouldn't raise. Beyond the onrushing Corolla, another vehicle was entering the lot—Next-door John! The .357 barked twice, like an angry pit bull at the end of its chain. Peg jumped to the left as the car went past; it did a ninety-degree turn to the right and rocketed past John as it headed for the street. The Corolla bounced onto Brook Road and had its left blinker flashing as it accelerated toward Route 3 North.

Chapter 37

Jordan Hospital
Room 201

T he calendar on the far wall proclaimed: "Today is Friday, April 4."
The antiseptic odor told Peg she was in a hospital.

"Ms. McCarthy, Ms. McCarthy, I'm Dr. Finn. I'm the trauma surgeon here at Jordan Hospital. You're very lucky. Damage from a stabbing with that type of knife is usually more severe. The blade near the handle has teeth. Those teeth got caught in a spot known as the scapula notch. The clavicle held the top of the blade in the notch on your right scapula. You know it as the shoulder blade. Very little damage. We pulled out a few bone chips but I don't expect any nerve or muscle damage. You're lucky."

"What time is it, Doc? When can I get out of here?"

"Well, Ms. McCarthy, it's nearly 10 a.m., and I think we'll keep you here until tomorrow morning. You lost quite a lot of blood. We want to monitor your condition for another day, perhaps two."

As Dr. Finn left the room, another gentleman entered.

"Ms. McCarthy?"

"Yes, I'm Peg McCarthy."

"Good morning. I'm Detective Jerome Slack of the Kingsbury Police Department. Could you tell me what happened at the railroad parking lot last night?"

"Good morning, detective. I took the 7:25 p.m. train from South Station. It took about an hour to get to Kingsbury Crossing. There weren't many passengers. When I got to my car, it had a flat tire on the left front. I called the owner of the car, Dr. Stuart Mirkin, and he told me he had a can of Fix-a-Flat in the trunk. He also called a neighbor to come to assist in case the tire wouldn't inflate.

"As I got the tire-repair kit from the trunk, another car pulled up, putting its lights on my flat. I recognized the driver as a fellow passenger on the train. She sat several rows behind me. She was pregnant. As I started blowing up the tire, the woman stabbed me from behind. Evidently, the blade was jammed, according to the doctor, between my clavicle and shoulder blade. She went back to her vehicle and approached with a larger knife—a machete. I reached for my fanny pack, which I had placed on the back seat, removed my pistol, and ordered the woman to stop. She continued towards me. I fired once. She dropped the machete. She started toward me again, and I fired a second shot. I believe the second shot hit her in the abdomen. Have you found her yet? If I hit her, she would need medical attention."

Detective Slack wrote all the details into a petite spiral-bound notepad with a dark-green leather cover. Expressionless, he didn't answer Peg's question. Slack didn't answer the question because he frankly hadn't looked for anyone the previous evening. He proceeded to ask, "Is that it?"

"No, the pregnant woman went to her car, reversed across the parking lot and then tried to run me over. I fired two shots at the vehicle."

Slack continued taking notes. "So, Ms. McCarthy, what you've just told me is that you fired four shots at your assailant. When you told her to stop, did you mention that you had a weapon?"

"No, I didn't take the time to explain that I had a pistol. The parking lot was well lit, and with a seven-inch blade in my back, I didn't spend much time with idle banter."

"Ms. McCarthy, please, no curt answers. By your own admission, you discharged a hand-held firearm four times at a possible attacker. Is that correct?"

"Yes, that's correct."

Peg could feel this discussion with Detective Jerome Slack turning into an interrogation.

Slack dabbed the end of his pencil on his tongue as if dipping a fountain pen into its well. "You said she dropped the knife when you told her to stop. Right?"

Peg paused and tried to respond without appearing upset. "No, she dropped the machete after I fired my pistol the first time."

The detective was still writing frantically. He continued to write as he asked questions, rarely making eye contact. Peg was feeling very uncomfortable with Slack. "Ms. McCarthy, where is your firearm now?"

"My assumption is that Dr. Mirkin's neighbor, who arrived as the assailant sped away, must have taken my pistol. I'm not sure; everything was rather fuzzy around the time the ambulance arrived."

Slack finally looked at Peg. He stopped his endless notation. He adjusted his blue clip-on tie, cleared his throat, and very officially proclaimed, "Ms. McCarthy, I'm going to need to investigate this further."

Three taps on the door preceded its opening. Another stranger entered ahead of a familiar face. The familiar face was Tim Snow.

Slack scowled. "Gentleman, you'll have to leave. There's official police business being conducted here."

Tim Snow and his unfamiliar companion entered the room and closed the door. They stood at the foot of the bed. Tim spoke first. "Peg, I just talked with the doctor. He says you're going to be okay. Stu will be here shortly; I just talked with him. He was here during the night but you were still sedated from the surgery."

A perturbed Slack reiterated his feelings. "You two are interfering with official police business. If you don't remove yourselves from this room immediately, I'll call for back-up and have you escorted from the premises. Do you understand?"

Slack's jacket was open at the waist. Both hands on hips. The array of equipment on his belt was more than enough to start a small war. Two phones, radio, 9mm Glock, mace, handcuffs—and that was only what was visible from the front. And keys. Keys, perhaps as many as twenty-five or thirty hung from a five-inch brass ring. The keys were strategically located on left side of Slack's belt, between his handcuffs and the holstered can of mace. Tim Snow and the stranger looked at Peg, then at each other. Broad grins developed. The stranger looked at Slack, scratched his left ear, and asked, "Excuse me, sir. Are you some kind of a cop?"

"I am Detective Jerome Slack of the Kingsbury Police Department. Who the heck are you?"

As the stranger reached inside his top coat, Slack's right knee buckled as if he expected a weapon to be drawn. Flashing his badge to Slack, the stranger began, "Well, Detective Slick, I'm Patrick Preston. I'm Director of the Boston Office of the FBI. This is Timothy Snow, Chief of Homicide, Boston PD."

Without missing a beat, Slack quickly tried to adjust to the situation. "Oh, I'm glad you're here."

Preston had his own notebook in which he began writing. Politely, but with sarcastic edge, he addressed Jerome Slack. "Officer Slick, why don't you get yourself a cup of coffee? This case will be under FBI jurisdiction. Do you have any evidence collected? If so, could you please get it?"

Jerome Slack started to stammer, "What do you mean, FBI jurisdiction? This isn't an FBI matter."

Pat Preston applied more pressure to the rapidly dissolving Detective Slack. "Patrolman Slick, make yourself useful. Call your headquarters and tell your chief, John Polio, that Pat Preston of the FBI will meet him here at Jordan Hospital as soon as possible. If you want, you can add that you are questioning FBI jurisdiction in this case. Was there any evidence collected last evening at the train station?"

Slack began to stammer. "Yes, it's out in my car, I'll get it."

Preston shook his head. "In your car! What kind of evidence protection is that?"

Detective Slack left Room 201 in what could be best described as a dejected scurry. As he exited Peg's room, Slack murmured, "What's the big deal? My car is locked up."

Preston explained to Peg that, technically speaking, she was attacked as a result of her investigation under the jurisdiction of the U.S. Customs Service. This, combined with the fact that he was a close friend of Tim Snow, prompted him to bring the resources of the FBI into this matter.

Dr. Bill Finn, Jordan Hospital trauma room surgeon, returned, carrying a large plastic Ziploc bag. The bag contained the knife that had been surgically removed from Peg's right collar bone area.

Preston and Snow examined the weapon without removing it from the bag. Snow asked, "Is it military? Looks like some kind of combat knife."

Preston looked at the knife from all angles. He handed the bag to Peg. She reluctantly accepted and also examined the seven-inch blade with its black canvas micarta handle and nylon wrist lanyard.

Preston scrutinized the knife again and said, "Yancy. It's a Yancy."

Tim looked at Peg, she at him.

"What the heck is a Yancy?"

Preston was studying the markings on the stainless steel blade, up near the tang. "The Yancy is a special graduation knife that an Army Green Beret candidate receives when he successfully completes Special Forces School. This isn't marked Yancy but it's made by the same company, John Oakes Knives, Scranton, Pennsylvania. I've met John Oakes. He's a genius with steel. These knives are so special that Oakes even puts a serial number on each. I'll be right back; I'm going to make a quick call to my office."

Peg's room door opened, and Dr. Stuart Mirkin, limping badly on the right, entered. Dr. Mirkin was all business, as if Peg's injury was the reason for his appearance, not that he came to see her. Here was the renowned forensic scientist, not her friend whom she had nursed back to health over the past month.

Almost everyone who had entered Room 201 this morning carried a notebook. All had the ability to jot voluminous notations at terrific speed into said notebooks. Mirkin was no exception. He asked, "Peg, can you roll to one side and show me the exact location of the entrance wound?"

Dr. Finn placed a group of five X-rays on the backlit viewing device on the far wall. Mirkin looked at each of the X-rays for about one to two minutes. Three of the X-rays had been taken prior to the removal of the seven-inch Yancy. The metallic blade provided sharp contrast as it passed through the notch and exited in the front. Using a metal ruler, Stu measured, re-measured, then measured again, wrote numbers, drew figures with lines and arrows. Preston reentered the room. Mirkin never noticed; he had entered the zone and would not return until his calculations were complete. Room 201 was rapidly reaching capacity as Detective Slack returned carrying the jungle machete wrapped in a towel.

Patrick Preston was shaking his head in disbelief. "Slack, don't you use evidence bags here in Kingsbury?"

"We got nothing that big. Sorry." After talking with his chief, Detective Slack had accepted his subservient role in this case.

Stu re-emerged into reality. He seemed surprised at the number of people in the room. Tim Snow stepped forward to introduce the world-famous forensic scientist to all parties. Snow asked, "What do you think, Stu?"

"Ninety percent probability that the assailant was male. Perhaps a little more than 90 percent. That's how I see it. Somewhere near five foot eight in height. Slight build. Weight appropriate with height, maybe 155 to 160 pounds. Oh, he's right handed."

Preston nodded before speaking. "You see all that in those X-rays, Dr. Mirkin? Very impressive! Can you tell me how you reached your conclusions?"

Stuart Mirkin was in his own world. The master of his craft. "According to Peg, when I talked with her on the phone this morning, she was squatting down, putting air into the left front tire when attacked. The amount of force needed to put that weapon in the location shown in the X-rays would be approximately 325 foot-pounds. The ulna and radius bones of the lower arm are, on average, 9 to 10 millimeters longer on a male. The rotation of these bones around the elbow joint generates the force. The shorter female arm would have to travel faster and/or farther to produce the 325 foot-pounds of force.

Additionally, the initial report states the assailant was pregnant. Pregnancy would shift the total force vectors even further away. My conclusion: the assailant was either a tall, muscular pregnant woman or a man of average size and stature. Peg, how would you describe your attacker?"

Immersed in the middle of this case, Dr, Stuart A. Mirkin was cool and clinical. Peg wondered what happened to her friend Stu. "She was of average height, five foot eight, maybe a little shorter. She appeared to be very pregnant. When she boarded the train, she even walked pregnant."

It was at that instant, when Peg stated walked pregnant, that she reached a very uncomfortable realization. She wondered if Sheriff Franklin Ames' unknown pregnant car thief and her expectant, machete-toting attacker might be one and the same. Maybe Stu was correct. Pregnancy would be an ideal cover and would fit the M.O. of this killer. Preston's cell phone rang; he excused himself and left the room. Less than three minutes later, he returned, looked at his watch and asked, "Anyone ever hear of a Dr. Julia Emig? My office called. We contacted John Oakes Company, and they said that 350 similar knives"—Preston lifted the Ziploc bag with the Yancy look-a-like— "were sold to a company in Helena, Montana. The company is called BlueSky Optik; they specialize in high-end military items. Knives, binoculars, military timepieces. Things like that. BlueSky looked up the serial number on the knife. Purchased on February 17, 2003. Customer bought the following:

One
John Oakes Knife, seven-inch blade, 11.4 ounce with sheath...........$325.00
Serial Number 7204
One
WWII New Zealand Jungle Machete......................................$60.00
One
WWII French Army Oral Surgery Kit....................................$65.00
One
Bulova 789 Wristwatch Self-Winding with Date...... ....$230.00

Customer paid with two bank money orders. One in the amount of $300 and the second in the amount of $380. The checks were purchased at Ryan's News & Convenience Store in Rockland, Massachusetts. Both bank checks were dated 2-17-2003. Items were shipped, via UPS, on 2-23-03 to Dr. Julia Emig, Saugus Dental Associates, 782 Market

Street, Suite 74, Rockland, Massachusetts. Does anyone know this Julia Emig?"

Preston had no way of knowing that half the room knew Julia Emig.

Peg was sipping cranberry juice. She paused and answered. "I know Dr. Emig, and I can tell you, to my knowledge, she is not pregnant. That was not Julia Emig who attacked me last night, and that is not her office address."

Preston was looking at the long, black New Zealand machete. "Look at this, Tim. Guess we know why he or she dropped this weapon."

About twelve inches from the machete's tip, along the top of the blade, a chunk of the metal was missing. A circular indentation surrounded the damage. "This must be where your first shot hit, Ms. McCarthy. It's a wonder the fragments didn't stop your attacker right there."

After examining the dented machete, Snow said, "Someone wants us to believe that Julia Emig or her deceased brother Carl was responsible for this purchase from BlueSky. I bet the Saugus Dental address is a mail drop, just like Scrimshaw and Stone. Did you notice they all begin with 'S'?"

Chapter 38

Diverging Roads

Within days of the attack, Peg was again sitting on the porch at Rocky Nook. The days were longer and warmer. Sarek and Peg took more frequent and longer walks along the beach. She and Stu, fewer and fewer. This wonderful house on the shore seemed to be more Peg's than his. Dr. Mirkin had entered a cocoon of his own creation.

Next-door John reiterates the feelings of all of Stu's friends. "I worry about him; it's all about his stinking job. There seems to be no room for anything or anyone else. The guy is a workaholic."

Dr. Stuart Mirkin became invisible at Rocky Nook while testifying in Los Angeles, Denver, San Antonio. Stu's workload had increased exponentially. When in Boston, he often slept on a reclining chair in his office.

Peg, in her continuing role with the Expos, made several trips away from the Kingsbury shore. On her last trip to Montreal, with additional documents from Marie Chance, Bellevue asked her to consider working for the Expos full time. The majority of Expos players were American but living in a city that was predominantly French-speaking. This presented issues that might be best solved by an American who was fluent in Canadian French. This would mean living in Canada, at least during the baseball season. She told Bellevue that she would consider it.

Sarek was spending more time at John's. The dog had his own travel bag for those times when both Stu and Peg were away.

What Peg was really thinking about was the fact that her stalker/assailant had, as yet, neither been located nor identified.

Peg did manage to fly back to Maryland over the Easter weekend to visit with her parents, sisters, nieces, and nephews. Each kid seemed to have grown a foot. Everyone in the family asked about the retirement party. Her standard response was "I'm working on it. I'm working on it. I have picked a date at least. Give me a little credit for that!"

April 19 was a state holiday in Massachusetts, Patriot's Day—the day the "Shot Heard Round the World" commenced the start of the Revolutionary War. This year, the nineteenth was the Saturday before Easter, and the holiday was celebrated on Monday, the 21st. It was also the day of the Boston Marathon. Tim Snow ran, as promised, but his pacing partner, Stu, was in Los Angeles. Peg's return flight from Washington, D.C., arrived at 11:30 a.m., and she was able to miss the traffic associated with the Marathon. The easiest method to get to Kingsbury from the airport was the Brockton & Plymouth shuttle bus. Better known as the B & P, this conveyance picked up and delivered passengers from each airline terminal and transported them to and from the South Shore with three stops. The terminus for this service was in North Plymouth, about five miles from Rocky Nook. A quick cell phone call, after passing through the Ted Williams Tunnel, to Next-door John assured an immediate ride from the bus terminal to home. John and Sarek were waiting as the long silver bus with the blue lettering turned into the North Plymouth lot.

"Where's Stu these days?"

"I'm not sure, John. Last I heard he was in L.A., working on a high-profile case. I'm worried about him."

The remainder of the ride to Rocky Nook was quiet, but both John and Peg had the same faces of concern. Concern for their friend, Dr. Stuart Mirkin.

Wednesday evening, at about 8:30 p.m., the phone rang.

"Hi, Peg, Stu here. When are you returning from Maryland?"

"Hi, Stu, I got back Monday at noon. How are you doing?"

"I'm okay. I'm awfully tired. I need a few days off. I'm coming home tomorrow. I'll be arriving at 1:45 p.m. Can you pick me up at the North Plymouth bus station?"

"Sure. Do you want me to pick you up at the airport?"

"No. I'll take the bus. I'll call you when I hop the shuttle. How did Tim Snow do in the Marathon?"

"He says he did okay. But I looked at his time on the Marathon website, and it was 2:57. I'd say that was better than okay. Wouldn't you?"

"Yeah. That's a real good time. About five minutes better than he did last year. Well, I'll call you tomorrow. Night-night, hon."

"Good night."

By the sound of his voice, Stu Mirkin was approaching exhaustion. Now Peg was really worried.

Thursday, April 24, was another beautiful spring day. Temperature in the mid-sixties. Just after two o'clock, Stu called to relay the fact that his B & P shuttle bus from Logan Airport was on its way to North Plymouth. Always ready for a ride, Sarek was the first to the car. Peg and Sarek arrived five minutes ahead of the bus. About twenty people got off the bus and were milling around the doors of the cavernous underbelly, waiting for their luggage. Stu was the last to come down the stairs. Peg was shocked. He seemed to have aged about ten years since she had seen him three weeks before. His limp was much more pronounced. Quickly, she left her car to help with Stu's bag. A hug revealed that he had lost considerable weight. His eyes sunken, he appeared to be physically exhausted.

"I'm home. Thank God."

"You hungry? Want to stop for something?"

"No. Let's take a ride over to Duxbury Beach. I need to get my feet and leg into the therapeutic salts of the ocean."

Stu opened an oversized envelope and started to review the contents.

About four miles east of the bus station, the road from North Plymouth had a three-way fork. The road to the right went to Rocky Nook; the left road was the main thoroughfare, part of State Route 53; the middle street was Landing Avenue, which was a connector between Kingsbury and Duxbury. About two miles from the three-way intersection, the road narrowed as it crossed the Jones River. Here, the Jones River was mostly saltwater as it was part of the Plymouth Harbor tidal estuary. There seemed to be activity at the bridge, and there, in the middle of the road was Patrolman Jerome Slack. He was waving his arms like a windmill and tooting his whistle like an overdue locomotive.

"Move it! Move it! Move it!" Slack was shouting as Peg and Stu started across the bridge. Peg couldn't resist. She slowed to a stop in the middle of the bridge and lowered the window.

"Hello, Officer Slack. What's going on?"

"Move it! Move it! Move it! Can't you're see you're tying up traffic?"

Glancing in the rear-view mirror and then looking ahead confirmed Peg's initial assumption: no vehicles in either direction. As the car approached the end of the bridge, she could see that all the action was on the far side of the river. The presence of several divers in wet suits, two wreckers with recovery cables into the water, Chief Polio of the Kingsbury Police, the Duxbury Rescue Ambulance, and the Commonwealth of Massachusetts Medical Examiner's van all pointed to a fatality in the water. It was at that very moment that Stu's phone issued its alert tune, the "William Tell Overture."

"Dr. Mirkin here."

"Hi, Stu Mirkin. This is Norman Blumberg, Medical Examiner's Office. Stu, I was wondering if you might be available for a forensic autopsy tomorrow?"

"What have you got, Norm?"

"Well, Stu, we got a soaker, but it might be more complicated. Are you anywhere near Duxbury on the South Shore?"

"Yeah, Norm. Look at the car just beyond the bridge behind you." Stu raised his right hand and wiggled his fingers.

"How did you know, Stu?"

"Just luck, Norm. We were going to Duxbury Beach. I just returned from L.A. at noon. We'll pull over, and you can fill me in."

It was obvious that Officer Slack did not recognize either Peg or Stu. With major discomfort, Stu Mirkin exited the car and started walking towards the scene.

"Hey! Hey! Hey! You can't park there! Sir, you'll have to leave. There's official police business being conducted here." Slack walked off the bridge toward Mirkin like a goose-stepping storm trooper, keys jingling with each step. "Hey! Hey! Hey! What's the matter with you? Are you deaf? I said you can't park there!"

Doc Mirkin was already entering the zone and was either ignoring Slack or was oblivious to his noise. Chief Polio ran up the embankment from the river to put an end to Slack's foolishness.

"Easy, Jerry, this is Dr. Mirkin. He's here at the request of the Medical Examiner. Hi, Dr. Mirkin. I'm John Polio, Kingsbury Police Chief. Please excuse Officer Slack; he's a bit too gung-ho, I'm afraid."

Mirkin just nodded as he descended to the water's edge. Norm Blumberg greeted Mirkin with a warm hand shake.

"Hi, Doc, long time, no see. Been a couple of years, hasn't it?"

"Hi, Norm, closer to three. It was the shallow gravesite in Miles Standish State Forest, right near Torrey Pond." Stu Mirkin had trouble remembering his own birthday but could remember every detail of each and every case in which he had ever been involved. "What's happening here, Norm?"

Blumberg had a twelve-foot square blue evidence tarp spread out on the shore, just above the normal high-tide line, weighted along the edges by stones. On the right side of the tarp was a large, square Ziploc bag. The contents of the bag included a maroon beret sewn to a blonde wig.

"Two kids fishing from the bridge snared this wig and cap. They thought they could see the vague outline of an automobile below the surface of the outgoing tide. When the local fire-and-rescue team arrived, the tide had turned and nothing was visible. The first diver confirmed a vehicle resting on its left side. The kid must have dropped his line right through the open window and hooked the wig. The divers confirm a body in the car. They're in the process of removing it. Might be tough to identify. Looks like the car has been in the water a while."

"Well, Norm, Peg and I are headed to the beach for a little solitude and contemplation. Besides that, I need to get my sore leg into the salt water. Where and when for the autopsy?"

"My office at the old Plymouth County House of Correction on Obery Street. You know, where the jail was located until they built the new facility on the opposite side of the highway? Is eight o'clock tomorrow morning too early?"

"The county farm?"

"Right, Stu. When they demolished the old place the county refurbished the newer portion of the building and built me an office, morgue, and autopsy lab."

"Okay, Norm, see you there at eight."

Stu limped up the embankment and slowly walked the seventy-five yards to Peg, Sarek, and the car.

"Have a nice day, Dr. Mirkin," Officer Slack offered.

Mirkin never noticed. The blonde wig and beret might be the big break in Peg's case. Stu didn't mention to Peg what he had viewed in the plastic bag on the blue tarp. He didn't mention his suspicions to Blumberg either.

Peg and Stu continued their short trek to Duxbury Beach. Just as they made the bend around Martin's Marsh, the rear bumper of a blue Toyota Corolla, with Connecticut license tag AB 417, was cabled to the surface through the murk of the incoming tide.

Chapter 39

Uca Pugnax

A gated compound contained the remains of three damaged vehicles. This protected area was about a quarter mile from the main building that housed Doc Blumberg's morgue.

"Stu, it's remarkable how Mother Nature will, often quickly, attempt to reclaim any object. You have to keep moving, Stu. That's the secret of extended life."

The blue Corolla was no exception to Blumberg's Rule. Several barnacles were already attached to the car's finish. A green slimy film was growing on all exposed glass, inside and out.

Mirkin walked around the vehicle several times. Saltwater still dripped onto the concrete pad. "How long do you think the car had been in the water, Norm?

"Probably no more than a month, Stu, looking at the barnacle count. The spring tides are still cool, so the underwater wildlife around the car was rather subdued. The occupant is in worse condition than his car. Note the two holes in the windshield—looks like large caliber rounds. They obviously were there prior to immersion."

Stu Mirkin had visited morgues all over the world. He found it amusing and amazing how alike these facilities were. Similar layouts, usually on the ground or basement level; identical cool, dank atmosphere; same equipment for the dissection of the deceased; familiar hum of the refrigeration equipment used to deter decomposition; all were found in morgues worldwide.

Blumberg positioned the autopsy gurney in front of Storage Vault Number 17 and stiffly pulled the handle. Slowly, a dark-green plastic body bag emerged from its cold repository. Blumberg and Mirkin, both wearing autopsy garb, latex gloves and face shields, guided the bag onto the mobile cart, and it was pushed into the bright lights of the Plymouth County Medical Examiner's work area. Blumberg unzipped the bag. The stench of human body decay and saltwater flowed from the body bag and mixed with the antiseptic atmosphere of the morgue. A pea-green tag was tied to the left big toe and matching information was written on a similar tag affixed to the zipper of the body bag.

_4-03-32_   Date___4-24-2003_____19___
case number

Name: _Unidentified Male_____

From: _Vehicle S.W. immersion-Landing_
Rd- Dux/Kingsbury Line-Jones River

Plymouth County Medical Examiner's Office

Mirkin was the first to speak. "That's interesting!"

The fully clothed body of the deceased was in sharp contrast to the exposed parts. The hands and skull were devoid of skin. Portions of the skull and finger bones appeared bright white when compared to the surrounding reddish/purple flesh.

"Uca Pugnax." Blumberg had a wide grin. "Uca Pugnax, Fiddler crabs. They go for the exposed areas first."

Mirkin, as always, slowly circled the table. He jotted into his notebook. Blumberg adjusted the suspended microphone as they prepared for the autopsy.

"Norm, you said male. What kind of outfit is this?"

"I checked that out yesterday when I brought him in. It's called the 'Empathy Belly' Pregnancy Simulator; it's used in childbirth education classes. Very expensive. Interesting part is that this guy had body armor under the maternity get-up. Guess the vest didn't help him much."

Dr. Stu Mirkin was ready. He quickly concluded that this must be the pregnant assailant that Peg had encountered at the Kingsbury Crossing lot exactly three weeks ago. Examination of the Empathy Belly and the bullet proof vest located a .357 slug, one of the four shots that Peg had fired. The body armor, at a distance of four to five feet from Peg's weapon, had done its job. The .357 round was neatly surrounded by the Kevlar webbing. Its pristine condition would be more than enough to match its origin to Peg McCarthy's .357 Smith & Wesson.

After removal of the Empathy Belly and the body armor worn under it, Norm Blumberg started to examine the entire corpse for scars, tattoos, and other distinguishing marks for prior or present wounds. "Hey, Stu, look at this." In the lower neck, just above the area that the bulletproof vest would have protected, was a wound about the size of a quarter. The appetite of the fiddler crabs had nearly obscured the entry.

Now that's a penetrating wound! Mirkin thought.

Blumberg cut while Mirkin held the two opposing flaps of flesh apart. From the bottom of the 5.75cm hole, Blumberg retrieved a black metallic object that was not quite circular. The seawater had already started its oxidation. "What the heck is that, Stu?"

"That is a piece of a New Zealand Jungle Machete, circa 1940."

Blumberg was in awe. "Stu, how do you know that?"

"The FBI has the rest of the machete with a missing spot on the top of the blade."

The phone rang three times before Peg could answer. The view from Rocky Nook was extra special this morning.

"Hello, Peg McCarthy here."

"Hi, Peg. Stu. I think we have your pregnant attacker. I'm with Norm Blumberg doing the autopsy on that soaker from Landing Road, the one that we saw yesterday."

"That's good news. Any clue as to who it is?"

"Sorry, Peg, no ID yet. Might be a while. The car was clean. We don't have a face to match and no prints either. His face and fingers are gone."

"Gone! What do you mean gone? Missing?"

"Yeah, Peg, missing. More like consumed. Fiddler crabs ate all the exposed tissue. You think you might be able to identify the clothes?"

"I doubt it, Stu. I didn't really notice anything other than the blonde hair, beret, and matching slacks. No magnetic signs on the vehicle?"

"Sorry, Peg, nothing that easy. We will have a dental chart and DNA. We also have a slug, looks like a .357 or close to it. He was wearing something called a pregnancy simulator and a bulletproof vest. One thing was interesting—he was wearing a watch, a Bulova 789 self-winder, that seems to match the one that Patrick Preston had on the purchase order that included the Yancy. The watch had stopped at 2:20 a.m., and the date indicated was April third, about three hours after the attack in the parking lot. Weird. Real weird. The car has two holes in the windshield but no other apparent damage. The vehicle doesn't look like it had be involved in any other incidents." Mirkin paused and when he didn't get a response from Peg he added, "Didn't you say Ames was looking for a mother-to-be car thief back in early March?"

"Right, Stu. I had the same thought about the expectant mom, when I was recuperating in Jordan Hospital. Last I heard from Sheriff Ames, that case was never resolved. A pregnancy simulator?"

"Birthing classes use them to give the wearer a sense of being pregnant. They are used in schools as well. They are expensive and only made by one company. It should be easy to track down. I'm going to call Tim Snow and fill him in on the autopsy. I should be home by one o'clock. Do you want to go to lunch down by the harbor?"

"That sounds great. See you at one."

Journal Entry
Thursday, April 24, 2003

Phew! My first break since, well, really, since January when this bizarre case began. I'm hoping the violence has finally ended, assuming that the assailant was working solo. The task now is to determine the identity of the killer and decipher any possible motive(s).

Why kill LaChance and why all the interest in Sarek? Sarek is snuggled up here on the couch with his snoot right against me. If I make a run to the refrigerator, he wants to be the first to know. Periodically, he looks up with his pleading brown puppy-dog eyes, just hoping for even a brief scratch behind the ears. Why would anyone be so interested in this adorable and loving, but still, mutt?

The list of casualties is long—LaChance, Buckley Roberts, Stu, the Banks family, Carl Wells, and me. I wish I knew the dead mystery man's identification. The latest turn of events has certainly shortened my potential suspects list!

Potential Suspect(s)

Mystery Assailant (male) wearing pregnancy simuluator and body armor. Finger prints and facial indentification eaten by crabs. Bizarre.

Well, I called the Grey Gables Mansion Bread & Breakfast in nearby Richford and reserved the whole house for the 4th of July weekend. It's absolutely beautiful. Built in 1890, it's only twenty-five minutes from North Troy. It sleeps thirteen, so everyone who wants to stay should be able to. They have an exquisite dining room that seats forty for a sit-down dinner. The catering menu looks fabulous! I think it will be perfect. Won't everyone be shocked when I tell them I'm actually making progress on this party!

I even purchased invitations! I'll send them out next week. I hope Jim and his wife can attend. I also mentioned the date to Stu, but you know him. His response: "We'll see."

Chapter 40

A Quiet Month Later
Thursday
May 22, 2003

P eg sprinted from the Rocky Nook porch to answer the phone.
"Hi, Peg. Tim here. How are things going? These next few weeks
must be the best time of the year to be down near the water."

"You got that right, Tim. Next weekend is Memorial Day and some
folks will be opening up the cottages for the summer. Any news on the
identification of my expectant assailant?"

"No, it's been a quiet month since the autopsy. The only match we
got was the slug from your pistol. We got plenty of DNA but nothing in
the database comes close. He had an extremely high level of mercury in
his liver. That's unusual. Also, the dental records are unusual. Very
unique work; looks like it might have been done at a dental college. I
did get a lead today from the Plymouth County Women's Health
Coalition. They purchased two of those Empathy Belly pregnancy
simulators about two years ago. They loan them out to schools and
other groups. They seem to be missing one. I have an appointment with
the director tomorrow at 2:00 in the afternoon."

"That's interesting. Where are they located?"

"Their office is in Cohasset. I thought I might meet you and Stu in
Cohasset for lunch at noon and then head over to their office. Interested?"

"Well, as usual, Stu is away; it's Washington, D.C., this time. I'll
call John to see if Sarek can visit for a few hours. Where are we having
lunch?"

"There's a new place, the Leaky Dory, right on the water. Let's try
that? Are you familiar with Cohasset?"

"Well, actually, in another life, I was a French teacher at Cohasset
High School. I know my way around town. I can't imagine it has
changed too much."

"Okay, Peg, see you at the Leaky Dory at noon."

The coastal community of Cohasset was affluent and aloof. This
wealth was emphasized by the fact that Cohasset was bordered by the

towns of Hull, Hingham, and Scituate. These three salt-marsh townships were in Plymouth County, while their well-heeled neighbor, Cohasset, was a partitioned enclave of Norfolk County.

Interesting, thought Peg, *the Plymouth County Woman's Health Coalition is not actually in Plymouth County. Interesting.*

The Leaky Dory was located near the bend where Mink Island Road intersected Jerusalem Way. Here, at Kimball Point, this newly constructed restaurant had the contrived artificial ambiance of a New England fishing village. A brown K-car, circa 1982, with the red-primer driver's door, announced the fact that Snowman had arrived early. The left rear hubcap was still missing. The red-primed door had a newly acquired gash that revealed the inner workings of the window cranking mechanism.

Tim was finishing his second helping of popcorn shrimp. There were three large glasses in the center of the table. One full, one empty, and one in-between.

Peg observed the culinary proceedings with a grin. "You thirsty, Tim? What happened to your door?"

"Moxie, Peg, Moxie. You hardly ever see Moxie on the menu. Here, have this one. I'll order another. Oh, the door? Friend of mine, Ed Egan, was digging a trench for a new retaining wall at my place. Caught it with his backhoe. Guess I parked too close. Got to call my cousin Marlene and have her ask her husband if he has another door. Maybe I'll go for green this time."

"I'll pass on the Moxie. It's not one of my favorites. So Tim, what's the story with the Empathy Belly?"

The Snowman was tossing down popcorn shrimp as if they were cashews. "I checked with the manufacturer located in Xenea, Ohio, the day after Stu called me with the autopsy details. There are twenty-seven Empathy Belly pregnancy simulators located in Massachusetts, eleven in Rhode Island, and five in New Hampshire. I started with the Boston locations and finally talked with everyone who has one. All were accounted for until yesterday." Tim Snow was flipping through his notepad. "I called the Plymouth County Women's Health Coalition on Monday, April 28, at 11:30 a.m. The person on the phone, a Mrs. Norene Rolle, stated that she has two Empathy Belly pregnancy simulators and that they were locked in a storage closet at their office in Cohasset. Mrs. Rolle called me back yesterday to notify me that both boxes, each of which contained one Empathy Belly, had been removed from the storage area for cleaning. The boxes had been stacked in the closet and, after examination this week, it was discovered that the bottom container was empty."

"That doesn't necessarily mean that my assailant was wearing their prosthesis, does it?"

"Nope, it doesn't. The manufacturer sews an identification tag onto each device. The one they recovered from the corpse in the Landing Street immersion didn't have its ID tag."

Peg and Tim left the restaurant parking lot in tandem. Peg followed Tim through Cohasset Center, up Souther Street, past Cohasset High School, where Peg McCarthy was a French teacher two-plus decades ago, and onto Route 3A. About a mile north on 3A, also known as Chief Justice Rachel Cummings Highway, was a fourteen-unit strip mall anchored by a Super Stop & Shop at its north end. The Women's Health Coalition office was located at the southernmost end of the complex.

Entering the office, Peg and Tim were greeted by the director Norene Rolle. She explained the function of the Health Coalition. Various pamphlets and brochures were exhibited on a six-foot-by-six-foot display rack, which was to the left of the entrance. *Smoking*, *Alcohol and Drug Dependency*, and *Exercise* were just a few of the titles available.

In the middle of the room were two hard-plastic, rectangular storage containers, each approximately 1½ by 1½ feet deep by 2 feet in length. The top of each container had a placard which simply stated:

Empathy Belly Pregnancy Simulator

Matt-Dorchester Manufacturing Company
Xenea, Ohio

Mrs. Rolle opened both boxes, the top swinging to the rear on its piano hinge. One of the boxes was nearly empty. "See, Detective Snow. This is how we found it. I keep careful records of who borrows these. Very expensive, you know. The last to borrow the missing unit was the Norwell Visiting Nurse Association. Loaned on September 22, and returned on October 17 of last year. Mrs. Mary Corkery, a volunteer who works Thursdays and Fridays, signed it out. The administrator of the Norwell Visiting Nurse Association, Mrs. Karen Cahill, picked up and returned the pregnancy simulator. She's very responsible, you know. I was here when she returned this box on October 17. It would be very unusual for me not to have examined the contents when it was returned. There are a number of accessories that are also in the box. I would have inventoried the boxes. I called Mrs. Cahill; it's her recollection that I carefully inventoried the contents while she was here. I just don't know how someone could remove the pregnancy simulator from its container without my knowledge."

"Mrs. Rolle, thank you for calling me when you discovered that the prosthesis was not in its box. You haven't noticed anything else missing or misplaced in the office?"

"No, Detective Snow, nothing. We've been here for nearly seven years and have never had a problem. There is a security system in all stores in this complex. There are only about five entry keys. Do you think I should have the locks changed?"

"Well, Mrs. Rolle, I don't think we should assume that you've been broken into. It might be premature to jump to any conclusions. Have you checked with all of your staff and volunteers?"

"Not all, one of our volunteers spends the winter in Florida and another is on vacation. Nellie Campbell, the one who winters in Florida, might be back now, but she doesn't return to work here until June first. Mrs. Gervais is on a cruise to the Caribbean; she'll be back next Tuesday, the 27th."

"Why don't you check with all parties who have access to the closet. Perhaps someone misplaced the Empathy Belly or loaned out the item and forgot to record the borrower."

"I doubt that, Detective Snow. My staff is very meticulous about what comes and goes in my office. Besides, why is the box here?"

"I don't know the answer to that question, Mrs. Rolle, but I'm sure that this matter will soon be settled. Again, thank you for calling me. Here's my card; please let me know if there is anything new when you talk with your staff."

Peg and Tim walked to the second row, where Peg was parked. Snow's multicolored Aries was farther down the lot.

"What do you think, Tim? Wild goose chase?"

"Ah, I don't know. Seems more likely that someone borrowed that thing and forgot to return it. Maybe someone borrowed it for a Halloween party. That would make for an excellent costume. Perhaps it was lost or stolen from whomever borrowed it. It seems if someone were going to go to the trouble of stealing it, he would have taken the whole thing, box and all."

As Peg's car turned left to exit the parking area, Tim came running back waving his arms. "Peg, I almost forgot. I got some stuff for Stu to look over when he returns. Pull down to my car. I'm in front of the pet shop."

There was a parking space three spots down from Snow's battered K-car, with the bent tail pipe that emitted sparks as it entered and exited parking lots. Peg noted that the tail pipe was about three inches shorter than it had been in February.

Putting the transmission into park, Peg noticed the store, directly in front of where she had stopped, was vacant, with a large "For Rent" sign in the window. The remaining glass was covered, from the inside, with faded yellow newspaper. Although the interior of the store was not visible from outside, the stenciled lettering of the previous occupant had not been removed from the glass. It read: Shore Dental Associates.

"Tim, look at this. This seems more than a little unusual. Stone Investigative Services, Saugus Dental Laboratory, Scrimshaw Security Service, Shore Dental Associates. I wonder if there's any connection? I wonder why and when they went out of business? The dates on the newspapers covering the windows go back to late February."

"Peg, let's walk back to the health office and ask Mrs. Rolle if she knows anything about this dental office."

Norene Rolle was carrying a large carton and heading back to her office from her car just as Tim and Peg arrived at the door of the Woman's Health Coalition.

"Mrs. Rolle, let me help you with that." Always a gentleman, Tim sprinted in the direction of the struggling director.

"Oh, thank you, Detective Snow. More brochures for the masses."

"That's okay, Mrs. Rolle, I've got the box. Do you know anything about the vacant office next to the pet store? The one with the "For Rent" sign in the window?"

"No, I rarely get to the other end of the complex. The best people to ask are at the real estate office, about seven doors up from here. They do the property management for the whole place."

The sign on the door stated "PHP Reality. We're Sorry. We are showing a home to a prospective buyer. We will return before ___ " The hands of the clock in the window were pointing to 3:30.

"Well, Peg, I've a 3:30 appointment with Anita Ivarson at the Ballistics Lab. Can you hang around until someone returns and let me know what you find out? Call me on my cell phone."

With more than forty-five minutes before 3:30 p.m., Peg entered the pet store next to Shore Dental Associates to look for something special for Sarek. Poor Sarek; he seemed to spend more time with Next-door John than he did at home. It sure was a lot easier having a dog back at the Customs Station.

Chapter 41

Tooth No. 10

At precisely 3:28 p.m., a candy-apple-red Blazer pulled into a parking spot two doors down from the PHP Reality Office. An attractive woman in her mid-thirties approached the office door, keys in hand. A flipping of the sign on the door announced the reopening of the office.

"Hi, I'm Neelia. Welcome to PHP Reality. How can I help you?"

"Good afternoon, my name is Peg McCarthy. I was wondering if you could give me any information about that vacant location next to the pet store?"

"It's small, 1400 square feet. We manage all the properties, but the owner has the final say about the type of business that leases each store. We've had several inquiries. Are you interested in renting?"

"No, no, I was wondering about the previous renter, Shore Dental Associates. Did the dentist go out of business?"

"Shore Dental was a dental supply firm. They handled all kinds of dental needs. You know—equipment, tools, anything a dentist would use. I guess there were three partners, and they split up. Business issues. They moved to Quincy back in February. They're still in business under a similar name, South Shore Dentist Supply or something like that."

"Well, thank you. Could I have one of your business cards?"

With a fifty-pound bag of Sarek's favorite treat on the backseat and a PHP Realty business card in hand, Peg was ready to head south on Route 3A for the fourteen-mile ride back to Rocky Nook when her cell phone rang.

"Hi, Peg. Tim here. Anything of interest about Shore Dental?"

"No, Tim, the company moved to Quincy back in February. Changed its name to South Shore Dental Supply. They sell equipment and supplies to dentists and orthodontists. I called their new phone number; they seem legit. I talked with one of the owners, a Bill Rudder. He said that the company moved to Hancock Street in North Quincy after one of the partners decided to end his involvement with the company."

"I'll try to visit Shore Dental in the next few days. Give me the phone number. You said the owner's name is Rudder?

"You got it, Tim. R-U-D-D-E-R. Bill Rudder. The number is 617-843-2121."

"Peg, did you say when Stu might be returning? I need to discuss that material I gave you."

"You never know, Tim. Stu said he would return by Memorial Day. He's speaking at a seminar in Falmouth on the 28th. I'll have him contact you as soon as I hear."

"Thanks, Peg. Talk to you soon. Bye."

Route 3A, although not the most direct route from Cohasset back to Rocky Nook, didn't have the hectic pace of nearby Route 3. With the exception of the usual congestion of Marshfield Center, the twenty-five minute ride was uneventful. As Peg pulled into the driveway, Sarek leaped off the porch and headed for the car. Canine intuition must have alerted him of his surprise parcel on the backseat.

Walking around the wrap-around porch to the ocean side, Peg discovered someone sleeping in a Stetson green Adirondack chair. Not Next-door John but Dr. Stu Mirkin. By all appearances, Stu was another five to ten pounds lighter than a month ago. Not good news. Not good at all. Stu obviously had not fully recovered from the February accident.

"Hi, Stu, I didn't expect you home today." Silence. "Stu, are you okay?" No response.

Mirkin didn't move until Sarek licked his hand.

"Guess I dozed off. What time is it?"

"Nearly five. Why didn't you call? I'd have picked you up."

"I called from the airport just after noon. When I didn't get an answer, I called John. He said you were meeting Tim for lunch. Any news?"

Peg explained the meeting with Norene Rolle and her missing Empathy Belly. "Tim sent this envelope for you. He said it's more dental information from the body that they pulled out of the drink."

"I don't know, Peg. This whole situation has me confounded. We have a body that is probably that of a killer. We have a collection of cadavers, which at last count included Bill LaChance, Buckley Roberts, and Carl Wells. Did I miss anyone? Did anyone have any details about Qaqish and his nephew? Then there's the attempt on Bill LaChance's daughter and her family, my accident in South Boston, and the assailant who attacked you. Basically, we don't have a clue to his identity. I must be missing something," said Mirkin as the trio entered the house.

Stu opened the large manila envelope and quickly crossed the threshold into the zone. Upon entering the large, spacious room that faced Plymouth Harbor, Mirkin viewed a dozen or so five-inch-by-eight-inch dental X-rays while holding each near the illuminated globe of a colonial style floor lamp. After shuffling through the stack of negatives for the third time, Mirkin pulled out three and placed the remainder back into the brown envelope.

"These three X-rays are the key, Peg. If we can find the dentist who performed the procedure on this one tooth—tooth number 10—we'll solve this entire matter." Mirkin paused. "Number 10, that's the lucky number." Mirkin looked at the X-rays once more. "See this, Peg? Look at this tooth. Tell me what you see."

Peg peered into the cloudy haze of the dental negative. "I'm not sure, Stu. They all look fairly similar to me. What am I suppose to be looking for?"

Stu circled one tooth with a black marker. "That one. What's different?"

"I don't know. The top of the tooth looks unusual. Is that a filling?"

"Gold foil. It's gold foil. Very expensive. It's odd that he has several amalgam fillings and one tooth that is gold foil. I wonder who his dentist was."

As Dr. Stu Mirkin continued looking at tooth number 10, Peg asked, "How did you get number 10? Is there a dental numeration system?"

Reaching again into the manila envelope, Mirkin pulled out a green dental form printed on heavy stock paper. The teeth of the chart were numbered, starting at the upper right rear with number 1 and continuing to number 16 on the upper left side of the illustration. The lower teeth were similarly numbered from 17 to 32. Number 10 was an upper tooth toward the front of the left side.

"Peg, I'm going to talk with a friend at Tufts Dental tomorrow. Maybe he'll have an idea how we can survey the dental community to identify these records."

"While you go to Boston, maybe I ought to talk with Julia Emig, who is more than a tad involved in this whole affair. She might have some ideas. Maybe she performs gold onlay procedures. It won't hurt to ask."

Yellow Pad Entry: #23 5-22-2003 5:23 p.m.
Called Dr. Julia Emig. She states that 10:00 a.m. tomorrow morning would be a good time to arrive at her Rockland office.

Stu will meet with dental professor Renee Bertram-Shannon at 8:30.

Stu rode with Peg from Rocky Nook to the Whitman Commuter Rail Station. This was the longest ride they'd had together since the day the body was pulled from the Jones River.

"Peg, I'm really thinking of taking the entire summer off. I'm just exhausted."

"That's the best idea I've heard in months. Are you going to get away?"

"I'm not sure. I need to slow down."

They pulled into the Whitman Station parking lot just as the South Avenue crossing signal came alive. If he had arrived a minute and a half later, Stu would have missed the train.

The five-mile ride to Rockland brought Peg to Julia Emig's office at exactly 9:55 a.m. The office looked the same as it had three months ago. Dr. Emig, in her white dental smock, greeted Peg as soon as she entered the office.

"Hi, Peg. How are you after your terrible ordeal? I've been following the story in the local papers. Do they have any clue as to who was in the vehicle that went into the water?"

"I'm doing much better. Thanks for asking. No one has an inkling about who my attacker might have been."

A couple of minutes of idle chitchat brought Peg to the real reason for visiting.

"Dr. Emig, do you have any patients who are dentists?"

"Well, when I need dental work, I go to Dr. Joan Eacmen in Norwell. She comes to me when she needs dental assistance. Oh, I did some work on old Doc Connelly before he retired to Arizona. Why do you ask?"

"Just wondering. Have you done many gold-foil procedures?"

Julia Emig chuckled. "Gold foil. Oh, yes, I've done one. just one. In fact, I have a gold foil tooth." She pointed to the left upper quadrant of her mouth.

"Which tooth number has your gold foil?"

Julia was obviously impressed with Peg's knowledge of dental procedures. "My gold foil is on number 7. Many would-be dentists have a gold-foil procedure on number 7 or number 10."

Dr. Emig explained the fact that often, in dental school, graduating students performed a gold-foil procedure on each other as part of their

Dental Certification Test. Usually, it was number 7 or number 10 because they seemed easier.

Stu had sent one of the three X-ray negatives that plainly displayed tooth number 10 of the body fished from the Jones River back in April. Peg handed it to Dr. Emig. "Does this dental work look familiar?"

"Well, Peg, that certainly is a fine example of gold-foil procedure. Is this an X-ray of your drowned assailant's teeth?"

Peg didn't explain to Dr. Emig that the Jones River dead body had very little water in his lungs, meaning he hadn't drowned and was basically dead when he drove off Landing Road into the estuary.

"Yes, that's one from a set of dental photos. Any ideas?"

"No ideas at all. Boy, I wish my former dental hygienist were around. She could remember teeth she had cleaned four years ago. She kept everything in a database; worked as a consultant for a software company that was developing a dental tracking system so the dentist and/or hygienist could get away from paper dental charts. She only worked for me part-time, usually on Thursday. I'm open Thursday evening until 8:30. Allison worked the entire day."

"Allison? Is that the dental hygienist?"

"Yes, Allison Smith. She worked part-time for me and four or five other dentists. Always trying to build up her software database." Dr. Emig was fingering through a file cabinet drawer that was identified A–D. "See? Here's a hard copy of what Allison had on her database. Look at the level of detail: every chip, inlay, onlay, extraction, wisdom tooth, crown, implant. She could complete a dental chart in less than a minute. She said this new computer program would be marketed in the next year. If she ever saw that gold-foil procedure of yours, it would certainly be in her records."

"Can you describe her? Where can I get in touch with Allison?"

"That's a good question; she left here abruptly back in March. She was a rather reserved sort. Just came in one day, picked up her belongings, and said she was returning to the area near the computer software company. She left me a business card with the address to mail her final check. I hope I still have the card. Dentex, the company Allison works for, called here looking for her right after she left."

Thumbing through a two-inch deck of cards, Julia Emig stopped about three-quarters of the way through the stack. "Here it is! I'll make a photocopy for you."

Allison Smith
Licensed Dental Hygienist
Software Consultant
Dentex Software Limited
257 American Legion Blvd.
Upper Darby, PA 19082
(610) 333-3168

Peg looked at the information on the business card. "Do you know if she's married? Boyfriend?"

"She never mentioned being married. My brother, Carl"—Julia Emig paused, took out a hankie and wiped her eyes—"I guess I should say my late brother. Carl was fond of Allison. He asked her out several times without success. He said he saw Allison and a male companion at a local restaurant. That was just before his death. He mentioned he spoke to Allison at the restaurant, and she appeared very depressed. I never found out what he meant by that comment."

As Peg left Rockland and headed into Hanover on Route 139, she wondered what Carl Wells meant by very depressed. She also wondered who Allison Smith was having dinner with.

Chapter 42

Sunday Morning
May 25, 2003

F ive-thirty a.m. is always too early for the phone to ring. It's never good news at that hour. Today was no exception.

"Good morning, Peg. Sorry to call you so early. This is Kate."

"Hi, Kate, I haven't heard from you in months. What's up?"

"Not good news. They rushed Dad to the hospital at midnight. Chest pains. They're doing tests this morning. He has all the classic symptoms of a blocked artery. Peg, are you there?"

"Yeah, Kate, I'm here. Let me get a few things in a bag and I'll get a flight out of Boston ASAP."

Stu and Sarek were out for their morning walk along the beach and then north about two miles to the point, where the Jones River spilled into Plymouth Harbor. The Landing Road Bridge, where the blue Toyota Corolla was winched out of the water a month ago, was about a half-mile further inland. The four-mile walk was usually a brisk one-hour excursion for Sarek, but, lately, it'd been taking Stu an extra fifteen or twenty minutes to complete. Peg was hopeful that Stu would soon regain his strength and his endurance would improve.

"Stu, I've got to catch a flight to Baltimore. My sister called. My dad is in the hospital. They don't know if it was a heart attack or something else."

"No other information?"

"No, he was admitted around midnight. They're running some tests this morning. Can you give me a ride to the B&P? I'm going to try to make an 8 a.m. flight."

"I can drive you to the airport."

"Thanks, Stu, but the bus will probably be quicker during the morning commute. They can use that HOV express lane on the highway."

"No HOV—it's Sunday," Stu quipped, as he tried to break the tension of the moment.

Peg and Stu were silent on the short ride to the bus terminal in Plymouth. As Peg exited the car, Stu tried to comfort her. "Please call me as soon as you have any news concerning your father. If you have any medical questions, just call me. If I don't have the answer, I'll find someone who does."

All Peg could say was "Thanks." She hugged Stu and climbed the steps of the bus.

The ride via the B&P to Logan and the flight to BWI were all uneventful but seemed to take forever. Peg's sister Mary was standing next to a loud stainless-steel luggage carousel marked BAGGAGE CLAIMS C. A huge clock under each baggage sign proudly announced in flashing red LED lights: Welcome to Baltimore-Washington International—the time is: 9:42 a.m.

"Welcome home, Peg. Sorry to bring you back under these circumstances. Good news. Dad had a comfortable night. They think he may need an arterial stent. They should know more by the time we get to the hospital."

Mary and Peg arrived at Anne Arundel Medical Center at exactly 11:00 a.m. Her sister Kate was in an absolute tizzy, while her mom was trying to keep everyone calm. Peg noticed how much her mother had aged in the past three months. Maybe she just hadn't paid attention on her last visit. The hospital atmosphere seemed to sharpen one's senses. Perhaps it was the bright lights and the extra oxygen that was in the air that made one more attentive.

Chapter 43

215-1130
8:33 p.m.

M om, Kate, and Peg had no sooner returned to Mom's home when Peg's cell phone started its tune. Caller ID indicated that it was Stu.

"Hi, Peg. Stu here. How's your dad doing?"

"Thanks for calling. He's doing much better. Three stents in two arteries. He'll be home in about four days."

"That's good news. How far are you from Philly?"

"Philadelphia? About two hours, maybe a little less. Why?"

"Oh, I thought I'd come down to give you some support with the hospital and all, and maybe we could take a ride to Upper Darby and talk with the people at Dentex Software."

"Did you call them?"

"Sure did. This morning. I was going to leave a message and was surprised when a James Campbelli answered. He's the CFO at Dentex. Said he'd rather not discuss the Allison Smith matter on the telephone. Seemed reluctant to give the smallest bit of information, but he did say he would discuss Smith's relationship with Dentex Software, if I were to visit him in the future. I'm thinking sooner than later. Maybe this is the break we've been looking for. I asked Campbelli if I could chat with him on Tuesday morning around 11:30. I talked with Tim Snow, and he says he'd like to come with me to talk to Dentex. Campbelli might be more inclined to provide information to a Boston detective. Maybe not, you never know. Tim and I could catch the 8:00 on Tuesday morning; you could pick us up at BWI, and then we could drive up to Philly. Tim needs to catch a flight back Tuesday evening. He has to be in Dorchester District Court first thing Wednesday morning."

"Okay, Stu. There should be an extra car around here. I'll meet you at Baltimore-Washington International at 9:30 a.m. on Tuesday, the 27th. Which airline?"

"Global Airways."

Peg's mother and sister Kate looked up as she put the phone down. Sister Kate had a grin that was more like a typical sisterly smirk. "And who might that have been?"

"Oh, that was Stu. He's coming down Tuesday morning. May I put him in the guest bedroom, Mom? And could I use someone's car for the day?"

"Oh, the elusive Dr. Mirkin. We finally get to meet him. Peg, we were beginning to wonder if he was just a figment of your imagination. This must be getting pretty serious for the busy Dr. Mirkin to make a special trip here."

"Well, Kate, I wish I could tell you it was serious, but he's just a special friend. Besides, he's coming here on business. We have to visit a company near Philadelphia. Also, he's not arriving alone. A Boston detective is coming with him."

The thirty-minute ride to BWI Airport gave Peg time to reflect on the events of the past couple of days. Her dad was much improved. In fact, he was up and out of bed, cautiously walking the long fifth-floor corridor of the Anne Arundel Medical Center. Modern medicine—remarkable.

Why is there always construction on the roads leading to our major airports? Peg thought as she pulled in front of the lower level doors of Global Airways at 9:25 a.m. Thank goodness, no Stu. No Tim. Just an officer of the Maryland State Police slowly walking down the line of cars, ticketing those with no occupants, telling others to "move on. No waiting." It was obvious that BWI was taking security precautions associated with 9/11 very seriously. Remember when traveling by air was a great adventure? Everything had changed.

As the Maryland State Police officer approached Peg's car, the terminal doors slid open and Stu and Tim exited into the bright Chesapeake sunshine. Characteristically, Mirkin was dressed in a charcoal-gray business suit with one of his favorite Garcia ties and carrying a long blue garment bag. Snow, more casual, had a blue gym bag with the logo of the Boston Police Detectives Union embossed on each side. Snow was immediately engrossed in a lively conversation with the Maryland State Police officer. They shook hands, and Snow threw his bag onto the rear floor of the car. It landed with a mighty thump. Tim jumped in and closed the door.

"Welcome to Baltimore. What are you carrying in the bag, Tim? Sounds like dumbbells."

Mirkin answered for Snow, as Tim was busy rummaging through the large blue gym bag.

"The darn bag is full of food. He has enough for a month."

"I need my nourishment. I've got a race in Idaho at the end of June. What a small world. That state cop has a sister who's married to a guy in vice. He's out of Precinct 7, you know, the one across the street from Dickie O'Doherty's in Southie."

Snow was already halfway through a container of yogurt while sipping on a bottle of some athletic drink that was the bright green color of a popular aftershave lotion. Probably had a similar taste.

"Peg, you want something?"

"Yeah, Tim. You have any Moxie?"

"No. Sorry. No Moxie. I got other stuff but no Moxie. That Moxie is hard to find, especially in eight-ounce bottles. Moxie's not that good when it's warm. Peg, I didn't think you liked Moxie?"

"I don't!"

At this hour of the day, the ride to Upper Darby was only an hour and fifteen minutes. Everyone pictured computer companies in large multi-building complexes with parking lots that held thousands of vehicles. The reality was that Dentex Software made Patricia Tremblay's Cajun Food Specialties of Ponchatoula, Louisiana look like a multi-national conglomerate. It was a two-story, white cement-block building with about ten or twelve cars parked in front. Stu Mirkin led the group into the building.

Upon entering the front lobby, they were greeted by a receptionist who was sitting behind a glass partition, which reminded Peg of a doctor's office. "Hello. Welcome to Dentex Software. How can I help you?"

"Hi, there, I'm Dr. Stuart Mirkin. I have an appointment with Mr. Camp—"

The door adjoining the office opened. "Hi, Dr. Mirkin. I'm Jim Campbelli. Come in to my office."

Stu made the necessary introductions. "This is Detective Tim Snow, Boston Police Department."

Tim offered his right hand for shaking and his left with his police identification. Badge on one side, photo on the other.

"And this is Agent Peg McCarthy, U.S. Customs Service."

An irritated Peg wondered, *Why does Stu continue to introduce me as Agent Peg McCarthy, U.S. Customs Service? I know. I know. Sometimes it's just easier that way.*

Campbelli offered them a seat—nothing fancy; the fold-up variety; the kind that has a soft cushion in the center. "This must be important for the three of you to come down from Boston. We were just getting ready to order lunch. Anyone hungry?" Campbelli held up a take-out bill of fare from Gino's Sandwich Shoppe.

Tim quickly reached for the menu.

"Well, Mr. Campbelli, Peg and I are in the Baltimore area on an unrelated matter. When you said you would rather not discuss any information on the phone, I understood completely. There are some things that just can't be discussed on the phone. What can you tell us about Allison Smith?"

Campbelli opened the center drawer of his desk and removed an employee identification card. "That's Allison Smith. She's been an employee of mine for nearly four years and I'm very concerned about her."

Both Snow and Mirkin had small notebooks and pencils in hand. As usual, Peg had her yellow legal pad. Snow was the first to speak. "Why do you say you are concerned?"

Campbelli was slow to respond. When he did, he selected his words cautiously. "This company develops software programs that are used by dentists in their practices. We usually have ten to twelve dental hygienists/data programmers that work across the country. We provide a generous stipend to those dentists who allow our people to work part-time in their offices. All of our personnel are state-licensed, and most reside in the state where they practice. Allison was different. She's originally from Florida. She is licensed as a dental hygienist in Massachusetts and Rhode Island, as well as Florida."

Mirkin looked up from his writing. "You said you were concerned?"

Campbelli also had a notebook, which he opened and flipped through several pages. "On Thursday, March 27, Allison called me saying that she was returning to the office on Monday, March 31. She explained that personal issues dictated her leaving the Boston area ASAP. I asked if she was leaving because of problems with one of the dentists that she worked for, and she responded, "Not exactly." We booked a room for her at a local motel. She said she was leaving early Saturday morning. Allison never arrived here from Massachusetts."

Tim Snow asked, "Is that the last time you heard from her?"

Campbelli flipped another page in his notebook. "I haven't spoken to Allison since Thursday, the 27th. However, she did submit her weekly report, as usual, on Friday evening. She never was late in submitting her reports; not late even once in nearly four years."

Snow continued writing. As he did so he asked, "Did you try to contact her relatives? Any friends? Does she have a phone?"

"Yes, I had Casey, the receptionist who greeted you, call Allison's cell phone number when she wasn't here on Monday morning. We called the number, at least once every day, for a week. We also contacted each of the five dentists with whom she worked. She has relatives in the Orlando area. We've been in contact with them on a weekly basis. Her aunt in Florida said she filed a missing persons report with the county sheriff's office in mid-April. I asked a friend of mine who works in the district attorney's office what we should do, and she says because Allison did not live in Pennsylvania, there wasn't much sense in filling out a missing person report here. I did give her Allison's vehicle plate number and she did run an APB on it. It's a leased car that we provide. Nothing. Nothing at all."

Campbelli continued to review his papers. "I don't know if this has anything to do with this case. On the 31st of March, the day that Allison should have been back here at the office, I received a call from an irate dental patient complaining that he did not give anyone permission to enter his dental records into our national database. He didn't give his phone number or location. I told him that our database contains no names or other data that could connect a patient with a record. I'm not sure if he believed me. I stretched the truth a bit just to get him off the phone."

"What do you mean stretched the truth?" Both Snow and Mirkin seemed surprised that Peg asked a question.

"Well, Ms. McCarthy, although our database doesn't list patient names, we can identify, if necessary, the dentist for which each dental record is filed. It should become very useful for law enforcement persons."

"How so?" asked Snow.

Campbelli turned and started entering information on his computer keyboard. "Let's say you have a set of dental records that you're trying to identify. Electronically, you could compare those dental records for a match with our database. We can even find possible matches of one tooth."

Mirkin stared deeply into the computer display. "You mean if I give you information about one tooth, you might find a match?"

"That's exactly what I mean, Dr. Mirkin."

Stu looked at Peg with a slight smile. "How about a gold-foil procedure. Does your database categorize those separately?"

Jim Campbelli was pounding his keys as if playing a concerto. "Nationwide, we've got sixty-one gold-foil procedures. What number tooth you looking for, Doc?"

"Tooth number 10."

Campbelli continued moving his mouse with one hand while typing with the left. "We've got twenty-six foil procedures for tooth number 10. Thirty-four for tooth number 7, and one for number 9. Perhaps that tooth nine is an error."

Mirkin was looking directly over Campbelli's left shoulder, and Snow was doing the same on the right side.

"You said you don't have any patient names, but could you tell if any of those foil procedures were patients of any of Allison Smith's dentists?"

"That's easy. Yes, two of those foil procedure patients were in Allison's database collection. Let me check. One was a patient of Doctor 1819. The other, Doctor 2133. Let me run these two doctor numbers. Number 2133 is Dr. Joan Eacmen of Norwell, Massachusetts, and Number 1819 is Dr. Ray Shurtleff of Abington. I don't recognize Shurtleff. I thought I was familiar with all of Allison's dentists. Oh, I see. She was at Dr. Shurtleff's office from July to December of 2000. I recall he retired at the end of the year. Dr. Collins, Joe Collins, took over Dr. Shurtleff's practice. Allison continued working with Dr. Collins."

Mirkin was already out of his chair and heading for the door. "Peg, toss me the car keys. I'll be right back."

Tim was still jotting notes when Stu returned with an already opened black leather document case. "Here's the full set of X-rays, including a panoramic view."

James Campbelli slowly looked at the X-rays and entered the information concerning the work done on each tooth. "I'm afraid I'm not as proficient as my field representatives. Ideally, we hope to have these X-ray images entered directly into the database. We are getting very close to perfecting that process."

After a minute or two of entering data, Campbelli tapped the ENTER key. The monitor blinked once and issued the following message:

Doctor # 2133......MATCHING DATA PERCENTAGE------5.4%
Doctor # 1819......MATCHING DATA PERCENTAGE-----96.1%

Campbelli sent all pertinent documents to the printer in the outer office. "Looks like that's a definite match. Your dental records match that patient of Shurtleff. I only entered the data of seven teeth. I'll bet if

I refined my search the percentage will be even higher. Any idea who it is?"

Stu Mirkin pondered the data on Campbelli's computer. He paused several seconds before answering. "No, we've been working these dental records for about a month. We seem to be getting closer. I wonder if Dr. Shurtleff is still around. How we can check that?"

Campbelli began moving his computer mouse. "Let me check to see if he's still a member of the North American Dental Association. A lot of dentists and doctors keep the affiliations after they retire. It's a social thing. Yes, sir, right here. Here's the only Ray Shurtleff listed. Everything is here."

Dr. Ray Shurtleff, DMD
145 Bogey Creek Road, Apartment 390
Boca Raton, FL 33344
213-454-7639

Campbelli electronically sent another document to be printed. "Doctor Mirkin, Detective Snow, use my phone if you want to try that number."

On the third ring to the Boca Raton number, an answering machine with a monotonic voice announced: "Hello, you have reached the Shurtleff residence. We are unable to answer the phone. Please leave your name, number, and a brief mess—Hello, give me a moment to shut off the answering machine. Hello."

"Good afternoon. My name is Dr. Stuart Mirkin. I'm calling from Pennsylvania. I'm trying to contact Dr. Shurtleff, who had a dental practice in Abington, Massachusetts. Do I have the correct number?"

"Oh, yes, you've reached Dr. Shurtleff's residence. Mrs. Shurtleff speaking. Sorry, but Dr. Shurtleff is at work. If you leave your number, I'll have him call you. It might not be until tomorrow. He has a bridge tournament in Jupiter tonight. That's the town, not the planet." Mrs. Shurtleff cackled at her joke. " I don't expect him home until after ten o'clock."

"Thank you, Mrs. Shurtleff, that would be fine. Did you say working? I thought the doctor retired."

"Dr. Shurtleff works part time. Three days a week. I wish he'd work more. He gets in the way around here. Thinks he's a chef. Terrible cook."

"I understand, Mrs. Shurtleff. Is the doctor still doing dental work?"

"Sort of. Not really dental. More like dentures. He works in a dental lab. They manufacture dentures. There's a huge need for that here in Southern Florida."

Mrs. Shurtleff started to chuckle again. Mirkin could only smile as he gave her his cell phone number.

"Okay, Dr. Mirkin, I'll give him your number. May I ask what this is in reference to?"

"I'm working to identify a set of dental records. They could belong to a former patient of Dr. Shurtleff."

"Oh, I see, you're *that* kind of a doctor. I'll give him the message. Don't be surprised if he doesn't return the call 'til tomorrow. You hear what I'm saying?"

After thanking Campbelli for his assistance and armed with significant information that could lead to the potential conclusion of this case, the trio headed to Philadelphia Airport, fifteen miles southeast of Upper Darby. Dropping Tim off at Concourse E, Peg and Stu turned left and were quickly back on Interstate 95, heading south toward Baltimore.

Chapter 44

Boca Calling

Journal Entry
Wednesday May 28, 2003
Dad is coming home tomorrow. We stopped at the hospital on the way back from Philly yesterday afternoon. Amazing how quickly the human spirit can recover from a surgical invasion. Dad was ready to get out last night. Said he had stuff to do.

Stu had his cell phone to his left ear as he came down the stairs. "Okay, Tim, yes, that is good news. We'll talk when Peg and I get back to Boston this afternoon. Want to do late lunch at Dickie O'Doherty's? I'll call you when we arrive. Bye."

"Good morning, everyone." It was obvious that Stu Mirkin had just received an encouraging report from Tim. "That was Tim. He said he had an hour to kill at the airport yesterday. He was able to talk with Allison Smith's aunt in Florida. He confirmed with the Osceola Sheriff's Department that a missing-person report was filed by Smith's aunt and uncle on April 3. The aunt says Allison's boss has had someone call often to see if there had been any news. She's very concerned. Tim said he also had an APB notice filed on Allison's car. By the time he reached Boston, they'd found the car. It was at a Logan Express Parking Lot in Braintree. It's been there for at least two or three weeks. He had the crime lab hauler pick it up last night. What smells so good?"

Halfway through Stu's first sip of coffee, his phone issued its alert tune.

"Hello. Good morning, Dr. Shurtleff. Hold on a second." Stu excused himself and went to the living room. "Yes, Dr. Shurtleff, I can hear you just fine. How are you enjoying retirement?"

"Oh, retirement is fine. I'm working three or four days a week in a dental lab. Dr. Mirkin, my wife tells me you're looking to ID a dental chart. How can I help?"

"We have a set of dental records that seem to match a former patient of yours. Several dentists south of Boston mentioned that they were involved in a computer software development program with a company called Dentex. We went to Dentex yesterday, and the match they came up with was one of your patients. We still don't know the identity of this person. Could we fax or overnight the X-rays to you? Perhaps you might have a clue."

"I have a pretty good memory, Dr. Mirkin, especially when it comes to teeth. Any unusual restorative procedures visible?"

"Yes, this guy had a gold-foil procedure."

"Maybe he was a dentist or at least a dental student?"

"That's possible. Why do you say that, Dr. Shurtleff?"

"Please, call me Ray. Everybody calls me Ray. I work on dentures now. Back when I was in dental college, we used to do a gold-foil procedure as part of our exam for the State Board of Dental Examiners. I think they dropped that requirement, mercifully so. We would pay someone twenty-five or thirty dollars to be the patient. We'd do anything to make or save a few bucks, like sell our blood, sit for a dental procedure, or go down to the Barber's College on Tremont Street just to get a free haircut. I remember the woman who sat for my gold-foil. Paid her twenty bucks. Maria Luscatonni. Her husband was a friend and fellow dental student. She only charged me twenty dollars because her husband was a friend. He had to find someone else to work on. They wouldn't let you work on a relative. What number tooth?"

"Number 10, Ray. Thanks for being informal. Please call me Stu."

"Number 10 gold-foil. Anything else interesting?"

"Hold on a minute, Ray. Let me get the X-rays. ... Peg, could you run up and grab that case of mine? I need the X-rays. ... Okay, Ray, he had amalgam work on numbers 17 and 18, as well as porcelain veneer on number 15."

"Stu, no extractions?"

"No, Ray, no extractions noted."

"Hm-m. This sounds awfully familiar. Check one more thing, Stu. Do your X-rays show an extra-wide gap between numbers 22 and 23?"

"Yes. Yes. A very wide gap between 22 and 23. Any ideas?" There was silence in Mirkin's phone. "Hello. Hello, Ray. Are you still there?"

"Oh, I'm still here. I know who this is Stu. Is he deceased?"

"Yes, Ray."

"Dr. Mirkin, those are the dental records of Santa Claus, and I knew him very well."

Mirkin placed his hand over the mouthpiece of his phone. "Peg, he says these are the dental X-rays of Santa Claus. Perhaps the old doc isn't as sharp as he first sounded. Maybe we now know why his wife wants him out of the house." Mirkin rolled his eyes as old Doc Shurtleff kept rambling.

"Doc Shurtleff, surely you jest? Santa Claus? Really?"

"No, Mirkin, not the real Santa Claus. What do you think I am? Senile? That's what I called him. Actually, I called him Shabby Santa Claus. I'm trying to think of his last name. He and I were bridge partners in a couple of tournaments. Very aggressive. Too aggressive. Mostly, I competed against him in mixed doubles competitions. My bridge partner, Kathleen Centorino, and I beat him and his wife in five or six tournaments in a row. He was always too aggressive. That was many years ago, before his wife died. He turned flakey after her death. Come to think of it, he turned flakey before she died."

Stu Mirkin was rapidly taking notes. "Was he a dentist, Ray?"

"Oral surgeon. Specialized in extractions. The guy could remove wisdom teeth like you wouldn't believe. Too bad—he developed the shakes the last few years. You know, shakes, looked like Parkinson's disease or something. Too bad—he's not that old. Wow, I know his name like my own. I just can't think of it. Scabby Santini, Shabby Santilatti. Something like that. I'll think of it. I'll call you back when it comes to me."

"Yes, Dr. Shurtleff, please call me when you think of the name. How old would you say this Shabby is?

"Oh, I'd say mid-forties or so. I'll call you when I think of his name."

"Okay, Doc. Thank you for your help. Good-bye."

Stu returned to the kitchen and his now cold coffee. "Well, Peg, I think we're getting closer. Old Doc Shurtleff thinks he knows those dental records. He just can't think of the name. Says it's something like Santini, Santotti. Sabby Santilatti. That ring any bells with you, Peg?"

Peg felt like someone had thrown a bucket of ice water over her. Goose bumps all over. Before she could utter a syllable Mirkin's phone chimed once again.

"Hi, Doc. Oh, you recall the name? Okay, I got it. Thanks again."

Peg and Stu spoke in unison: "Sebastian Santagati!"

"Peg, you know this Sebastian Santagati?"

"He's the traveling oral surgeon that Julia Emig, the dentist in Rockland, used for tooth extractions. He suddenly stopped practicing right after his son died of leukemia. But why, Stu? Why?"

"I'm sure the reasons why will come to light. We need to get back to Boston ASAP. Let's get to the airport. Perhaps we can get switched to an earlier flight. I'll call Tim."

Chapter 45

M. Villanueva Monument Co.

The 10:00 a.m. flight returning to Boston was at about half capacity. As Peg and Stu exited the ramp into the bright lights of Gate 38—Terminal C—Logan International—Boston, a familiar voice boomed across the crowd.

"Peg, Stu, over here. You have any luggage?" As usual, Tim Snow was in perpetual motion. He was also carrying a small bag of his energy snacks. "Anyone want some grapes? How about one of these new low-carb chocolate bars? Let's go. I've got a state trooper watching my car. I'm double-parked."

As Mirkin flung his garment bag over his right shoulder, he asked, "Get out of court early, Tim?"

"Continued, Stu. Continued until the end of July. That should be my middle name. Continued. I was in and out of court in forty-five minutes. The new Dorchester Court, right near the bridge. You know the bridge that goes over the Neponset River into North Quincy. I figured, while I was in the area and had a little time to kill, I'd go over and talk with South Shore Dental Supply. Peg, I met with the guy that you talked with on the phone, Bill Rudder. Been in business over ten years. Moved out of Cohasset back in February. Said he and his partner bought out a third investor; said the third guy had turned into a real pain. He said the guy is a nutcake. The third investor owned the building. One of the main reasons for moving to North Quincy, in addition to increased storage, was to get away from this guy. Care to guess the third investor's name?"

Peg looked at Stu, and he at her. "I don't know, Tim. Neither Norene Rolle nor Neelia, the manager of PHP, ever mentioned the name of the owner of the strip mall in Cohasset. Anyone we know?"

"The name Rudder gave me wouldn't have rung any bells, except that Stu gave me the same name on the phone, from Baltimore, this morning. Dr. Sebastian Santagati."

"Odd that we went from the end of January to almost the beginning of June with nothing, and, suddenly many pieces of the puzzle are fitting together. Guess we know where he got the Empathy Belly. He owned the place and must have had his own key."

The three headed out through the departure section of Terminal C to Tim's battered Aries. Tim veered to the left to pick up a copy of today's *Boston Post*, dropping three quarters on the counter. "Too bad we didn't solve it a bit sooner. Look at this. Must be a slow news day."

The back page, the one that is the first page of the sports section, announced in bold 18-point type:

Instead of the Hall of Fame "No Chance" LaChance Enters the Cold Case File?

"So, Tim, thanks for picking us up. Where are we heading?"

"I figured I'd give you guys a ride home. We can stop and get a bite to eat on the way, and we could also stop at Santagati's house in Marshfield, take a look around, see if anyone is home. We'll get a court order to search tomorrow."

Route 123 was a meandering two-lane country road that connected the villages of the coastal South Shore. It was portrayed as an east/west thoroughfare but often went north/south. In several sections of this strange little highway, the signs were marked EAST-123, but a vehicle compass would indicate due west.

Less than a mile out of Norwell Center, on the right, was Bridge Street. Aptly named, about 300 yards from Route 123, Bridge Street crossed the brackish portion of the North River. During the heat of the summer, if the tide was right, a horde of teens could be found diving off the bridge into the estuary below. The yellow warning sign, "Diving from Bridge Is Not Permitted," had lost the word "Not."

"There it is! First house on the left after the bridge." Tim pointed to a large Victorian that faced the North River. The home was about 100 feet above and 300 feet back from the water's edge. The North River was the boundary between Norwell and Marshfield. After crossing the bridge, the road bent sharply left. At this bend was a narrow dirt driveway that could easily be missed. About a quarter-mile down the dirt driveway, there was a triple fork. The path to the right was marked with a large V. The center one had a square sign displaying the name "Burke." The driveway to the left was unmarked. "Must be this way." As always, Snow didn't drive the Aries as much as he aimed it.

Careening down the driveway, as usual carrying a tad too much momentum, the multi-colored ex-MWRA inspection car bottomed out on the gravel as it made its final approach to the Santagati home. Its bent tail pipe gouged a deep trail in the dirt driveway.

In the back seat, Peg was holding on as they passed between two stone columns, each emblazoned with a large Gothic 'S' in granite.

"Watch it, Tim!" Mirkin was gripping the armrest with his right hand and grabbing the dash with his left. Snow jammed his foot on the brakes as they narrowly avoided and slid up beside an older green Chevrolet rack-body truck, which was heading out in the opposite direction. The truck appeared to be of mid-1950s vintage and was in pristine condition. Printing on the door of the Chevy declared "M. Villanueva Monument Co., Hanover, MA." It was obvious that the driver and his co-worker were more than a little annoyed by the near collision with Snow's Aries. Tim quickly exited the car and approached the truck.

"I'm Detective Tim Snow, Boston PD." Snow opened his identification wallet. "Can I ask you a couple of questions?"

Mr. Villanueva explained that he had just delivered two granite grave markers and one monument to the Santagati property.

Snow began writing on his small note pad. Mirkin, who had joined the discussion, was also writing.

Peg asked, "Mr. Villanueva, just what is the difference between a grave marker and a monument?"

"A grave marker is flat with the ground; a monument is above the surface. You know, like a tombstone. A lot of newer cemeteries only allow grave markers. It makes it easier to mow the grass."

Mirkin looked over the top of his half-rimmed glasses. "I didn't think you could bury on private property in Massachusetts."

"You can't bury humans except in an approved cemetery. Pets are different. Some towns prohibit pet burial except in a pet cemetery. Marshfield doesn't have such an ordinance. None yet anyway. Give 'em time. These days there's a law against everything. Any more questions? I got to get rolling—got another delivery." Villanueva gestured to the rear of the truck to a large polished black headstone bearing the name "Ralston."

Tim glanced at the Ralston. "Pets, you say, Mr. Villova? The stones you delivered were for pets? You sure?"

"It's Villanueva." He patted his hand on the driver's door lettering. "Villanueva."

"Sorry."

"Pretty sure. Muffy and Buffy are usually pet names. Besides, Mr. Santagati had us pickup a pet casket down at the Oceanview Pet Cemetery in Manomet and bury it here. I'm not sure if it was Muffy or

Buffy. He said he promised his son, before his son died, that he would have both pets buried together. One was here and the other at Oceanview."

"You buried the pet today, Mr. Villanueva?"

"No, we did that back in late March, early April. I know it was spitting sleet the day we went to Manomet. Cold. Awfully cold. And raw. We placed the pet in the hole, on top of the other casket. Santagati said he'd take care of back filling. We delivered the gravestones today."

"You placed the Oceanview casket on top of the other one? Same plot?"

"Common thing to do. As long as you dig the hole deep enough for the first casket, you'll have no trouble putting another on top at a later date. They do that often in regular cemeteries. Santagati must have dug the hole himself. He's got a tractor with a backhoe attachment behind the garage over there. Good customer. Paid cash."

Villanueva depressed the clutch and started the old Chevy. Mirkin and Snow were still in writing. Snow stopped. "Thanks a lot, Mr. Villanueva. Okay to call you if I have any other questions?"

"I'm in the book." He patted his hand on the driver's door lettering. "Villanueva, right on Route 123 where it crosses Route 53. Oh, Detective Snow, nice car."

"Thanks. ... I wonder what he meant by that? Let's take a quick look at the gravesite. We've got to get out of here; I'm hungry."

As Villanueva described, about 200 yards from the garage, near a group of maples were the two stone grave markers, BUFFY and MUFFY, side-by-side. The larger monument was about two feet away:

ERECTED
IN MEMORY OF
ERIK SANTAGATI,
WHO DIED ON
JANUARY 18TH IN
THE YEAR OF
2003.

AGED: 11 YRS,
3 MTHS, 2 DAYS

BASEBALL WAS HIS LIFE.
SO YOUNG, SO SAD.

The engraving was not unlike epitaphs found on stones in ancient graveyards across New England.

"Let's go. I'm starved. I wonder what's really in that grave? I'll call the court to modify the search warrant to include digging up poor Muffy and Buffy."

Chapter 46

Detective Meredith Skiffington
and
NBC, ABC, CBS, & Fox

S tu left early for his conference at the Vineyard Sound Inn in Falmouth. Three—no, four—TV communication trucks were parked along Bridge Street near the entrance to Santagati's driveway. By all appearances, the story had broken. Satellite dishes pointed toward the heavens. Several uniformed officers stood in front of two yellow sawhorse barriers in the driveway. Thanks to Tim Snow, Peg was expected. A local radio reporter with a portable recorder pushed a microphone into her car.

"Are you the lady who's with U.S. Customs?"

"Not I! I'm retired." Oh, how long Peg had been waiting to say that. Disappointed, the reporter scurried to another vehicle now stopped on Bridge Street. Several neighbors and part of the swimming gang from the bridge had gathered along Bridge Street to witness the hubbub.

The Massachusetts State Police Mobile Crime Lab was parked near the garage next to the Tim's Aries. Peg walked the short distance to the gravesite. A green John Deere backhoe was scooping the first layer of sod and topsoil from the area above Buffy's marker.

"Good morning, Tim. You're getting an early start. I see the press knows that something's up."

"Yeah, it's hard to keep things quiet, especially when you're getting court orders etc. I talked to the manager of the Manomet Pet Cemetery. He said Santagati came down on or about March 26 and paid him $150 to exhume the casket of Santagati's dog, Buffy. Needed it done right away. Gave him an extra twenty dollars if he could have it done by Friday noon. The dog was buried in Manomet about three years ago. Said, at the time, the oral surgeon bought two caskets. One for Buffy and another for a pet to be named later. Interesting!"

With the drone of the Deere, the dig proceeded. Who would have guessed? Pet caskets. The excavator operator stopped. "Hey, Detective Snow! I think we're getting close. I think I see something."

Five sets of eyes strained into the 3-foot-by-5-foot pit. Besides Tim, the only other person Peg recognized was Woy Lee, the Boston PD crime scene photographer. Barely visible, the white top of the pet casket was at a depth of just under two feet. Tim jumped into the hole with a broom. Sweeping revealed: Fitzgerald Pet Casket Co., Greenville, NC 27836.

"Okay, see if you can remove the dirt around the perimeter of the box. We need to get to the casket under this one."

A couple more minutes of digging and the second pet casket beneath the first became visible. Snow and a female detective from the state police, one Meredith Skiffington, jumped into opposite ends of the hole and hoisted the top casket onto the grass at the edge of the gravesite. The pet casket was measured.

"Four feet long by two feet wide and eighteen inches high," Skiffington called out to the others standing around the white plastic box. "Looks like it's sealed with some kind of gray duct tape. Want me to break the seal?"

"Just a second." Woy Lee was snapping photos from all angles. "I want pictures before, during, and after opening. Okay, open it up."

If anyone felt queasy, it didn't show. Peg sure wasn't looking forward to the grand opening of Buffy's remains. Skiffington cut the two-inch sealing tape along the seam formed by the lid and the plastic box marked Fitzgerald Pet Casket Co. Woy Lee's Nikon F continued clicking. Skiffington flipped the lid onto the manicured turf. Peg wasn't sure what to expect inside the casket. The skeletal remains of a large sized dog, a worm-and-bug-infested carcass, or a rotting mass in its third year of decay. She mostly expected the pungent smell of Santagati's beloved pet, Buffy.

None of these possibilities proved true. When State Police Detective Skiffington opened Buffy's cover, what was revealed was a rather large, mostly black dog curled in a ball, as if sleeping with its head lying on a crepe-fringed pillow. There was no noticeable smell. Woy continued clicking.

"Doesn't look like it's been opened since Manomet sealed it up four years ago." Snow poked around Buffy's remains looking for evidence that may have been hidden in the interior. He looked up. "Any guesses what we might find in the second box?"

The top of the second pet casket was measured at thirty-nine inches below the surface. Snow spoke to the backhoe operator as he climbed out. "Bob, trench around the bottom casket so about ten to twelve inches are exposed. We'll open that one right where it sits in the hole."

Snow continued writing details into his notebook. Skiffington—younger and probably more technologically attuned—entered data, both verbally and with a stylus, into a handheld recording device.

Tim gestured with his arm to move away from the noisy tractor. "Hey, Peg, Mirkin sleeping in this morning?"

"No, he's speaking to that group down the Cape in Falmouth. He'll be here as quick as he can. What, or should I say who, do you think will be in casket number two?"

"You never know, Peg. They got their own Next-door John in this neighborhood, just like you at Rocky Nook. He was over this morning. Burke. Irvin "No 'G,' Thank You" Burke. Been here thirty-four years. Said Buffy spent more time at his house, sleeping under the porch, than she did at home. Said the dog came over for a cheese snack two or three times a day. I bet old Buffy died of clogged arteries. He also said he never knew Santagati had any other pets. I wonder who Muffy is."

The four-cylinder of the John Deere went to idle. Bob shut the machine off. It became quiet. Real quiet. Woy's Nikon was whispering the only sounds. Click … Click … Click.

"All set!" Mrs. Lee stepped away from the ever-deepening burial bunker. This time Detective Skiffington needed assistance getting into the hole. She cut the sealing tape, lifted the cover, and threw it out of the pit onto the ground, landing on Peg's left foot. Nothing was visible in the casket, just a blanket filling the void of the box. She lifted the cloth revealing a cat with a red collar.

"Looks like a Himalayan." Skiffington ran her gloved hand around the interior of the pet casket. "Nothing, Snowman. Just a dead cat!"

"Damn. I was so sure there would be a connection. I thought we'd find some evidence, maybe even a body or two." Snow tossed a handful of dirt into the hole. "Peg, kick that cover back to Meredith. Anybody got any duct tape?"

"Tim, I wonder why this cover is different from the first? I bet they're not even interchangeable. This one is thicker. No name on top either."

Tim Snow held the casket covers side by side. "They are different. Damn."

Snow took out his phone, accessed the recent call key, and pressed redial. "Hello, Edgar. Edgar Molson, please. Hi Edgar, Tim Snow, Boston PD. I have a quick question for you. Those pet caskets that

Sebastian Santagati bought from you. Yes, four years ago. Were they identical? No, not in size. Manufacturer? One of them has Fitzgerald Pet Casket Co., Greenville, NC 27836, embossed on the lid. The other one has a blank lid. I see, you only buy from Fitzgerald. Always have. Still do. I see. Okay, you check; I'll wait." Snow removed the flip phone from his left ear. "Molson's checking to see what the covers say that he has in stock. Okay, Edgar. Yeah, I'm still here. How many did you say? Nineteen? Wow! Three different sizes. All nineteen have Fitzgerald Pet Casket Co. on the lid. Okay Edgar, thanks a lot." Tim peered into the final resting spot of Buffy and Muffy. "Okay, Skiffington, out of the pool. We've got a little more digging to do. Bob, keep digging. We've got to look under that second casket."

The trench around the second pet casket was expanded both in width and depth. Bob stopped when casket number two was fully exposed. Snow and Skiffington carefully slid into the grave. Only Snow's head was above the hole. He and Skiffington lifted the box to the top. Deputy Hadfield, of the Plymouth County Sheriff's Department, and Peg pulled the second coffin out of the pit and placed it next to casket number one.

Woy Lee's camera continued to record the proceedings.

From his seat on the back of the John Deere, operator Bob issued a warning. "Be careful, Detective Snow, that hole's getting pretty deep. Hard to tell how stable the earth is. Wouldn't want it to collapse on you."

Snowman and Skiffington were kneeling at the bottom of the hole, which was at the five-foot-depth mark.

"Someone hand me the shovel and the broom." Snow scraped the bottom with the blade of the shovel. "Something's here. Peg, can you hear that hollow sound?" Skiffington was tapping the broom handle into the dirt. "Help us out of here. We've got more digging to do."

The long bucket-arm of the John Deere reached deep into the final resting place of Buffy and Muffy. Lord only knows what, or who, might be buried here. Twelve, fourteen, then sixteen large scoops of dirt were added to the nearby expanding mound.

With Woy Lee still taking pictures, Tim announced, "We've got a third coffin. Fitzgerald Pet Casket. This hole is getting deep. We better wrap a chain around this one and hoist it out with the backhoe."

Snow kept adding information to his notepad. The crowd of onlookers expanded to about ten. Anyone with any jurisdiction over anything seemed to have a representative: State Police, Plymouth County Sheriff's

Department, Boston Police. Tim looked up from his notes. "Wow! We seem to be gathering quite a group. Let me introduce those of you I know. First, I'm Tim Snow, homicide, Boston PD." Snow started the intros counterclockwise. "The lady with the blue jumpsuit is Detective Meredith Skiffington; she's in charge of this excavation scene. Homicide, Mass. State Police. Next is Mrs. Woy Lee, photographer, Boston PD. Then Deputy Russ Hadfield, Plymouth County Sheriff's

Department. Our shovel operator is Bob. Bob, what's your last name?"

"Gates!"

Snow continued, "Thanks Bob. Bob Gates, Marshfield DPW. Peg McCarthy, U.S. Customs. Did I miss anyone?"

"Hi, I'm John Leonard, chief of the Marshfield Police, and this is Zack Robbins, detective, Marshfield PD."

Snow wrote all the names into his notebook, and Skiffington filed them electronically. It seemed to be a dead heat in their recording competition.

Snow beckoned to Chief Leonard. "Chief, Gates, the shovel operator, says the DPW has some steel plates used for road repair. Could you ask if we could borrow one large enough to cover this hole? I don't want anyone falling in. Also, ask if they might have an old tarp? I want to cover his dirt pile. We'll sift through it when we fill the hole. Oh, Chief, thanks for the detail at the driveway. If you need relief, Hadfield says he can get you a couple of officers from the Sheriff's Department. Let's seal this place off. Nobody on the Santagati property. It's okay for the neighbors to use the driveway. Oh, Chief, let your guys out on the road know that we're expecting a Dr. Stu Mirkin. Let him through when he arrives. Thanks."

Chief Leonard was already on his radio.

"Oh, Chief, one more thing. We'll have to brief the press. Where's a good place without causing too much commotion?"

Bob already had the third pet casket neatly aligned with the others. Skiffington was riding the bucket back into the hole.

"We've got something else, Tim." Skiffington, with her orange work gloves, carefully wrapped a chain around what appeared to be a four- to five-foot length of white four-inch PVC drainpipe. Bob lifted the bucket, Skiffington, and the dangling pipe out of the grave. Deftly, he placed the pipe next to the caskets.

Skiffington wondered, "Any guesses as to what might be in the box or the pipe?"

Snow wondered. Everyone wondered. Skiffington once again took out her Swiss Army jackknife, opened the 2½-inch blade and cut the tape. When she finished, the tape was neatly sliced so that part was attached to the lid and the rest to the casket.

"That looks good. I think we can dust for prints later."

Click … click … click. Woy moved around the row of white plastic boxes and the accompanying PVC pipe.

"If we find any latent prints, it will surprise me. Everything associated with this case has been clean, real clean." Snow spoke as he wrote. "Meredith, do the end caps on that pipe look glued?"

"Sure do. Both ends have that purple PVC adhesive oozing out."

"Figures. We'll have to open it up in the truck or back at the lab. Let's open the box."

Click … click … click.

Neatly placed in the final pet coffin was an adult female, legs bent back at the knees and torso pushed forward at the hips. The body was fully clothed. There were no signs of trauma, with the exception of bruising around the neck.

Skiffington carefully examined the corpse. "Looks like ligature strangulation, probably some kind of cord. Tim, any idea who this might be?"

"I'm about 99 percent sure it's Allison Smith. Hard to get a height estimate with her all folded up like that. I can say who, but I can't say why."

Chapter 47

Lab Reports

Within hours of the discovery of the body in the pet coffin, the initial autopsy report confirmed Snow's suspicions. Indeed, the deceased was Allison Smith, and she had been strangled with a cord that had been doubled over. As usual, there were no prints on any of the three pet coffins, none on any of Santagati's tools or on the red-and-white International Harvester tractor (the piece of equipment that 'Sabby' Santagati used to dig the graves).

Skiffington requested and received assistance from the Massachusetts State Police Training Academy in Framingham. At about 9:45 a.m. on Friday morning, a twenty-six-passenger, blue-and-gray school-type bus arrived at the Santagati property. Fifteen recruits exited the bus and stood at attention as Skiffington outlined the details of the crime scene. As the recruits were breaking rank, Bob Gates of the Marshfield DPW was leaving the scene on his green John Deere, having lifted the rectangular steel plate from the gravesite. Wide-eyed, the fifteen rookies stared into the hole. In a long line, they walked around the coffins of Muffy and Buffy as Skiffington explained what was found.

"There were three pet coffins, buried one atop the next, in this grave. The top two were pets, and the bottom casket had a human victim. We almost missed the final coffin. Look at the depth of that hole. Any questions?"

The fifteen officers-in-training, along with their instructors, searched the entire exterior of the Santagati estate, from the driveway entrance with its two stone columns emblazoned with a Gothic 'S' to the boat dock where the property went into the water of the North River. Nothing!

After a brief tour of the crime lab truck, the student cops enjoyed a thirty-minute break for lunch. The afternoon proceedings included splitting the group into thirds and assigning each unit a task. The groups rotated assignments throughout the afternoon. Group A relieved the Marshfield police officers at the head of the driveway out on Bridge Street. Gone were the TV trucks. Gone were the river rats, back to their perches on the bridge as they prepared for an afternoon of diving into the incoming tide. Group B was stationed near the two stone columns. Group C was given the first shift of sifting the hundred or so cubic feet of dirt through a fine screen mesh, as it returned to the hole to cover the replaced remains of Buffy and Muffy. The yield from three and a half hours of sifting was four 3½-inch cut nails (circa 1800), a half-dozen pieces of broken porcelain, and a child's marble. Items of interest which might pertain to this case. None.

At exactly 3:45 p.m., a smallish dump truck bearing the seal of the Town of Marshfield and the lettering of the Dept. of Public Works entered the backyard, followed by Bob Gates on his backhoe. Extra soil from the dump truck was shoveled into the gravesite. Filling the missing three feet of earth only took a few minutes. Other than the outline of a few tire treads and a rectangular patch of sod, the scene appeared as it had on Wednesday afternoon. As Villanueva described, about two hundred yards from the garage, near the group of maple trees, were the two stone grave markers, BUFFY and MUFFY, side by side, and a larger monument about two feet away which stated: Erected in Memory of ERIK SANTAGATI, who died on January 18th in the year of 2003, aged 11 years, 3 months, 2 days.

The Massachusetts State Police Crime Laboratory was housed in one of the many buildings that were part of the former South Weymouth Naval Air Station. Early Saturday morning brought a select group, by invitation only, to view the contents of the four-foot-six-inch section of white PCV tubing that had been buried below Allison Smith's casket. The room had nearly fifteen school chairs, the ones with the pull-up writing area. All but two of the desks were for right-handed writers.

Parties present included:

Tim Snow—Boston PD; Detective Meredith Skiffington—Massachusetts State Police; Woy Lee—Boston PD; Dr. Stuart A. Mirkin; Margaret "Peg" McCarthy; Patrick Preston, FBI—Boston Office; and Dr. Norm Blumberg—Plymouth County Medical Examiner.

"Good morning, all. I'm Carl Gustafson, director of the Massachusetts State Police Crime Laboratory. This is Mr. Robert Modrak, latent print deputy for the Commonwealth of Massachusetts. You all seem to know one another." Gustafson continued, "To bring everyone up to speed, we are all here to discuss the alleged Santagati homicides; three occurred in Massachusetts, two possibles in Rhode Island, and one, the first of the series, which took place in Vermont in January of this year. Additionally, the perpetrator seems to be

responsible for at least three assaults with intent. Two assault victims
are here today. Peg McCarthy, retired director of the U.S. Customs
Service Station at North Troy, Vermont, discovered the first homicide
victim, Mr. William LaChance, near the Vermont/Canadian border. Ms.
McCarthy was stabbed in early April. The second assault victim is Dr.
Stuart A. Mirkin. Dr. Mirkin is a medical doctor and world renowned
forensic scientist, who was run off the road in Boston on February 18.
Any questions thus far?"

Gustafson handed a folder to Norm Blumberg. "Norm, could you
pass these around? This is the first of several handouts that I'll
distribute today. We are not going to discuss, at length, the possible
rationale that may have turned a successful oral surgeon into a
pathological predator. However, Dr. Blumberg did the initial autopsy of
a saltwater immersion victim who was recovered from the Jones River
in Duxbury on April 24. That body was recently identified as Dr.
Sebastian Santagati. The toxicology results indicated an extremely high
level of mercury in Dr. Santagati's organs, especially the liver, kidneys
and brain tissue. It has not been determined how, or why, these mercury
levels were elevated. We do know that up until about fifteen years ago,
dental students, dentists, and their patients were exposed to mercury in
amalgam fillings. Take a minute to read that fax."

Date: 5-31-03
To: Carl Gustafson—Director, Massachusetts State Police Crime
Laboratory
From: Dr. Nina Johannson—University of Massachusetts Medical
College
Re: Phone conversation of yesterday (5-30-03)

Mercury poisoning is not usually caused by ingestion of the silvery
liquid that we associate with antique thermometers, meteorological
instruments, and medical equipment such as sphygmomanometer (the
device used for measurement of blood pressure). Liquid mercury, if
swallowed, passes through the body without absorption.

However, inhalation of mercury vapor over a long period may
cause a condition referred to as mercurialism, which is characterized by
fine tremors and erethism. Tremors may affect the hands first, but may
also become evident in the face, arms, and legs. Erethism may be
manifested by abnormal shyness, blushing, self-consciousness,
depression or despondency, resentment of criticism, irritability or

excitability, headache, fatigue, and insomnia. In severe cases, hallucinations, loss of memory, and mental deterioration may occur. Concentrations as low as 0.03 mg/m3 have induced psychiatric symptoms in humans.

Mercury poisoning was a particular hazard in the early 1900s, especially among the millinery and dental professions.

Please call if you have any additional questions.

The door opened and a cart with a coffee urn atop was pushed into the room. Gustafson returned carrying a box of donuts and a large bag of bagels. "Coffee's on. A tad late." The group moved in unison toward the coffee wagon and donuts.

Someone in the back offered, "Hey, Gus. One dozen doesn't seem enough for this mob. What, no Bavarian cream?"

Gus Gustafson waited until people were heading back to their seats. "Bob Modrak will brief us on the fingerprint status. Bob, the floor is yours."

"Good morning. We had a very busy day yesterday. Three of us scoured the Santagati residence top to bottom. Inside and out. As you might expect we didn't find much in the way of latent fingerprints. We did find some possible DNA samples, mostly hair. It will be a few weeks before we receive the results. There were no prints on the three pet coffins, none on the backhoe, none on the body of Allison Smith. Everything was clean. It's as if Santagati was toying with us. I wonder if he wore latex gloves 24/7. Santagati, never served in the military, didn't have a police record, and never had a firearms identification card. Therefore, there are no official prints to use in comparison and, as Norm Blumberg will attest, there are no prints on the corpse of Santagati. While immersed, all exposed parts of Santagati's remains were consumed by Uca Pugnax—fiddler crabs."

"That's a unique method of fingerprint removal!" came from the rear of the room.

Modrak paused, poured himself a cup of coffee. Added cream. Looked over at Detectives Snow and Skiffington. Then continued, "The four-and-a-half foot PCV tube that was placed in the gravesite had no external prints. The contents are a much more interesting story. Here's a list. Take a look."

The contents of a second manila folder was circulated to the gathering.

Evidence Voucher:
4-foot-6-inch white PCV capped tubing removed from gravesite at 631 Bridge Street, Marshfield, Mass., on May 29, 2003.

After external inspection, the tubing was opened using a band saw. The cut was at a distance of approximately two inches from the end of the tube, marked 'A' on the end cap.

Contents List

ITEM #	DESCRIPTION
1	Colt, semi-auto pistol, marked 'Calibre .455,' Ser. No. W23749
2	Box of ammo, marked 'Calibre .455,' 3 rounds inside
3	Typed document titled: 'Letter of Explanation,' signed S.S., dated 4-1-03
4	Receipt for (1) Pet Casket from EdEk Company, Olive, VA dated 1-14-03
5	Rental Receipt for Ford P.U. from Jteck Corp., Hanson, MA dated 2-2-03
6	2 small plastic bottles marked "No Chance" LaChance Hi-Heat Hot Sauce; 1.75 fl. oz. (50 ml) Prepared by Cajun Food Specialties; Ponchatoula, LA
7	Rental Receipt for Toyota Corolla from Jteck Corp., Hanson, MA dated 3-21-03

Gustafson interjected, "It looks like Santagati kept these items as mementoes of his escapades. His Letter of Explanation gives an overview of his rationale for the killings. Bill LaChance, his first victim, was not Santagati's intended target. His primary purpose in this whole affair was to eliminate LaChance's dog. He was obsessed with killing that dog. He was under the assumption that LaChance carried those little bottles of hot sauce to put on his dog's food. Everyone knew—it was in all the papers—that LaChance's dog, Sarek, had that hot sauce with every meal."

Everyone knew? Guess that's everyone but me! thought Peg.

Modrak continued his presentation. "We did find a couple of prints on the items in the tube. On the pistol, near the serial number, there is a perfect thumbprint. Interestingly, in the home on the den wall was a large photograph of a World War I aviator. Evidently the pilot in the photograph, standing in front of his Nieuport, is the grandfather of Santagati. The photo is tagged "Captain Elmer S. Tilden—21 Confirmed Kills—Croix de Guerre, Médailles Militaires, and Légions d'Honneur—Lafayette Escadrille April, 1916, to February, 1918." Tilden is wearing a holster; the part of the automatic that is visible in the photo is similar to the Colt that was in the tube. Out of curiosity, I dusted the photograph. Wouldn't you know? Right on the holster was a perfect thumbprint that matched the one on the pistol. Just like it was placed there to taunt us. We're trying to have the photo enhanced to compare the weapon in the photo with the Colt in the tube. Unusual caliber, you know, a .455 British. Another clean print was found on the reverse side of the Letter of Explanation."

"Thanks, Bob."

Gustafson shuffled through his papers. "Santagati's Letter of Explanation is interesting. It's not a confession but rather his reasons for what happened. Santagati didn't know if his letter would ever be located, but in case it was, he wanted to brag how he had committed the perfect crime. According to his letter, he inadvertently poisoned LaChance in an effort to assassinate the dog. He shot Buckley Roberts because he wouldn't divulge the dog's location. We know now that Roberts didn't know, or even care, where the dog was located. Santagati explained that poor Carl Wells happened to walk in on him as he, Santagati, was stealing the picture of LaChance and his dog from the wall of Dr. Julia Emig's waiting room. Allison Smith became a victim when Santagati learned that her detailed dental records could identify him. He probably destroyed her records not knowing that she filed them electronically each week. Ms. McCarthy, Dr. Mirkin, I guess your connection to this case was reciprocal. Both of you were looking for Santagati as you tried to solve the crimes, and he was looking for you because of your connection to the dog. Interesting. Complex thing, the human psyche. Here's an overhead of Santagati's letter. This briefing is confidential. We'll have a press release early next week."

Letter of Explanation

In the unlikely event that this letter is discovered, I, Sebastian Santagati, would like to offer this brief explanation. I can only hope that any possible discoverer of the contents of this burial site has the necessary intellect to sort the facts and reach the obvious conclusions.

This entire affair was never planned to be a crime, but occasionally the alignment of the stars and other ethereal phenomena can bring misfortune to many a deserving party. In this case, the arrogance of one Mr. William Emeril "No Chance" LaChance lead to his demise and as well to the untimely death and misfortune to others who had no business being involved.

My initial encounter with Mr. William Emeril "No Chance" LaChance was, one could say, simply by chance. As an oral surgeon, I performed extractions and other difficult oral procedures for nearly two dozen dentists scattered about south coastal Massachusetts. Mr. LaChance was a patient and friend of one of my dental colleagues, Dr. Julia Emig. I received a phone message from Dr. Emig on November 14 stating that she was adding an additional patient, Mr. William E. LaChance, to her extraction appointments scheduled at her office for Saturday, November 16, 2002. For Mr. LaChance, Dr. Emig had requested an extraction procedure for tooth number 32, the lower right third molar, which was mesially impacted. During the extraction procedure conducted on 11-16-2002, Dr. Emig and I concurred and concluded that tooth number 16 was also mesially impacted and an additional appointment was made for its extraction on Saturday 1-11-2003. I asked LaChance for an autographed picture for my dying son Erik, a photo promised, however never delivered. A simple request for a terminally disposed son. LaChance stated, "Sure, I'll send that here to Dr. Emig's office." Never delivered. So sad. This fact combined with that sanctimonious image of LaChance and that mangy canine hanging brazenly on Emig's wall of "honor" were the final narcissistic actions by this hackneyed charlatan that caused his demise and downfall. Hall of Fame. Such a hoax. LaChance, and only LaChance, was culpable for these proceedings. He had not a scintilla of decency, or he might have received my plenary indulgence and absolution.

I blame LaChance as much as I blame his shark-like agent, Buckley Roberts. May they, and LaChance's stinking dog, all rot eternally in hell.

Signed this 29th day of March, 2003, by Sebastian Santagati, DDS, DMD, MSD, MPH, PC.

Chapter 48

Saturday July 5
The Grey Gables Mansion
Richford, Vermont

The weekend was absolutely perfect! The weather was gorgeous— not too hot, sunny, blue sky, and not a cloud to be seen. Everyone came: Peg's whole family made it, Jim and his wife, all the gang from North Troy, and, of course, Stu.

The kids had a blast having their own room and sleeping on bunk beds. The staff was very gracious, making sure everyone had everything they needed. A delectable dinner of filet mignon and lobster was enjoyed by all, and then it was time for the embarrassing toasts.

Stu, in his usual take-charge fashion, started the festivities by suggesting a Peg Roast. Boy, plenty of people offered a plethora of embarrassing Peg stories. Jim started with a good ol' JFK story that Peg had long forgotten. Everyone was laughing so hard it hurt! Sisters Kate and Mary chimed in with a few entertaining childhood stories.

"That's just not fair!" cried Peg. "They have nearly fifty years of material!"

Peg was afraid this could go on all night! Mom and Dad got in a few jabs of their own. It was remarkable how well her father recovered after his surgery.

The gang from the Customs Station was without mercy as they portrayed North Troy as the center of international crossings and intrigue between Canada and the U.S.

Oh no! It was Stu's turn. Peg was nervous and her thoughts were racing, "We've only known each other six months. Who knows what he will say. He can, on occasion, be a bit bizarre. Okay, a couple of Sarek stories. That's not too bad. But wait, he's not done. A gift. The first of many from the table nearby. A simple card."

Peg read the card out loud: "Congratulations Peg! Yours truly, Stu."

She examined the box, a jewelry box. The long, rectangular type. She opened the box with a slight hesitation. A beautiful gold chain with a pendant.

"Will you marry me?"

She wanted to accept Stu's marriage proposal but couldn't speak. Then as a single tear rolled down Peg's cheek, she answered a simple "yes."

Chapter 49

"It's the Top of the First."

B elieve it or not, ladies and gents, boys and girls, it's the top of the first inning of the sixth meeting of the 2003 baseball season between the New York Mets and the struggling Montreal Expos."

"This is your WMET sportscaster, Rich Cleary, assisted by my able statistician, cohort and sidekick, D.W. Cederquist, bringing you our radio broadcast from Montreal's Olympic Stadium on the fifth day of July. Well, Ceder, this is your first trip to Olympic Stadium in Montreal, right? Bienvenue."

"Thanks, Rich. Yes, this is my first visit to Montreal. Last year, when the Mets came north to Canada, I was sidelined with an appendectomy. This sure is a pitcher's park with 350 feet down the foul lines and 404 feet to straightaway center field. A pitcher's park with lots of foul ground. We can only dream what No Chance LaChance would have accomplished here at Olympic Stadium. And we are ready to go."

"Attention-n-n-n-n—Leading off for the New York Mets, playing second base, number 17, Paul-l-l-l Natola-a-a-a-a. Number 17, Natola-a-a-a-a-a-a-a-a-a-a-a."

"Ceder, what do you think? Would LaChance have made a big difference here at Montreal?"

"Well, Richie, my friend, as you know, I was a huge LaChance fan. You and I miss him; Montreal misses him; baseball misses him. Last year with the Mets, No Chance had a 10–2 record at this point in the year. The Expos are already 9½ games behind the Braves. You do the math."

"You're right, Ceder, No Chance's statistics spoke for themselves. LaChance is certainly headed for the Hall of Fame in Cooperstown. Here's the first pitch of the game. Outside, ball one. Looking in the Baseball Encyclopedia, LaChance was already in the top twenty-five in almost every pitching category."

"Paul Natola has had a good year, hitting .287, fifteen strikeouts, thirty-six walks, twenty-one stolen bases. Fouled off to the right, just behind the Expo's dugout. One ball/one strike."

"Rubbing the baseball, Expos pitcher Steve Heney is ready, winds. A slow roller to short. Ed Harris gloves it. Over to first. One away."

"Attention-n-n-n-n! Now batting-g-g-g-g, the center fielder, number 6, Bob Oliver-r-r-r-r-r-r-r-r-r."

"Ollie Oliver was thinking of retirement during the off-season due to his chronic hip problem. Feeling better, thank you. Ollie's been in all fifty-three games, eleven home runs, thirty-nine runs batted in."

"Rich, did you watch the news this morning? They think they've finally solved the LaChance murder."

"No, Ceder, I didn't catch the morning news. I was working out in the hotel health club. You really should try to get in shape, Ceder. We ought to put together a show about the illustrious career of Bill LaChance for our weekly sports talk show, Sports Beat, right here on WMET on weekend nights starting at 7:00. That's Saturday and Sunday at seven o'clock in the evening. Strike one to Ollie."

"Interesting. Perhaps we can get some of LaChance's friends and teammates. We could do a whole program on LaChance's philanthropic activities. Funny, you really don't know how complex an individual is until after his passing. Rich, I had you on my list of possible suspects after that big blowout you had with No Chance on the Sports Beat show last November."

"That's not funny, Ceder. Oliver is going through his predictable gyrations between pitches. Cracking his knuckles. Adjusting his knee brace. Ollie's got more padding than an NHL goalie. Now he's back in the box. Here's the pitch. It's a well-hit ball to deep centerfield; Digger Walsh is going back, back. Does it have enough? *Gone!* It has a more than enough. Wow! That's about a 390-foot line-drive! Ollie's really in the groove. It's one-zip, Mets."

"Now-w-w-w battin-g-g-g-g-g-g-g—the first baseman, Dennis McHugh-h-h-h-h-h. Number 44, Dennie-ie-ie-ie-ie-ie McHugh."

"Den McHugh at the plate. Raised his average some thirty-two points since May 15. Now hitting a solid .316 with fifty RBIs. If we hurry, maybe we can get the LaChance show ready for the All-Star Weekend Show. A lot of people would like to hear the No Chance LaChance story, Ceder. Ball one, outside to McHugh."

"That's a great idea! Did you read that Major League baseball is going to have a LaChance moment at the All-Star Game? Some people think LaChance should be inducted into the Hall of Fame now, without the five-year waiting period."

"Oh, sorry, Ceder, I guess I must have missed that. Ball two."

"Yeah, you were probably in the health club."

"That's not funny, Ceder. Heney looks in. Catcher Gregory flashes the sign. Home plate umpire MacEachern looks like he's sitting on Gregory's right shoulder. The pitch, strike one. *Wow!* Ninety-three miles per hour on the gun! Two balls, one strike. Heney looks in for Gregory's sign. Shakes off the first, now the second, and the third. Ryan Gregory is trotting to the mound. Gregory says nothing as Steve Heney, glove to mouth, tells his catcher what his next offering will be. Gregory heads back to the plate and has a couple of words with home plate umpire Gerry MacEachern. Another couple of words to McHugh and we are ready. The wind up, the pitch. Swinging strike two. Ninety-seven miles per hour! Looks like Heney is getting loose. Any listeners out there? If you know of anyone who might have been even remotely connected with Bill LaChance, I'd like to invite them on our show on Saturday, July 12, at 7:00 p.m., right here on WMET. Ceder, you'll start on that in the morning, right?"

"You got that, Richie. Hey Rich, maybe we can get LaChance's dog to come on the show?"

"That's not funny, Ceder."